First World War
and Army of Occupation
War Diary
France, Belgium and Germany

17 DIVISION
51 Infantry Brigade
South Staffordshire Regiment
8th Service Battalion
6 July 1915 - 23 February 1918

WO95/2007/2

The Naval & Military Press Ltd
www.nmarchive.com
Published in association with The National Archives

Published by

The Naval & Military Press Ltd

Unit 10 Ridgewood Industrial Park,

Uckfield, East Sussex,

TN22 5QE England

Tel: +44 (0) 1825 749494

www.naval-military-press.com

www.nmarchive.com

This diary has been reprinted in facsimile from the original. Any imperfections are inevitably reproduced and the quality may fall short of modern type and cartographic standards.

© Crown Copyright
Images reproduced by permission of The National Archives, London, England, 2015.

War Diary	Pommiers Redoubt	02/08/1916	04/08/1916
War Diary	Bn Support & Delville Wood	05/08/1916	09/08/1916
War Diary	Delville Wood	09/08/1916	10/08/1916
War Diary	Fricourt	11/08/1916	11/08/1916
War Diary	Buire	12/08/1916	14/08/1916
War Diary	Gezaincourt	15/08/1916	16/08/1916
War Diary	Bouquemaison	17/08/1916	18/08/1916
War Diary	Bienvillers	18/08/1916	11/09/1916
War Diary	Hannescamp	12/09/1916	21/09/1916
War Diary	Mondicourt	22/09/1916	22/09/1916
War Diary	Remaisnil	23/09/1916	23/09/1916
War Diary	Yvrencheux	24/09/1916	30/09/1916
Heading	8th South Staffs Regt War Diary October 1916 Vol 16		
War Diary	Yvrencheux	01/10/1916	02/10/1916
War Diary	Frohen-Le Grand	02/10/1916	08/10/1916
War Diary	Hebuterne	09/10/1916	14/10/1916
War Diary	Sailly Au Bois	15/10/1916	18/10/1916
War Diary	Doullens	19/10/1916	21/10/1916
War Diary	Ville Sur Ancre	22/10/1916	26/10/1916
War Diary	The Citadel	27/10/1916	31/10/1916
Heading	War Diary 8th South Staffordshire Rgt. November 1916 Vol 17		
War Diary	Montauban	01/11/1916	15/11/1916
War Diary	Meaulte	15/11/1916	16/11/1916
War Diary	Hangest	16/11/1916	16/11/1916
War Diary	Riencourt	17/11/1916	30/11/1916
Heading	D.A.G. Base Herewith War Diary of 8th Battalion South Staffordshire Regt. for month of December 1916		
War Diary	Riencourt	01/12/1916	12/12/1916
War Diary	Corbie	12/12/1916	25/12/1916
War Diary	Carnoy Camp	26/12/1916	31/12/1916
War Diary	Carnoy	01/01/1917	02/01/1917
War Diary	Guillemont	03/01/1917	03/01/1917
War Diary	Trenches	04/01/1917	06/01/1917
War Diary	Carnoy	07/01/1917	13/01/1917
War Diary	In Line	13/01/1917	13/01/1917
War Diary	Carnoy Camp	14/01/1917	15/01/1917
War Diary	Moricourt	16/01/1917	25/01/1917
War Diary	Prontray	26/01/1917	31/01/1917
Heading	D.A.G. Base Herewith War Diary of 8th Battalion South Staffordshire Regt. from 1-2-17-28-2-17		
War Diary	Bonfray	01/02/1917	01/02/1917
War Diary	Bouleaux	02/02/1917	02/02/1917
War Diary	Line	03/02/1917	06/02/1917
War Diary	Bronfay	07/02/1917	07/02/1917
War Diary	Bouleaux	08/02/1917	09/02/1917
War Diary	Line Sailly-Saillisel	09/02/1917	10/02/1917
War Diary	Line	10/02/1917	11/02/1917
War Diary	Bronfay Farm	11/02/1917	13/02/1917
War Diary	Bouleaux Wood	13/02/1917	14/02/1917
War Diary	Line	15/02/1917	15/02/1917
War Diary	Line Sailly-Saillisel	15/02/1917	16/02/1917
War Diary	Maltz Horn	16/02/1917	17/02/1917
War Diary	Bronfay	17/02/1917	18/02/1917
War Diary	La Neuville	18/02/1917	28/02/1917

Type	Location	Start	End
Heading	D.A.G Base Herewith War Diary of 8th Battalion South Staffordshire Regiment from month 1at to 31st March 1917		
War Diary	La Neuville	01/03/1917	01/03/1917
War Diary	Rubempre	02/03/1917	12/03/1917
War Diary	Gezaincourt	13/03/1917	13/03/1917
War Diary	Maizicourt	14/03/1917	14/03/1917
War Diary	Regnauville	15/03/1917	21/03/1917
War Diary	Buire-Au-Bois	22/03/1917	22/03/1917
War Diary	Beaudricourt	23/03/1917	31/03/1917
War Diary	Oppy	01/04/1917	01/04/1917
War Diary	Beaudricourt	02/04/1917	04/04/1917
War Diary	Moncheaox	05/04/1917	06/04/1917
War Diary	Givenchy Le-Noble	07/04/1917	07/04/1917
War Diary	Noyellette	08/04/1917	10/04/1917
War Diary	Arras	10/04/1917	13/04/1917
War Diary	Railway-Triangle	13/04/1917	21/04/1917
War Diary		21/04/1917	25/04/1917
War Diary	Beaudricourt	25/04/1917	30/04/1917
Operation(al) Order(s)	Operation Orders by Lieut. Colonel W.A.J. Barker D.S.O. Comdg. 8th Bn. South Staffordshire Regiment	22/04/1917	22/04/1917
Miscellaneous	Dear Collins	24/04/1917	24/04/1917
Heading	D.A.G. Base. Herewith War Diary of the Battalion under my command for month of May 1917		
War Diary	Beaudricourt	01/05/1917	01/05/1917
War Diary	Huts	02/05/1917	03/05/1917
War Diary	St. Nicholas Camp	03/05/1917	15/05/1917
War Diary	Green Line	15/05/1917	16/05/1917
War Diary	Cadiz Trench	16/05/1917	16/05/1917
War Diary	Green Line	17/05/1917	20/05/1917
War Diary	Railway Cutting	20/05/1917	22/05/1917
War Diary	Green Line	22/05/1917	24/05/1917
War Diary	Cadiz Trench	25/05/1917	27/05/1917
War Diary	Green Line	27/05/1917	30/05/1917
War Diary	St. Nicholas Camp	31/05/1917	31/05/1917
Heading	D.A.G. 3rd. Echelon Herewith War Diary of 8th Battalion South Staffordshire Regiment for month of June 1917		
War Diary	Mondicourt	01/06/1917	21/06/1917
War Diary	St. Nicholas	21/06/1917	29/06/1917
War Diary	Front Line	30/06/1917	30/06/1917
War Diary	Front Line N. of Scarpe	01/07/1917	03/07/1917
War Diary	Trenches	04/07/1917	09/07/1917
War Diary	Trenches (Green Line)	10/07/1917	13/07/1917
War Diary	Green Line	14/07/1917	15/07/1917
War Diary	St. Nicholas	16/07/1917	22/07/1917
War Diary	Front Line	23/07/1917	25/07/1917
War Diary	Chemical Sub-Sector	25/07/1917	28/07/1917
War Diary	Front Line	29/07/1917	31/07/1917
War Diary	Chemical Sub-Sector	01/08/1917	01/08/1917
War Diary	Support	02/08/1917	04/08/1917
War Diary	Railway Cutting	05/08/1917	12/08/1917
War Diary	Lancaster Camp	13/08/1917	16/08/1917
War Diary	Front Line	17/08/1917	22/08/1917
War Diary	Greenland Hill Sector	22/08/1917	23/08/1917
War Diary	Gavrelle Switch	23/08/1917	24/08/1917

War Diary	Hudson Trench	25/08/1917	31/08/1917
Heading	D.A.G. Base.		
War Diary	Hudson Trench	01/09/1917	01/09/1917
War Diary	Lancaster Camp	02/09/1917	09/09/1917
War Diary	Front Line	10/09/1917	10/09/1917
War Diary	Chemical Works Sector	10/09/1917	12/09/1917
War Diary	Front Line Chemical Works Sector	13/09/1917	18/09/1917
War Diary	Reserve Line (Lemon Trench)	19/09/1917	23/09/1917
War Diary	Gavrelle Switch	23/09/1917	23/09/1917
War Diary	Arras	24/09/1917	24/09/1917
War Diary	Simencourt	24/09/1917	25/09/1917
War Diary	Beaudricourt	26/09/1917	04/10/1917
War Diary	Saulty	04/10/1917	05/10/1917
War Diary	Herzeele	05/10/1917	08/10/1917
War Diary	Suez Camp	09/10/1917	09/10/1917
War Diary	Whitemill Camp (Elverdinghe)	09/10/1917	10/10/1917
War Diary	Whitemill Camp	10/10/1917	10/10/1917
War Diary	In Support (Namor Crossing)	11/10/1917	12/10/1917
War Diary	Front Line	13/10/1917	15/10/1917
War Diary	Caribou Camp	15/10/1917	16/10/1917
War Diary	Piddington Camp	17/10/1917	21/10/1917
War Diary	Licques	22/10/1917	25/10/1917
War Diary	Proven Patiala Camp	26/10/1917	27/10/1917
War Diary	Boesinghe	27/10/1917	27/10/1917
War Diary	Baboon Camp	28/10/1917	30/10/1917
War Diary	Patiala Camp Proven	30/10/1917	31/10/1917
Miscellaneous	Report On The Advance of The 8th Battalion South Staffordshire Regt In The Attack On The Morning of The 12th October 1917	15/10/1917	15/10/1917
Miscellaneous	A Form. Messages And Signals		
Heading	D.A.G. Base. Herewith War Diary for the Battalion under my command from November 1st to November 30th.1917		
War Diary	Patiala Camp Proven	01/11/1917	01/11/1917
War Diary	Wormhoudt	02/11/1917	08/11/1917
War Diary	Piddington Camp Proven	09/11/1917	13/11/1917
War Diary	Bridge Camp Elverdinghe	14/11/1917	19/11/1917
War Diary	Front Line	20/11/1917	22/11/1917
War Diary	Huddleston Camp	23/11/1917	24/11/1917
War Diary	Huddleston Camp & Caribou Camp	25/11/1917	25/11/1917
War Diary	Caribou Camp	26/11/1917	01/12/1917
War Diary	Bridge Camp	02/12/1917	04/12/1917
War Diary	Poodle And Pitchcott Camps	05/12/1917	09/12/1917
War Diary	Licques	10/12/1917	11/12/1917
War Diary	Mentque	12/12/1917	14/12/1917
War Diary	O 16 a Camp Barastre	15/12/1917	20/12/1917
War Diary	Havrincourt Wood	21/12/1917	21/12/1917
War Diary	In Line.	22/12/1917	25/12/1917
War Diary	Tank Trench & Tank Support	26/12/1917	30/12/1917
War Diary	Old British Front Line	31/12/1917	31/12/1917
Heading	D.A.G. Base. Herewith War Diary for the Month of January 1918		
War Diary	Old British Fr. Line	01/01/1918	03/01/1918
War Diary	In Line K 8 a 90.40-K 9 b 20.40	04/01/1918	04/01/1918
War Diary	In Line K 8 a 90-40-K 9 b 95-90	05/01/1918	09/01/1918
War Diary	Bde Support	10/01/1918	14/01/1918

War Diary	In Line	15/01/1918	19/01/1918
War Diary	Saunders Camp Haplincourt	20/01/1918	22/01/1918
War Diary	Saunders Camp	23/01/1918	25/01/1918
War Diary	K 32 Q2	26/01/1918	31/01/1918
War Diary	In Line K 10a 50.25-K 11a 00.00	01/02/1918	06/02/1918
War Diary	Saunders Camp	07/02/1918	23/02/1918

WO 2007/2

17TH DIVISION
51ST INFY BDE

8TH BN STH STAFFS REGT

JLY 1915-FEB 1918

Battalion became 7 Entrenching Bn

51st Inf.Bde.
17th Div.

8th BATTN. THE SOUTH STAFFORDSHIRE REGIMENT.

A U G U S T

1 9 1 5

Attached:

Appendices Nos.
2, 3 & 4.

WAR DIARY or INTELLIGENCE SUMMARY

Army Form C. 2118

(Erase heading not required.)

Instructions regarding War Diaries and Intelligence Summaries are contained in F. S. Regs., Part II. and the Staff Manual respectively. Title Pages will be prepared in manuscript.

Place	Date	Hour	Summary of Events and Information	Remarks and references to Appendices
RENINGHELST	1.VIII.15		Orders received during night of 31 July/1st Aug to stand by to move at any moment. Orders received that Brigade will move to Bivouacs in Squares H.23 d & 6 (Ref. sheet 28/40000) B Coy still remain in the trenches. 1 casualty slightly wounded.	
H.23.b.	2.VIII.15		B Coy still remain in the trenches. 1 casualty (wounded) reported from D Coy (machine gunners) Marched into Bivouac at 3 A.M. B Coy relieved from trenches arrived in Bivouac at 10.30 on night of 1st VIII.15. 1 casualty reported (wounded) Machine gun team (1 m + gun) relieved from trenches. 1 casualty wounded.	Appendix 2.
" "	3.VIII.15		Remaining gun team relieved from trenches.	
" "	4.VIII.15		Two Platoons A Coy intended for 24 hours [fatigue] duty with the trenches attached to the 5th Bn (9th West Riding Regt.)	
" "	5.VIII.15		Two Platoons A Coy returned from trenches 1 casualty wounded; 2 Platoons C coy intended to trenches for 24 hours later attached to that Bn with march tonight back to RENINGHELST.	
" "	6.VIII.15		Orders received at 8 p.m. that Bn will march tonight back to RENINGHELST. Bn. marched out at 11.30 p.m. 2 Platoons D Coy proceeded to trenches for 24 hours [tour] attached to 9th West Riding Regt.	
RENINGHELST	7.VIII.15		Bn. marched into camp at 2.45 A.M. 2 Platoons C coy returned from trenches. Orders received that Bn. must be ready to move at ½ hours notice.	
" "	8.VIII.15		Bn. still standing by to move at ½ an hours notice. General Officer Commanding visited trenches of 50th Bde. About St Eloi. Senior Officer visited 50th Bde trenches. C.O. returned from trenches about 6.30 p.m.	

Army Form C. 2118

WAR DIARY
or
INTELLIGENCE SUMMARY
(Erase heading not required.)

Instructions regarding War Diaries and Intelligence Summaries are contained in F.S. Regs., Part II. and the Staff Manual respectively. Title Pages will be prepared in manuscript.

Place	Date	Hour	Summary of Events and Information	Remarks and references to Appendices
REMINGHELST	9.8.15		Remainment in Camp.	
"	11.8.15		C. Coy proceeded to take over section of trenches about ST ELOI (trench C1) from Coy of SOUTH LANCASHIRE Regt. Capt. S.S. POMEROY wounded at ST ELOI by rifle bullet while marching up the KRUISSTRAATHOEK - VOORMEZEELE Road. Trenches were heavily sniped by the enemy.	
"	12.8.15		Remained in Camp.	
"	13.8.15		Remained in Camp.	
"	14.8.15		Machine Gun Section proceeded to trenches to take over.	
"	15.8.15		Battn. proceeded to take over trenches about ST ELOI (see operation order No. 3) Relief commenced 9 p.m.	Operation Order No. 3 = Appendix B.
VOORMEZEELE	16.8.15	12.50 AM	Relief completed. During day casualties 1 man killed, 4 wounded. Snipings during night, apparently from behind front line trenches L.B.	
"	17.8.15		All quiet during morning & afternoon. About 9.15 p.m. bombardment by Minchin started by enemy. Trench mortar used. Col. Ewan answered & often you. Enemy died down about 11.10 p.m. Casualties during the 24 hours. W/S. 2 men killed & Eght wounded. About 2 a.m. on night 18-19, they kept up shelling & sniping during the day. Sgt. Kelley L.S.L. & 3 other three bomb & rifle grenade into our trench. Sgt. Kelley & 3 others machine gun crew were killed by one such grenade. Rifle Grenades from enemy's trenches considerably improved.	
	18/8/15		For 24 hours 4 killed & 12 wounded.	W/S

Army Form C. 2118

WAR DIARY
or
INTELLIGENCE SUMMARY
(Erase heading not required.)

Place	Date	Hour	Summary of Events and Information	Remarks and references to Appendices
Voormezeele	19/8/15		Day quiet. D Company relieved A Company in P3 & P1 & Trenches. A Company going into "Support" in R3 & R4. About 9 p.m. P2 was heavily shelled with high explosive & shrapnel & trenches in several places. Both wires from Q1 & Q2 cut; Trenches slight. 1 man killed & 3 men wounded. W.J.D.	
	20/8/15		Morning & afternoon quiet. At 5 p.m. Engineers exploded countermine in trenches & enemys mine. Engineers are of opinion that greater was successful. Several mining during the night. Casualties for the 24 hours 1 men killed & 2 wounded. W.J.D.	
	21/8/15		Trenches especially becoming into them were lost over. A great deal of work done on the front line. Sniping & gun fire during the day inconsiderable as usual. Enemys counter-mine exploded between the German & British lines. This was immediately followed by a short but sharp bombardment by their gunners our Artillery replied & information having been received from the front Companies that we had unlimbered a.a Germans the gunners were instructed, & the incident closed. Quiet night with exception that at 11 p.m. we bombed the enemys many Catapult & fired several rifle grenades. Casualties 2 wounded. W.J.D.	

WAR DIARY or INTELLIGENCE SUMMARY

Army Form C. 2118

Place	Date	Hour	Summary of Events and Information	Remarks and references to Appendices
VOORMEZEELE	22/8/15		Quiet day & night. Guard his post	WYP
	23/8/15		Quiet morning. 2 p.m. Enemy fired several rifle grenades leading to general reciprocal measures. Naval supply during afternoon & night. Casualties 3 wounded.	WYP
	24/8/15		Comparative quiet on our front. Lincolns on our left shelled good bombardy with H.E. shells. In the afternoon enemy used rifle grenades & bombs. About 4.15 p.m. they exploded a mine about 40 yards east of the Bruance on front B. R3. No material damage done. During the night enemy occupied the crater made by above premature & now it appears to be part of its & N/O D defence. 6 wounded.	WYP
	25/8/15		A lot of work appears to have been done by enemy in crater. At about 9 a.m. enemy started heavy bombardment with shrapnel & H.E. shells on trenches R3 & R2. Parapets & parados in places blown to bits. Only the hardwork put in during the last week set improvements saved the company from very heavy casualties. About 300 "Whizz-bangs" & 70 or 30 crumps Derry afternoon a Coy believed D which was however discharged a hour later. It took about 1½ hours to get our howitzer above trenches. Nothing on reply resumed during morning & afternoon. Shells & 13 wounded.	WYP

1875 Wt. W593/826 1,000,000 4/15 J.B.C. & A. A.D.S.S./Forms/C. 2118.

WAR DIARY
or
INTELLIGENCE SUMMARY

(Erase heading not required.)

Army Form C. 2118

Place	Date	Hour	Summary of Events and Information	Remarks and references to Appendices
Voormezeele	26/8/16		Comparative quiet during the morning. During night 25/26 work parties had about 150 rounds shrapnel over during day, no casualties. Our Listons spoting two communication trenches. Our artillery were placing shrapnel + H.E. well on to aforementioned trenches. Telephone communication into forward O.O. both closed + has been much put forward cancelled. W/P. 1 man killed.	
	27/8/16		At 10.30 am our artillery starting firing on craters, moored + works in juxtaposition. The Companies in R3 - R1 had previously been withdrawn to supporting trenches. Guns used by us 4.5" m Rs, 6" mortars + 8" + 9.2" in the afternoon with shrapnel, + R.G. many H.E. in all directions. Little damage replied by shelling our evacuated trenches. AP+4 Now to our trenches. At 8.30 pm 6th Dorset Regt started relief of 97, 07 the S. Staffords. Enemy continued shelling trenches both H.E. & shrapnel. No H. Relief delayed considerably. One man killed 2 + 2 wounded. Owing the period Companies so relieved marched back to Bosinghe Lines & to Pen. 176, 177, 178. WJ/B	
Reninghelst	28th 1st		Battalion in Brounke Huts, Vandry Volgue Bow law + Nancy bivouacs.	W/D

A P P E N D I C E S Nos. 2, 3 & 4.

B Coy. Tour of instruction in trenches Appendix 2
Ref. Map. Sheet 28

B Coy proceeded on 27th July for a tour of instruction in the trenches, & were attached to the 5th Bn. SOUTH STAFFORD Regt. The trenches occupied by this Bn. are situated in square I 35 a, the left of the Section is on the railway cutting, & looks onto Hill 60, the line of the Section of trench runs generally S.S.W. On the night of the 27th July there was nothing to report, 2 casualties occurred - wounded. On 28th July nothing to report. On the morning of 29th 2 men were slightly wounded, nothing to report. At dawn on 30th big bombardment started by enemy & was followed by enemy attack on left outside the section occupied by 5th Bn. British counter attack took place at 2 p.m. 1 casualty wounded. Another bombardment followed by enemy attack took place at dawn on 31st + a further attack at dusk, both attacks outside 5th Bn. Section, 2 casualties in our M.G. Section. On evening of 1st Aug. at 9.20 p.m. enemy made abortive attack also outside section.

During their tour in the trenches B Coy was subjected to several heavy bombardments & were unable to leave at the end of 3 days as had been arranged, they were eventually able to get out on the night of 1st August & rejoined the Battn. at H 23 b. According to report by Major R.G. RAPER Comdg B Coy, the men behaved excellently & showed coolness & steadiness under fire.

Copy No.

OPERATION ORDER No. 3
by
Lt. Col G.N. GOING.
Comdg 8th South Staffs. Regt.
RENINGHELST.
14.8.15.

Ref. Sheet 28/ 1
          40.000

Information. 1. The Battalion will take over the trenches about ST.ELOI from the 50th Bde. tomorrow night.

Rendezvous. 2. The Battn. (less 2 Coys) under Major R.G. RAPER will rendezvous at 8.15 pm. tomorrow at cross roads H.16. d.1.1. where guides will meet them.
Trench guides will meet Coys. at PRINCESS PATRICIA'S CEMETERY N.I.31.c.
Order of march to rendezvous. A.D.B.
After leaving KRUISTRAATHOEK the Battn. will move in parties not larger than 1 platoon.

Allotment of 3.
trenches.

Section.	Coy.	Garrison of trenches.
Right Section. Q.2 and Q.1 (a)	C	Q.2 2 platoons. Q.1(a) 2 platoons.
Left section. Q.1 (b) R.3. R.2	A	Q. 1(b). 1 platoon R.3 2 platoons. R.2 1 platoon.
Support section. No. 3 Barricade. Right Breastwork. R.4 and R.7	D	No. 3 Barricade) Right Breastwork) 1 platoon R.4 1 platoon. R.7 2 platoons

Reserve. B Coy will be in reserve at VOORMEZEELE

Rifles. 4 All rifles will be loaded with 5 rounds in the magazine and cut off closed before the Battn. marches out of Camp with the exception of the Coy. in reserve (B Coy).

Reports on 5. O.C. Coys. will report to Bn. HdQrs. immediately the
Relief. relief of their section of trench is complete.

Stand to. 6 For half an hour after the relief of the trenches is complete all Coys. will stand to arms without removing any of their equipment (including packs). After this period O.C. Coys. will satisfy themselves that every man knows the position he has to occupy and that all sentries and parties have been posted and detailed, packs will then be removed by sections under platoon arrangements.

Patrols. 7 Officers patrols will not be sent out except by order of the Commanding Officer

Reports. 8. All reports will be sent by wire, in the event of the wires being broken, reports will be sent in duplicate by 2 orderlies.

Trench Standing 9. Attention is called to Bde. and Battn. Trench
Orders. Standing Orders.

Issued at 6 pm.

                                                          Capt.
Adjutant 8th South Staffs. Regt.

Copy No. 1
" " 2 to "A" Coy.
" " 3 " "B" Coy.
" " 4 " "C" Coy.
" " 5 " "D" Coy.
" " 6 " "M.G. Officer.
" " 7   War Diary

Copy No. 6

OPERATION ORDERS No. 4
by
Lieut Colonel G.N. GOING.
Comdg. 8th Bn. South Staffs. Regt.

Ref. Map
VOORMEZEELE
10,000

1. Information.   The Battalion will be relieved tonight by the 6th Battn. Dorset Regt.
   The relief will commence at 8.30 p.m.

2. Guides.   Guides from each Platoon will meet the relieving Coys. at P.P.C.L.I. Cemetry at 8.30 pm. and the Coys. will be lead into the road running along the NORTH wall of the Convent I.31.c.6.9. under cover of the Convent wall. Platoons will be lead from this point past the LINCOLN H.Qs. to the trenches. One officer per Company will accompany the Platoon guides to the rendezvous.

3. Relief.   Q.1 (a) and Q.2 Trenches.
   Relieving Coy. will be lead by guides at 8.30 pm. by Platoons VIA Q.3 to Q.1 and Q.2. Two minutes between each Platoon.
   Relieved Coy. will evacuate by same route by platoons.
   R.3 and R.2 and Q.1(b) will be lead by guides at 8.40 pm by platoons VIA R.7 and R.4. Relieved platoons evacuate by same route.
   R.4 and R.7, Relieving Coy., will be lead to Battn. H.Qrs. and remain there till relief of front trenches is reported complete. They will then be lead down by platoon guides.
   Reserve Coy. and H.Qrs. (with exception of orderlies) will concentrate at CONVENT when they will be relieved at 8.30 pm.

4. Rendezvous.   Platoons will concentrate behind KRUISTRAATHOEK (Battn. dumping ground), from which place Coys will march independently to RENINGHELST.

5. Reports.   O.C. Coys. will report to Battn. H.Qrs. when the relief of their Coys. is complete.

6. Trench Stores.   Coys. will hand over Trench maps, trench bags and trench stores to relieving Coys.

Capt.
8th South Staffs. Regt.

Copy No. 1   "A" Coy.
"   "   2   "B" Coy.
"   "   3   "C" Coy.
"   "   4   "D" Coy.
"   "   5   H. Qrs.
"   "   6   War Diary.

51st Inf.Bde.
17th Div.

Battn. disembarked
Boulogne from
England 15.7.15.

8th BATTN. THE SOUTH STAFFORDSHIRE REGIMENT.

J U L Y

(6/31.7.15)

1 9 1 5

Attached:

Appendix 1.

WAR DIARY
or
INTELLIGENCE SUMMARY

(Erase heading not required.)

Army Form C. 2118

8th Bn. South Staffordshire Regt.

Place	Date	Hour	Summary of Events and Information	Remarks and references to Appendices
Perham Down Camp	4/7/15		Orders received that 17th Division was about to proceed overseas. The Bn embarkation officer thereupon left for Southampton.	
Perham Down Camp	10/7/15		Secret document re detrainment of trains received. No. C.B./17D/24A	
Perham Down Camp	12/7/15		Advance party proceeded by road to Southampton.	
Perham Down Camp	14/7/15		The Battn. marched out at 5 p.m. entrained for Folkestone at 6 p.m. & 6.30 p.m. Embarked at 10.50 p.m. for Boulogne.	
Boulogne	15/7/15		Arrived Boulogne 1 A.M. marched to rest camp. Capt W. GIBSON accidentally wounded in the left arm by accidental discharge of automatic pistol.	
do.	16/7/15		The Battn. marched out at 1.30 A.M. & entrained at Pont Brique for LONDRES marched to billets at ACQUIN arrived at 10 A.M.	
ACQUIN	18/7/15		The Battn. marched out of billets at 5.45 A.M. via GUEMES - SETQUES - ARQUES - ERBLINGHEM - WALLON-CAPPEL (20 miles) commanded by G.O.C. shifted on the 1st morning of the Bn. A new adj put out. Next into billets. Complimented by G.O.C. shifted on the first morning of the Bn.	
WALLON CAPPEL	19/7/15		The Battn. marched out of billets at 9 a.m. to EECKE. Billetted in town near EECKE. Capt A.W. FARMER sick sent to 51st F.A. Ambulance.	
EECKE	20/7/15		Inspected by General Sir H. Plumer Commdg 2nd Army. General addressed himself very pleased with the afternoon studying & turn out of the Battn.	
"	24/7/15		Received orders that Bn. will move to TRENINGHELST on night of 25/26 July & will be in Corps Reserve.	

1875 Wt. W593/826 1,000,000 4/15 J.B.C. & A. A.D.S.S./Forms/C.2118.

Army Form C. 2118

WAR DIARY
or
INTELLIGENCE SUMMARY

6th Bn. South Staffordshire Regt.

(Erase heading not required.)

Instructions regarding War Diaries and Intelligence Summaries are contained in F.S. Regs., Part II. and the Staff Manual respectively. Title Pages will be prepared in manuscript.

Place	Date	Hour	Summary of Events and Information	Remarks and references to Appendices
EECKE	28/7/15		Battn. marched out of billets at 8 p.m. Route - EECKE - BERTHEN - WESTOUTRE - HEKSKEN - RENINGHELST arrived in camp at 1. A.M.	
RENINGHELST	29/7/15		B Coy proceeded to the trenches, attached to 137th Bde. 46th Divn, for 3 days tour of duty.	143 Report re movement noted see Appendix 1.
"	30/7/15		B Coy ordered to remain in trenches, as owing to existing conditions in the neighbourhood of YPRES they could not be withdrawn. 2 casualties (wounded) reported June 24/25/26/11	
"	31/7/15		B Coy still unable to be withdrawn. 2 casualties (wounded slightly at duty) reported from 5th B.W. with the 51st B.A. Orders received that the 6th B.A. would move up into reserve on night of 1st/2nd August.	174

1875 Wt. W593/826 1,000,000 4/15 J.B.C. & A. A.D.S.S./Forms/C.

Appendix 1.

Report on poisoned Water.

It is certain from indisputable evidence & from analysis of the water, that the Enemy has poisoned the water of the DIEPENDAELBEEK which rises in their lines between ST ELOI & VOORMEZEELE thence into the moat of YPRES. The poison used is arsenic.

Extract from Routine Orders by

Brig Genl. R.B. FELL comdg 51st Bde

27.XII.15.

51st Inf.Bde.
17th Div.

8th BATTN. THE SOUTH STAFFORDSHIRE REGIMENT.

S E P T E M B E R

1 9 1 5

WAR DIARY or INTELLIGENCE SUMMARY

Army Form C. 2118

Place	Date	Hour	Summary of Events and Information	Remarks and references to Appendices
Reninghelst	1/9/15		Bn. in Onl Company resting. One Company at Scottish crowd on Engineer fatigue. One man wounded by stray bullet.	
"	2 & 3		Raining.	
"	4		Raining all day.	Wyp.D
			Fatigue during the day. Relieved 6th Dorset at Voormezeele at night. Relieving twenty stores Three Coy communicating Trenches knee deep in water & mud. Relief complete without casualties at 12.15 a.m.	
Voormezeele	5/9/15		Raining most of the day. Trenches & all dennis, polios very bad. Efforts by all hands to drain & rebuild dug outs etc. Worked away. Parties carrying stones etc has to later 85 timber Revet- pells up trenches & walk passage Trenches. Very little firing.	Wyp.D
			2.0 Casualties	
"	6/9/15		Fairly quiet all day. See bomb onstery on common (city) Trench. A pakapet with 6 bns. boxes 10/11/12. One accident 8 own 1 killed & 3 wounded.	Wyp.D
"	7/9/15		3 am. quiet until about 9/0 am. then enemy sent up Rif Lit & lit mortars followed by rapid fire from about 3 Batteries. Enemy showed on our support Trenches. 3 wounded J.J.	Wyp.D
"	8/9/15		Comparative quiet. Very little shelling Crumblis pel.	Wyp.D
"	9/9/15		- ditto -	Wyp.D

WAR DIARY
or
INTELLIGENCE SUMMARY
(Erase heading not required.)

Army Form C. 2118

Instructions regarding War Diaries and Intelligence Summaries are contained in F.S. Regs., Part II. and the Staff Manual respectively. Title Pages will be prepared in manuscript.

Place	Date	Hour	Summary of Events and Information	Remarks and references to Appendices
Voormezeele	10/9/15		Very little doing until about 5.30 p.m. One French mortar then fired several rounds at Enemy's work. That broke lite Machine Gun emplacement opposite. Enemy replied with sharp shrapnel & heavy enfilade gun. One shrapnel killed 4 men & wounded 9 another. Casualties in day 4 killed 1 wounded.	W&D
	11/9/15		In the morning at about 8 a.m. our French mortar gun played on Enemy trenches. Reply in form of several minenwerfer but 9.30 a.m. Reply grenades from our two front companies but the sufferers. What was for the time being closed up by the presence of our Telegrams in Enemy and Army by the rest of the day. Casualties 1 killed & 5 wounded	W&D
	12/9/15		Confusion quiet all day. Relieved by 6th Dorset R. & at 10.10 p.m. Back to end at Renninghelst	W&D
Renninghelst	13/9/15		At rest cleaning up. Baths not yet ready. One company (A) to scottish trans for work	W&D
	14/9/15		Bath. open & used by all available men	W&D
	15/9/15		Early. Bombers, machine guns Sct. & signallers working all day	W&D
	16/9/15		state	W&D
	17/9/15			W&D
	18/9/15		Inspected by General Plumer	W&D
	19/9/15		Still at Renninghelst	W&D
	29/9/15		Bomb throw in Dummy. Relieved 6th Dorset at Voormezeele. Coy. Lt. Col. Rawnghelst at intervals of 10 minutes starting at 4.30 p.m.	W&D

WAR DIARY or INTELLIGENCE SUMMARY

Army Form C. 2118

Place	Date	Hour	Summary of Events and Information	Remarks and references to Appendices
Voormezeele	21/9/15		In the morning our Trench mortars [?] fired a retaliation with 12 after [?] grenades. Very little "enemy's" artillery reply. Billings fire [?] Nichols [?] [illegible]	W.P.
	22/9/15		[1/slightly wounded?] [illegible] on him from [illegible]. Quite day our artillery opened bombardment on Enemy's [illegible] trenches at fronts B, R1 & R2 at 7:4:pm. Enemy replied [illegible] trenches at [illegible] 11th W.12 – Enemy doing very little damage. Pretty controllable.	W.P.R
	[illegible]		Enemy [illegible] on [illegible] [illegible] [illegible] 4.p.m. French [illegible] a [illegible] Dl French, Rd accurate [illegible] trenches 2 Sep.11/15 [illegible] L.C.S	W.P.R
	23/9/15		Bombardment quiet all day. Snipers and guns appear to be getting less active. Casualties	W.P.R
	24/9/15		Hardly a shot fired in the morning. Our artillery bombarded enemy's trenches from 4.pm. to 5.pm. Enemy retaliated but only a shew to [illegible] from at mouth His batt. Batteries on our front v our [Target gun?] Casualties nil.	W.P.R
	25/9/15	3.30 am	Our guns opened on Enemy; trenches in direction of HOOGE. Field guns in front. Our French opened a few smoke [illegible] on grounds between 73rd H.Qrs & front. French with cohesive intention of establishing [curtain?]. Enemy	
		4.10 am	our artillery commenced fury on trenches 18 on front, on Enemy Bombardment night about 4.am. But British attack was launched near HOOGE. Very [illegible] our Infantry commenced rapid fire on Enemy but to give impression of [preparation?]	
		5.30am	[illegible] attack. What was in any church [illegible] so D.C.G [Phosphorus?] bomb that has been prepared was not used. On our right the [illegible] & men just had [illegible] places in [position?] for going to [illegible] gas attack. The [illegible] [illegible] [illegible] on our own Trenches, that put the [illegible] immediate Bomb-burst by Enemy's [illegible] men down &c Casualties	W.P.R

WAR DIARY or INTELLIGENCE SUMMARY

Army Form C. 2118

Place	Date	Hour	Summary of Events and Information	Remarks and references to Appendices
VOORMEZEELE	25/9/15 (cont)		During the whole time, Enemy never once fired guns larger than Field guns. Enemy M.G. Snipers ever have been v. the town & were firing friends. HOODE. Unprecedented quiet prevailed as far as snipers were concerned after the bombardment. Lieut. S.R. Edwards buried in PPCLI Cemetery Voormezeele in the afternoon.	W&P
	26/9/15	Evening	Enemy exploded mine directly in front of A3 Trench. No damage. Rest of day quiet. Consolidation road.	W&P
	27/9/15		Slightly increased artillery on part of Enemy. Considerable amount of French artillery & more sniping than usual. Casualties 2 men wounded.	W&P
	28/9/15		Comparative quiet. Lieut. Boyd wounded by sniper. Battalion relieved at 7pm by 6th Devons. Relief complete at 9.15pm. Casualties 1 Officer & 3 men wounded. Bn marched by 10pm/3am via to Reninghelst. Reninghelst heat.	W&P
Reninghelst	29/9/15		At rest. Reninghelst heat all day.	W&P
	30/9/15		Preparing to move during morning. Bn moved out at 4.15.5pm to march via Ypres Salient to relieve 1st Sherwood Foresters. Reninghelst head of Column Reliof Abeele 6.5pm Enemy opened very heavy shell H.E. & Shrapnel on supporting troops & all approach roads. Sherwoods had a considerable casualty list, mainly Bn Officers Lieut Coleridge killed. Two runners were serving by enemy Belief Complete 12.30am No. 5. Staffs. & Grenadiers. Trench Warleen over Pros 31, & 32 with support of Reserves.	W&B

1875 Wt. W593/826 1,000,000 4/15 J.B.C. & A. A.D.S.S./Forms/C.2118.

51st Inf.Bde.
17th Div.

8th BATTN. THE SOUTH STAFFORDSHIRE REGIMENT.

O C T O B E R

1 9 1 5

WAR DIARY or INTELLIGENCE SUMMARY

Army Form C. 2118

Place	Date	Hour	Summary of Events and Information	Remarks and references to Appendices
Canal Bank nr. Verbrandenmolen	1/10/15		Quiet morning after relief. Continued sniping but little firing for Canal. 1 man killed.	
	2/10/15		Continuous sniping. Enemy have found rifles aimed to graze over our front parapet. At 4.30 pm Enemy started to send over aerial torpedo on front machine & rifle grenades retaliated. Through the night beated up by the Belgian guns. Our barrage puts D. trench which are just close to ours, one & ground were heavy. Casualties. 3 men wounded.	
	3/10/15		Sniping as usual. Occasional hand & trench mortar. Our artillery replied to Enemy rifle sniping during night. Casualties. 1 man killed & 1 man wounded.	
	4/10/15		Co-operation quiet. A Coy relieved by A Coy 2/8th Black Watch. Coy relieved by 9.15 pm & billeted at Reninghelst. Casualties 1 man killed Night.	
	5/10/15		Quiet in the morning. About 12 noon Infr/pion reported that Enemy had got into our foothill Sap. Pioneer officer accompanied by Head Bombes make reconnaissance. Non Shayh & there find on top Wood to bomb & bombes Organized in case Enemy exploded mine. Charge prepared by Engineers placed in creen Enemys Sap head so they looked for Tend at 3 PM No Exchange to Enemy. Though Enemy were only 12 yds distant. Bn relieved by 1/th Royal Scots at 8.30 pm Relief complete 11.30 pm & marched to billet at La Clytte.	

Army Form C. 2118

WAR DIARY
or
INTELLIGENCE SUMMARY

(Erase heading not required.)

Instructions regarding War Diaries and Intelligence Summaries are contained in F.S. Regs., Part II. and the Staff Manual respectively. Title Pages will be prepared in manuscript.

Place	Date	Hour	Summary of Events and Information	Remarks and references to Appendices
In Bly d.	6/10/15		Sa 6/10/15. During the day. At 5.p.m commenced march to Eecke arriving 12. m.n.	WyD
Eecke	7/10/15		Bn billet. 2 Senior Officers of every Bn in Div. driven about to Steenvoorde to meet Corps Commander who took opportunity of saying good bye to the 14th Division & wishing his Corps	WyD
"	8/10/15		All Ranks farewell. Bn resumed construction of Bombing	WyD
"	9 & 20/10/15		Remained in billet. Constant parades in the Attack; bombing, bayonet exercise, Bayonet fighting etc At 4 p.m on 20th Bn & Brigade moved to G.18 Sheet 28 near Vlamertinghe arriving 10.p.m	WyD
Bn Vlamertinghe	21/10/15		Under canvas in Camp until the afternoon. At 5.p.m, Bn left camp and marched to Transche Sanctuary Wood to relieve 13th Kings Liverpool Regt. Relief completed at 11.30 p.m. No casualties.	WyD
Sanctuary Wood	22/10/15		Quiet in the morning. At 2.30 p.m Enemy commenced shelling with heavy shells vicinity of Trench 6 - occupied by D Coy & vicinity of Bn Hqrs. Retaliation called for & given by our Artillery. Shelling continued on both sides until about 4.30 p.m Casualties our o/r/s	WyD
"	23/10/15		Peaceful morning. Trenches shelled on & near by Bn Ok mens & our horses traversed. Heavy shelling occurred about 11 p.m. Our Artillery for an hour	WyD
"	24/10/15		Information & Enemy Shelling & Infantry movement in the afternoon & Evening. Possible Barrier between Zy	WyD

WAR DIARY
or
INTELLIGENCE SUMMARY

Army Form C. 2118

Place	Date	Hour	Summary of Events and Information	Remarks and references to Appendices
Sanctuary Wood	25/10/15 – 26/10/15		Usual shelling from both sides. Snow, sleet and very little shelling following. Trenches in bad condition and owing to rain all trenches very much knocked about. Casualties 1 man wounded.	WyD WyD
"	27/10/15		Raining most of the day. Parapets all falling in & being rebuilt. Officer of 12th Munsters Regt came round trenches to make themselves acquainted as they are taking over on the 29th. Shelling as usual. Casualties 1 man killed 3 wounded	WyD
"	28/10/15		Still raining. Snow & Sleet. Shelling B 12 & H mortars ku arrived. Cooked spanned the trenches & returned. Prior being shelled & thrown out. Officers of the Sligo – out. 1 offn & 1 n.n.o. & 10 men casualties 2 wounded	WyD
"	29/10/15		Shelling as usual. Siege-running in the morning. Bn relieved in the evening by 12th Munsters Regt. Relief arrived 2½ hrs late. Bn first coy Bn not appearing until 11.15 pm. & the remainder much later. Relief completed at 1.15 am. 2nd Bn marched back by coys independently through Ypres & Vlamertinghe	WyD
Vlamertinghe	30/10/15		Billets. Bn inspected arrived tout. 6.30 am	WyD
"	31/10/15		Two coys taken for Vatigues for R.E. Remainder resting	WyD

51st Inf.Bde.
17th Div.

8th BATTN. THE SOUTH STAFFORDSHIRE REGIMENT.

N O V E M B E R

1 9 1 5

Army Form C. 2118

WAR DIARY
or
INTELLIGENCE SUMMARY

(Erase heading not required.)

Instructions regarding War Diaries and Intelligence Summaries are contained in F.S. Regs., Part II. and the Staff Manual respectively. Title Pages will be prepared in manuscript.

Place	Date	Hour	Summary of Events and Information	Remarks and references to Appendices
Flametinghe	Nov 1 1915		In and Billets. Running all day. Two days leave taken for P.E. Vulogne etc. Remainder of Bn still working up.	
	2/11/15 – 5/11/15		Bn still in Rest billets. One or two Conferences taken during the day. etc under R.E. Remainder doing physical drill, Company, drill, inspection clothing, put cli etc.	WyD
"	6/11/15		Preparing to relieve 12th Yorkshire Regt at Somehow Wood at 1.30pm orders received cancelling move.	WyD
	7/11/15 – 9/11/15		Rest billets. Working parties & work as usual.	WyD
Railway Wood nr Ypres	10/11/15		Bn marched out at 1.45pm en route for Railway Wood east of Ypres. Halted at White Chateau outside Krulshoek for an hour & a half for the Regiment & Cookers Cookers & French artillery. Menin Gate at 6.15pm. Guides of 1st Bn. The Buffs met Bn here & Companies proceeded to relieve the former. Relief completed at 8.55pm without casualties though enemy were firing a considerable number of HE shells during the period Crossed in Rl.	WyD
"	11/11/15		Communicating Trenches in appalling condition. A great snowy & water. Went deep at French, heavy, heavy & almost in many parts on both sides very heavy. Quiet between our bombers & enemy. In the two following nights Cpl in 7 practically no less on day time. Casualties 1 killed 3 wounded.	WyD

WAR DIARY
INTELLIGENCE SUMMARY
(Erase heading not required.)

Army Form C. 2118

Place	Date	Hour	Summary of Events and Information	Remarks and references to Appendices
Railway Wood	12/11/15		Rained all day. Trenches falling in in fact, as they are built. Communication trench found 1½' strong knee thigh deep in mud & water. Considerable sniping by artillery in morning increasing in afternoon. Bombs thrown by both sides at night. Casualties 1 killed, 1 missing (believed killed) & 6 wounded.	
"	13/11/15		Still raining. Guns busy on both sides in the morning. Our heavy Artillery commenced at 2.30 pm shelling enemies trenches in front of H20 with object of driving them to same state as our own. Before a quarter of an hour had elapsed enemy evidently began to find conditions in their trenches after being shelled not preferable & commenced coming over the top to seek shelter in rear of Railway Wood & taken up positions in same. Several hundred of enemy appeared to get "the wind up". Some hundreds to escape from enemy shelled and ran for shelter on the Very light was sent up & rapid fire of the Trenches on Bn right held by 8th York & Lanc. Regt. Reoccupation of trenches effected without incident. Casualties nil and gun wounded	W.Y/D
"	14/11/15 15/11/15		At Grenadines Afternoon. Artillery on enemy's H.Q. & surroundings. Organised Intelligence Retaliation but not so heavy as yesterday. Casualties 4 wounded.	W.Y/D
"	16/11/15	×	Shelling from both sides all day. Casualties 2 killed 9 men wounded.	W.Y/D

WAR DIARY or INTELLIGENCE SUMMARY

Army Form C. 2118

Place	Date	Hour	Summary of Events and Information	Remarks and references to Appendices
Railway Wood	17/11/15		Perpetual shelling from both sides. Penny mood of the day "Minniewerfers."	
"	18/11/15		Shelling intermittent during morning and afternoon. Abt 5 p.m. enemy sent heavy minenwerfer fire and 10 such bombs shells into enemy's trench. These were the first in which were supposed to be our enemy's Supt Point. A certain amount of Thirtre fire have however to fly. Bn were relieved by 4th Border Regt, the relief being completed at 8.35 p.m. from Bn marched back to rest billets at H.19.C. arriving about 11 p.m.	WD
Rest Billets H.19.C. Between Ooderdom and Vlamertinghe	19/11/15 to 23/11/15		Camps in tented huts. Bn much of fatigues. Both machine gun officers unsuitable. Very bad feet in sight. B 21 & 22 condition B. Games. Thirtey improved. Every day when weather permitted Coy. Hy practice carried out. Parades & inspections on the "Helmet", Rifles, boots, clothing, feet etc. When possible, Baths open at Poperinghe & between ?. Bn by Companies in Rotation. Hot's performed continually	
"	24/11/15		Relieved for by Bryd & Divman. Bn paraded at 3 p.m. & marched by Companies to Ypres thence to Railway Wood to Reliance of 4 Border Regt. Relief completed 9.45 p.m. Two N.C.Os. a man wounded.	WD

WAR DIARY or INTELLIGENCE SUMMARY

(Erase heading not required.)

Army Form C. 2118

Instructions regarding War Diaries and Intelligence Summaries are contained in F.S. Regs., Part II. and the Staff Manual respectively. Title Pages will be prepared in manuscript.

Place	Date	Hour	Summary of Events and Information	Remarks and references to Appendices
Railway Wood near Ypres	25/11/15		Fairly quiet in the morning. At 1.70 pm our trench mortars commenced firing on enemy's crater in front of I.20. Enemy retaliated with trench mortars. Our Artillery then opened & destroying the afternoon there was considerable exchange of rifle fire. Our Trench Mortars threw 6 bombs. 1 died.	
	26/11/15		Usual firing in the morning. Our trench mortars fired a few rounds at noon. At noon our heavy Artillery fired seven out of ten rounds. Enemy's hvy well observed & a lot of rounds. Retaliation resulted & our heavy batteries were called on to take part. There fire was absolutely magnificent. Nearly all the shots fell onto our own trenches. Most of the enemy's lines were knocked out. General Casualties 3 wounded.	
	27/11/15		The usual shell firing on both sides. Ant. bombardment of enemy's infantry trenches heavy. Afternoon. Enemy placed a lot of heavy shells on our trenches at 5.30 a.m. Casualties 4 wounded.	
	28/11/15		Fairly quiet in morning. Usual shelling in the afternoon. Enemy brought the howitzers up towards new crater, battery & trench mortars fired on this place in the evening. Patrols could not get any information of anything. Casualties killed 1, wounded 1.	

WAR DIARY or INTELLIGENCE SUMMARY

Army Form C. 2118

Place	Date	Hour	Summary of Events and Information	Remarks and references to Appendices
Railway Wood near YPRES	29.XI.15		Heavily shelled during morning & afternoon. Cambridge road suffered most being heavily shelled for some 5 hours. B Coys. were also shelled during the same period but not so heavily. One Machine gun Platoon relieved by that of Border Regt. Casualties 1 killed, 11 wounded.	
"	30.XI.15		Heavily shelled during morning and afternoon. Cambridge Road & RAILWAY WOOD being the areas to suffer most. One gun retired & for HQ tins the dugs shelling first down but began again vigorously in afternoon & heavy shelling. B Coys relieved by Border Regt. & when our guns ceased firing. Bn. relieved by YORKS Rampants. Casualties. 5 killed 4 wounded.	

51st Inf.Bde.
17th Div.

8th BATTN. THE SOUTH STAFFORDSHIRE REGIMENT.

D E C E M B E R

1 9 1 5

WAR DIARY or INTELLIGENCE SUMMARY

Army Form C. 2118

Place	Date	Hour	Summary of Events and Information	Remarks and references to Appendices
YPRES RAMPARTS	1.XII.15		In rest billets in YPRES.	
"	"	11	Remained in billets. Lt (A) Going went sick. Command of Bn. taken over by MAJOR. R.G. RAPER.	
"	"	III — VI.	Remained in billets.	
"	"	VI	Batt'n relieved 7th Bn Border Regt. in trenches about RAILWAY WOOD. Relief commenced 6 p.m. Complete. 8 p.m.	
Railway Wood	VII		Usual shelling by own guns and retaliation by enemy during morning and afternoon. Casualties wounded 2.	
"	VIII		Heavy shelling to our North during early morning, afterwards about 5.20 AM batt'n HQrs about 6.20 AM. Usual shelling during morning & afternoon. Some enemy shelling during evening. Major H.A.J. Rocke returned last 4 today and assumed command of the Bn. Casualties N.i.l.	

WAR DIARY
INTELLIGENCE SUMMARY
(Erase heading not required.)

Army Form C. 2118

Place	Date	Hour	Summary of Events and Information	Remarks and references to Appendices
Railway Wood	9.12.15		Heavy shelling in the north again by both sides about 5 p.m. Morning quiet. In afternoon enemy shelled CAMBRIDGE ROAD incessantly. J.M. evening coys in firing line (D & A) were relieved by coys in support (B & C). Casualty one wounded gere.	
	10.12.15		Very wet all day. Ten shelling than usual by day by both sides. Capt. Stephenson joined Brigade staff to take over duties as staff captain. At 10 p.m. midnight, & at intervals throughout one hour up to dawn enemy shelled very heavily for periods of about 15 minutes each time CAMBRIDGE ROAD, F13, Railway, HELL FIRE CORNER & BATT^n H.Q.S were all shelled. Our artillery did not retaliate. All wires were broken. Casualties (KILLED) one & wounded one him. Lt G.C.R. Gleadge assumed duties of acting adjutant family gebc	
	11.12.15		Shelling by both sides during morning. CAMBRIDGE road heavily shelled about 1 p.m. & trench & dug-outs damaged. Gun gear retaliated for shelling of 10.12.15 at 10 p.m. & midnight. Casualties killed two & wounded one gere	
	12.12.15		Morning fairly quiet. The enemy shelled CAMBRIDGE road at Rear of 11.35 a.m. for about two hours & used heavy guns retaliated. Rest of the day very quiet. During bombardment of CAMBRIDGE road 2nd Lt SANDERSON, 7th BORDER REG^t was killed & 2nd Lt HYNE, 8th So Staff^d wounded. Casualties 7.35 p.m. 1 officer & 1 man wounded. The 7th Border reg^t relieved (all) killed very quiet & complete	

1875. Wt. W593/826 1,000,000 4/15 I.R.C. & A. A.D.S.S./Forms/C. 2118.

WAR DIARY or INTELLIGENCE SUMMARY

Army Form C. 2118

Place	Date	Hour	Summary of Events and Information	Remarks and references to Appendices
H 19 b	13/12/15 to 18/12/15		Batt⁰ remained in rest billets at H 19 b. Casualties 1 killed & 1 wounded	(2nd Lieut. T.M. Puddifoot (Coy) gone)
(ALWAY WOOD)	18/12/15		Batt⁰ relieved 7th BORDER REGT. The night was very quiet and relay complete at 7.15 p.m. Batt⁰ marched in 16 officers & 573 other ranks strong. Casualties nil.	
	19/12/15.		At 5 a.m. bde informed us that a gas attack was being made against French north of us. At 5.30 a.m. enemy began a very heavy bombardment. At 5.30 a.m. to 6.15 a.m. orderly Coy in F.13 (reserve trench) moved up railway to CAMBRIDGE RD to reinforce & got through with 6 men (wounded). At 5.45 a.m. all wires were cut. At 6.15 a.m. orderly from bde arrived & informed us that gas was being heavily felt in YPRES. Bombardment ceased at 8.15 a.m. 6 in. guns retaliated all the time very heavily from lde Batt⁰ HQs but the coys in fire & support trenches. They Gas was distinctly felt at Batt⁰ HQs. At 2.15 p.m. enemy commenced a heavy bombardment of our support trenches, damage was on the right of our frontage however. The evening was quiet up to 8.30 p.m. enemy reported on our left at 9 p.m. & the enemy commenced firing lachrymose shells all round Batt⁰ HQ & 11½ S & 11½ X line. This was continued all through the night & a barrage shells 10.30 p.m. gas was established. (Casualties 4 killed & 14 wounded).	
	20/12/15		Enemy continued to fire lachrymose shells 6.30 p.m. & gas was up along the Ypres on other left. At 7.15 a.m. the wind veered round to the South & shelling ceased. D coy in F.13 reinforced CAMBRIDGE RD at 11 a.m. & was withdrawn at 3 a.m.	BDC

WAR DIARY or INTELLIGENCE SUMMARY

Army Form C. 2118

Place	Date	Hour	Summary of Events and Information	Remarks and references to Appendices
Railway Wood	20.12.15		Remainder of day was quiet in firing line but intermittent shelling of Batt⁰ HQS, Railway & MENIN ROAD continued all day. Wind gradually changed up to N.W. during afternoon & Batt⁰ was warned that a gas attack might be expected. Night exceptionally quiet in firing line but Batt⁰ HQ & shelled all night with shells of every calibre including lachrymose. Casualties 8 wounded. B & C Coys in firing line were relieved by D & A Coy respectively.	
	21.12.15		Morning very quiet wet & misty. Practically no shelling by either side. At 10.58am enemy working party was observed during morning. At 11.30am an enemy machine gun was opened at no⁰ gate & S⁰ men in front of A¹ Cage??? Machine gun bombarded enemy trenches intermittently were seen to fall. Our artillery from 5pm to 7pm as a relief was suspected to be proceeding. Casualties 1 killed & 1 wounded. SEPE	
	22.12.15		A quiet day. A suspected enemy M.G. emplacement I.12.a.4.5 was shelled with success by C79 ballery & direct hits obtained. Casualties 1 man wounded at duty BOC	
	23.12.15		Morning very quiet. Our artillery shelled enemy trenches for about an hour in the afternoon and drew very little retaliation. A very wet & quiet night. Our trench mortars & m. guns were relieved by 9pm & tp m. experimentally. Casualties nil SEPE	

WAR DIARY or INTELLIGENCE SUMMARY

Army Form C. 2118

(Erase heading not required.)

Place	Date	Hour	Summary of Events and Information	Remarks and references to Appendices
Railway Wood	24/12/15		The early morning was quiet. About 10.30 a.m. A1 was heavily trench mortared + it H.W.A System very severely wounded. Remainder of day very uneventful. The battn was relieved by the 7th BORDER Regt. A very slow relief was completed at 8.25 p.m. The batln marched back to rest camp at G.17.b.4.5. Casualties 1 Officer wounded	see Appendix
Rest Camp G.17.b.4.5	25.12.15		Christmas day was celebrated as well as the circumstances would permit. The men were given a good dinner + Eng. pray. encouraged. 2nd Lt W.A. Siffer died of wounds received 24.12.15	see Appendix
	26 27 28 29 30		Batln at rest camp G.17.b.4.5 Regt. The bombers + machine gunners relieved the Border bombers + m.g. 1 man wounded during the bombers + Taube dropped four bombs in vicinity of camp. No damage done. A German Taube dropped four bombs in vicinity of camp. No damage done in our area. The batln relieved the 7th Border Regt. Railway Wood A very quick + quiet relief complete at 7.25 p.m. A very quiet night. Casualties nil	see Appendix
Railway Wood	31		A quiet day. At 11 p.m. + midnight our Artillery fired heavily for about 5 minutes to ring in the New Year. Enemy did not retaliate. At 10.15 enemy started to trench mortar H30 & Cambridge R's very heavily. Our field-guns retaliated at once + at 11.15 a.m. H.T.R. guns turned on with good effect. Our trench-mortars also retaliated with effect. (Casualties)	see Appendix

J.T.G. Banks Major
1st Battalion S. Staffordshire Regt.

Army Form C. 2118

WAR DIARY
or
INTELLIGENCE SUMMARY

(Erase heading not required.)

Instructions regarding War Diaries and Intelligence Summaries are contained in F.S. Regs. Part II. and the Staff Manual respectively. Title Pages will be prepared in manuscript.

Place	Date	Hour	Summary of Events and Information	Remarks and references to Appendices
Railway Wood	31/12/15		Enemy also used minenwerfer as well as trench mortars. Casualties 8 killed and 11 wounded.	

Sir J. Stafford's
Vol:

Miss Brown (1) T.7

Jan

17
51- Rate

WAR DIARY or INTELLIGENCE SUMMARY

Army Form C. 2118

Instructions regarding War Diaries and Intelligence Summaries are contained in F.S. Regs., Part II. and the Staff Manual respectively. Title Pages will be prepared in manuscript.

(Erase heading not required.)

Place	Date	Hour	Summary of Events and Information	Remarks and references to Appendices
RAILWAY WOOD YPRES	1/1/16	noon	Enemy did not show any activity after his heavy bombardment of the morning. A message from Bde Hdqrs for working parties was received. Our days were very busy repairing damage all night.	
SALIENT	2/1/16	6pm	After a very squally wet but uneventful night our trench mortars and field How's SOC gun commenced an organized bombardment of enemy trenches in front of our lines. About 10 mins fire of 50 rounds each of Hows opened with shrapnel on enemy communication trench, several bombs were made in enemy front line. Enemy retaliated was slight + ineffectual Casualties 1 man wounded at R.E.Pk Duty	
	3/1/16		A quiet night followed by some desultory shelling. In the morning O 3pm enemy commenced to whiz bang A1 & Camp Hoo & CAMBRIDGE RD. At 3.20 pm 2nd L/C Russy was killed in action & 2/Lt Ballow wounded by shell fire from W frontiers heavy gun gave a good amount of retaliation. Right quiet Casualties one officer killed one officer wounded 5 OR wounded 1 OR wounded at R.E.P.C	
	4/1/16		Been in fire line as usual. Relieved by NORFOLK REG't bombers + gunners relief was complete by 8 P.M. An uneventful relief day. Snipers getting busy but not having luck in the salient. Our only casualties out of the salvo to shew was 1 man killed 10 R. wound and 5 S. Rc.t. to Rly Dugouts in the evening. Battn R.H.Q goes to camp	
HILL 6/1/16		Battalion marched out of camp at 12 midday to Poperinghe Station where it entrained for St OMER arrived St OMER about 8 P.M + marched to billets at Serques Lt Col N Gorring assumed command of the batt.	

Army Form C. 2118

WAR DIARY
or
INTELLIGENCE SUMMARY
(Erase heading not required.)

Place	Date	Hour	Summary of Events and Information	Remarks and references to Appendices
Serques	7/1/18 to 31/1/18		General re-organization & recuperation effected. Two drafts received during this period. A number of men were sick about a mile from the billet. Smoke Hy, bombing, company training, Musketry, Lewis gun training etc. and was practised. Several Officers & NCO's were sent to the various Schools V.e bombing, signalling, Machine gun, to get further training.	

J.V.Gort Lt. Col.
Comdg 8th Bat. S. Staffordshire Regt

1 2 6

8th South
Staffords
17/3/15 (5)
Vol 8
for rep

WAR DIARY or INTELLIGENCE SUMMARY

Army Form C.2118

8th S Staff Coy

Place	Date	Hour	Summary of Events and Information	Remarks and references to Appendices
SERQUES	Feb 5th	5 pm	Batt⁰ carried out tug & ball-bearing in rest billets. Lt Col Going promoted to Temp Brig-General on 5th & took over command of 76th Bde. Major W.A.J. Rawlins assumed command of regiment. que.	
Rest Camp H.3.d.	6th		Batt⁰ marched out of SERQUES at 2.15 a.m. Entrained at ST OMER for POPERINGHE. Marched from there to rest camp H.3.d. Batt⁰ GODEVARSVELDE. Marched (out of bivouac) & tho rather went up to th trench some night & took over from bombers. Mg/s & specialists of 8th Batt KING'S OWN REGT. & 8th Batt KING'S OWN ROYAL REGT. Relief complete	
Trench VERBRANDEN-MOLEN	7th		Batt⁰ took over trench from KING'S OWN ROYAL REGT. Guns silent. Casualties NIL. que. by 9.15 pm. A quiet night.	
	8th		A quiet morning. At 2 pm our bombarded enemy with rifle grenades. They retaliated with grenades & whizz-bangs but artillery active from 3.30 pm to 4.15 pm. Casualties 3 wounded. Otherwise nothing.	
	9th		Trench glittering with staff officers all the morning killing by enemy snipers behind Trench 37 about 3.15 pm. 6in guns bombarded Hill 60 & the Caterpillar from 2 pm to 4 pm. Casualties 1 wounded (10th)	
			A lot of wire put out as soon as moon went down. Snipers of the enemy busy from about 8 pm to 10 pm. The enemy threw bombs into the enemy lines about 10 pm. We threw bombs from enemy Trench 33, 34. Casualties NIL. Bomber 1 wounded. was no retaliation. P.C.	

WAR DIARY or INTELLIGENCE SUMMARY

Army Form C. 2118

Place	Date	Hour	Summary of Events and Information	Remarks and references to Appendices
Verbranden -Molen Trenches.	10.2.16		A lot of shelling all day. Trenches 36, 34, 33 & Reserve Wood round Batt? H.Q.s were all shelled. Our artillery gave a lot of retaliation. About 3 p.m. our heavier engaged their batteries + silenced them. A quiet evening. Casualties killed N.O.R. wounded 7 O.R.	T.O.R. 9/RC
	11.2.16		A quieter night than usual. About 10 a.m. Ratr H.Qrs were heavily shelled by 9 crumps. Morning after that quiet. About 3 p.m. a very intense bombardment was begun with north of us. At 5 p.m. news of a german attack up north was received. At 6 p.m. we found about 70 rifle grenades in the enemy hands. There was no retaliation. A Cpl - Cumming M.R. of our 4 Coy & 4 night & artillery activity by both sides.	9/RC Cumming M.R.
	12.2.16	1 p.m. to 3.30 p.m.	A quiet morning. Enemy artillery bombarded 33, 34 + 37 (Reserve Wood) was relieved by Border R. 1 killed + 1 wounded pass bombardment. Our bombers, machine gunners + snipers were organized.	Canadian
	13.2.16		A quiet night. At 9 a.m. enemy commenced why - trench of the Ravine, trenches 33 + 34 H.E. crumps, H.E. shrapnel, gun whizz bangs was delayed motars were active the whole morning. Rifle Grenades were employed but was effective when it came. Nil + wounded 2 SRO for retaliation as well as our heavy guns.	

WAR DIARY or INTELLIGENCE SUMMARY

Army Form C. 2118

Place	Date	Hour	Summary of Events and Information	Remarks and references to Appendices
VERBRAN -DEN MOLEN TRENCHES	14/7/15	morning	There was intermittent shelling of trench mortaring the whole morning by the enemy. They appeared to be registering all over our trenches. Our artillery retaliation was not very effective.	fire
		2.45pm	Enemy commence trench mortaring the Ravine and Trench 33	fire
		3.30pm	An intense bombardment of all our trenches & RESERVE WOOD and the RAVINE commencing	fire
		4.30pm	Bombardment particularly on Ravine. Enemy artillery was getting up ammunition light from the firing line. Every trench shell was nearly then 3.5.9 + 5 in especially type	
		6pm	Our retaliation was quite ineffective	
		6pm	Two mines exploded by enemy. Our counter-mines in companies zone 80x	
		6.15	An orderly from officer i/c of this enemy advancing against Trench 33 (R Coy) fire + that 5 Coy. Shire very much crowded. CO. gave up to investigate and a duplicate message sent to Bde for reinforcements. Lt E.H. PORTER reported killed	
		6.35pm	Orderly from R Coy reports no enemy in front 33. Casualties very heavy (orderly for Stretcher to BEDFORD HOUSE two returns. The platoon of R Coy for message waters	fire
		7pm	CSM Duel R Coy reports no enemy by rail at Ravine, but that enemy is advancing up Ravine. I have got up 2 Coy of 1 Lancaster on south by second Light A Coy by all men then to get to 8 Hy round Gap.	
		7.15pm	The CO returns to trenches. No enemy push, 2 guns hit in Ravine & another Defeated afort musketry	fire

1875 Wt. W593/826 1,000,000 4/15 J.B.C. & A. A.D.S.S./Forms/C. 2118.

WAR DIARY or INTELLIGENCE SUMMARY

Army Form C. 2118

Instructions regarding War Diaries and Intelligence Summaries are contained in F. S. Regs., Part II. and the Staff Manual respectively. Title Pages will be prepared in manuscript.

(Erase heading not required.)

Place	Date	Hour	Summary of Events and Information	Remarks and references to Appendices
9.30 of cutters Hrs Mulwn Head	14/3/16	7.30pm	A light wd. Wounded evacuated + all P.A.A. & bombs sent up	
		7.35pm	1 coy 4th Lincolns under Capt LEGA RD report. They are sent to 34.S + 24 out of raynes fore.	
		8 p.m.	1 coy 7 BORDER reg't report for duty. They are sent to right end of Z line + R9	re-buried per
		8 pm	1 coy 7 BORDER reg't report for duty. He is up later	
		8 pm	A lull. Enemy reported consolidating his position right half of trench 35 to trench 37 inclusive.	
		6.11 pm	to have taken from including the BLUFF	
		11.30pm	Counter-attack launched at 8.45 pm. Enemy commences very heavy wire bombardment gere	
		11.45pm	Heavy m.g. + rifle fire opened on our trenches. But of communication with all coys	
		12.15am		
		12.30 am	Orderly communication with late gere cut + unable to establish a orderly dispatched to find + but for runner gene	
		1pm	full + unable to get Communications established with	
		1.30am	Our field guns upload firing that artillery who have informed two pars to B Coy + too to H.Q. enemy are tee bombs arrive from	gun
		1.45am	Lt SAYLY reports that he is short of bombs. Enemy are 2 bays serious casus on	

WAR DIARY or INTELLIGENCE SUMMARY

Army Form C. 2118

Place	Date	Hour	Summary of Events and Information	Remarks and references to Appendices
HERBRANDEN MOLEN	15/16		Walthew gots and hold all the demands of trench 33. A stop has been built by our bombers in trench 33, but counter attack held up for want of bombs. Bett informed. JMC	
		2 am	Lt BIRREL & our loth bombers carry up there at once set up trench 33 to deal with situation. JMC	
		3.30 am	A working party of 50 men from 7th BORDER REGT & Reserve Coys (sic) to make trench 29, 30 & 31 at 4.30 am. All quiet in our trench. JMC	
		4.10 am	Wire from 16th Bde that two was able to obtain and is to make new trench 29, 30 + 31 at 4.30 am.	
		5.30 am	Enemy's Heavy & Light Enemy has worked bombing post in 32.5 as usual 5 to 6 ravine held by LINCOLNS & BORDER REGT including lot of BIRKEL ridge. JMC	
		6.10 am	Lt Smyth of 7th BORDER down but broken knee reported stop in 33.5	
		6.15 am	Enemy resumed heavy bombardment of (RESERVE WOOD) with Crump. Our artillery gave with retaliation. JMC	
		8.25 am	Situation reported to bde genl over phone. Enemy left casualties — 6 officers and 120 men. JMC	
			Remainder of day very quiet. Enemy attacked to our front & been repulsed heavy casualties being inflicted. JMC	

WAR DIARY
or
INTELLIGENCE SUMMARY
(Erase heading not required.)

Army Form C. 2118

Place	Date	Hour	Summary of Events and Information	Remarks and references to Appendices
YPRES (BRAND) -MULLEN Trenches	15.6.16	8 pm	Bombardment by our artillery of general enemy front line commenced. JWC	
		8.30 pm	Our field guns opened fire. Nature 2x + 2.8 trenches JWC	
		8.55 pm	Our bombardment & enemy retaliation most intense JWC	
		9 pm	Counter attack launched. Lost of communication with all coys	
		9.35 pm	2nd Lt Wheatcroft our officer report that BORDER attack on south of ravine has failed but that 2nd S. STAFFORDS attack is progressing slowly.	
		9.50 pm	Lt MORGAN 7th BORDER REGT reports his attack on south of ravine has failed	
		10 pm	Two bombs arrive from 1st SPRE	
		10.15 pm	Enemy toc emma intense bombardment & open rifle + m g fire SPRE	
		10.30 pm	Rate slowed to be responsive. BORDER bombers + reinforce our trenches with them SPRE	
		10.40 pm	2nd Lt. BARLOW reports that we have been only able to reach edge of the enemy have mg in his skip with splinter of our fire, having succeeded all Lewisses began to a spot which forged to get beyond. The shape all men seemed to reach is a distance have been held by rifle + m g fire. A bright moon to prevent of any surprise rush. SPRE	

WAR DIARY or INTELLIGENCE SUMMARY

Army Form C. 2118

Place	Date	Hour	Summary of Events and Information	Remarks and references to Appendices
Neubauten - MOLEN	15/2/16	11 p.m.	Preparation made to try & rush enemy's ship when moon goes down	PMC
	16/2/16	12.56 a.m.	The dressing station struck direct hit from an 8 inch shell. About 12 men L/B. Gough RAMC + L/C Y Birrell killed. Orderlies sent for another doctor. While the wounded...	FMC
		1 am	Q Bell & Lieutenant no news from right. Pale informed of position	Sere
		3.30 am	Final plans made for assault on enemy's ship when snow gone down	Sere
		4.5 am	Schulzen bay unwilled. Intense rifle fire on my far enemy right. Two ZEPPELINS reported flying in a N-W direction	Sere
		5.40 am	Attack on enemy's ship. Council of under 2/Lt L/S ELLIOT 2nd Lt L/S Pomfret... Capt. Mac-Smith shots whets attack failed. 2/Lt ELLIOT wounded. Attack was with a view of succeeding but orders were not close enough to 2/Lt ELLIOT who died. Attack to support him. Pake informed. Casualties	Sere
		7 am	Bath relieved by 7th BORDER Sgt Riley Hoppen 40 A See Bath proceed by...busses to...camp 1+31 st	Sere

WAR DIARY
or
INTELLIGENCE SUMMARY
(Erase heading not required.)

Army Form C. 2118

Place	Date	Hour	Summary of Events and Information	Remarks and references to Appendices
H 31 d	17th to 29th Feb		Batt. reorganising in rest camp. 19th inst. Major J. HALL-BROWN 10th Sherwood Foresters was attached to batt. + assumed command. Officers casualties were replaced + Batt. brought up to war establishment of officers. One draft of 38 O R received. From 23rd to 9th the whole batt. was employed on working parties on alleviate sights for R.E. for work on new defence works. On night 28/29th during one of these working parties one officer was wounded, one O R killed + 4 O R wounded. On 29th inst. Major General PILCHER C.B. C.B. 17th Div. paraded batt. + congratulated them on their gallant work in action during 14th 15th + 16th inst. Feb	

29.2.16

(signature)
Major
Lieut Colonel
Comdg. 8th Service Bn. So. Staffs. Regt.

HEADQUARTERS,

17TH DIVISION.

Herewith report by Major W.A.J.Barker,
Commanding 8th South Staffordshire Regiment,
on Operations of 14th and 15th February.

This throws more light on subject dealt with in private letter to G.O.C. to-day.

H C Grandly Capt
for Brigadier General,
16/3/16.   Commdg. 51st Infy.Brigade.

Headquarters,

51st. Infy. Brigade.

Following is report on attack made by enemy on night of 14th & 15th. Having been sent to hospital on night of 17th, I was unable to render a full report before.

1. Battalion was occupying trenches 33, 34, 35, 36, 37 (VERBANDEN MOLEN Area). Total length about 800 yards.
These trenches, with exception of 37, had supporting trenches in rear varying from 50 to 100 yards distance.
Behind these supporting trenches was a reserve trench in very indifferent condition with good bombing stops or strong points at the junction of communicating trenches.
In front of the fire trenches, the barb wiring was particularly bad and in some places was non-existant.
It had however been worked on by the Battalion during its 7 days occupation.
There was a considerable amount of barbed wire in front of support and reserve line.
Battalion bombers and machine gunners had been relieved by a similar number of the 7th BORDER REGIMENT bombers and machine gunners on the preceding night.
There was also 1 machine gun belonging to 7th LINCOLN Regt. in trench 34 and 1 in trench 33 S.
Total strength of Battalion (including BORDER specialists) was 683.

2. **Preliminary Bombardment**
The enemy commenced trench mortaring (apparently registering) about 2-45 p.m.
At 3-30 p.m. an intense bombardment of all our trenches, RESERVE Wood, The Ravine was started.
It was maintained till about 6 p.m., being especially heavy from 4-30 p.m. onwards.
At about 6 p.m. 2 mines were distinctly heard and felt to have been blown.
These did not appear to be very close and I thought at the time that they were probably in front of the SHERWOODS trenches.

3. **Communication**
(a) Early in the bombardment, communication by wire was broken with trenches 33, 34, & 35.
Later those with 36 & 37 went and in spite of every effort to re-establish them, which was occasionally successful for a few minutes all communications had to be carried on by runners.
(b) The line to Brigade was cut about 5-45 p.m.
An indirect line was temporarily established via the regiment on our left and the 50th Division who communicated with 51st Brigade.
At 5-27 p.m. I was successful in getting a message through to Brigade by this means, stating all other communications had been severed and that the bombardment was still very intense.
In the meantime, insspite of every effort of the forward observing officer, the wires communicating with artillery had gone.

Conditions prior to attack.
1. By about 5-45 p.m. the front trenches, 33, 34 and part of 35 had been so knocked about by trench mortars as to be almost unrecognisable.

2.

The supporting trenches to these had been even more severely damaged.

The ground in rear, especially round Battalion Headquarters, had been very heavily bombarded with heavy artillery.

Trees were lying about in all directions. Certain communication trenches which had originally had over-head cover had been blown in and were quite impassable.

Communicating trenches leading from the rear to the front were in many cases destroyed in parts.

Some of the bombing stops in the reserve line were blown in and barbed wired had been blown into the trenches.

A heavy smoke was hanging over trenches 33, 34 & 35 making it impossible to view the situation in front.

This was so unpleasant that Lieut. Dixon left the trenches and went in front to see if enemy were massing for attack.

The trenches on left (36 & 37) were not so severely dealt with.

The casualties had been very severe.

The Attack

At a little after 6 p.m. the enemy left their trenches and attempted to cross over.

They were met by rapid fire and machine gun fire from guns in trenches 33 s. & 35.

The gun in 34 had been put out of action during the bombardment.

They were unable to make a lodgement in any part of the line with the exception of the right of 33.

In the first instance they were ejected by the men in this part of the line who under an N.C.O. made an immediate counter-attack with bombs. What happened here afterwards I am unable to say as these men all appear to have been Killed.

Opposite trench 34 at a point where the German trenches are extremely close, the enemy made an attempt to dash across, were met with a fusilade of bombs and retired.

Messages during attack

Immediately attack was launched (about 6-10 p.m.) the O.C. trench 33 sent a runner down informing me of the fact.

I forwarded this information via 50th Division at 6-15 p.m. This was as soon as it could be written out

At the same time another message was sent by runner to Brigade with same information and asking for reinforcements A duplicate of this message was sent by another runner at 6-20 p.m.

I considered that in view of the fact that our casualties had been very severe and the line to be held was long, these reinforcements were very necessary.

I immediately took all available men from Headquarters and proceeded to front trenches. On arrival in trench 35 I was informed 35, 36 & 37 were intact. Information about 34 & 33 was conflicting.

I proceeded along these trenches and having got near the head of ravine, met a party of Germans bombing down our trench.

Unluckily I was hit by one of the bombs.

We immiately immediately formed a stop and sent for bombs and bombers to be concentrated at this point.

I returned to Battalion Headquarters about 7-15 p.m. and immediately sent a detailed report.

During my absence the Adjutant had forwarded 2 other messages, giving the situation as it was reported to him by various runners and asking for stretcher bearers.

3.

Reinforcements

At 7-30 p.m. a Company of LINCOLNS arrived as reinforcements and at 8 p.m. a Company of BORDERS.

Counter-Attacks

At 11-30 p.m. a counter-attack was delivered along trench 33, the Company of the LINCOLNS taking part, with 32 as their objective. This Company launched its attack from 32 S. This attack was unsuccessful.

During remainder of night all troops were employed in rebuilding the firing line.

At 9 p.m. the following day another counter-attack was launched.

That from the South side of the ravine was unsuccessful. That along trench 33 succeeded in recovering several bays from the enemy. An attempt was made by Lieut. Elliott to make a surprise attack outside the trench. He was wounded whilst doing so and did not succeed. During the night a shell dropped on our dressing staion and killed all the wounded in it.

Owing to the fact that the ground between our supporting line and fire trenches was wired, counter-attacks had to proceed along communicating trenches which in places were non-existant.

16-3-16.

W.J. Barker
Major,
Comdg. 8th South Staffords Regt.

Dear General Pilcher,

In answer to the two questions you asked me

(1) How it was the enemy was able to come out of his trenches in daylight without being observed or fired at by Infantry or Machine Guns, and

(2) The time taken by Battalion Commanders and Brigadiers to find out what was going on on their fronts.

I enclose you a statement which I think will do something towards clearing up the matter

It was not daylight when the Germans attached, but was dark - at 6 p.m. The enemy were observed, and were fired upon by all Infantry & Machine Guns still capable of doing so.

I feel certain that the Infantry attack did not take place until after 6 p.m., and not at 5.45 p.m. as stated. Major Barker commanding the South Staffords heard at his Headquarters at 6.15 p.m. by means of a runner that the German Infantry were attacking. This report was sent to Brigade Headquarters by a runner, and a duplicate message was sent through the 50th. Division.

I at once sent him up reinforcements. / Co Lincoln

Major Barker went up to his front trench himself, where the men were carrying on rapid fire. The Machine gun in 35 was in action, as was also the Machine Gun of the 7th. Lincolns in 33 S. - the Machine Gun in 34 had been buried by shells.

Major Barker is certain that he heard two mines, and believes that he heard a third.

The fire trenches were in ruins, and the smoke along them was so dense from the bombardment, that one of his officers went through it to find out if there were any Germans behind.

From all enquiries I have been able to make it would appear that the 8 officers and 162 men which the Sherwood Forresters had in their front trenches were all killed or buried alive by mines and heavy Trench Mortars.

Lieut. Tollemache, of the Sherwood Forresters, who was in a front trench (29) says he was buried for three or four hours, and was then helped out by Germans. Lieut. Millward, who is also a prisoner and has also written, says he was buried in trench 30 and that he first came to his senses in a German dressing station.

The Machine Gun in 33.S was buried by a shell, was got out and was buried again the next morning. The gun in 34 was buried, but dug out and again came into action. The machine gun in the LOOP TRENCH was blown up by a mine. The machine gun in the BLUFF TUNNEL was so damaged that it could not be used. The machine gun in 32.S did excellent work until its piston rod broke. The machine gun in 31.S did good work when the enemy advanced about 6 p.m. The machine gun in 30.R was buried by a shell. The gun in 35 opened fire about 6 p.m. All these guns were Lewis Guns.

To return to the Sherwood Forresters, Lt. Nichols, 10th. Sherwood Forresters has reported as follows :-

He was in 31.S throughout the bombardment, which started at 3.20 p.m., and was very severe. The smoke was so thick that the front trenches, which were from 1/200 yards in front, were not visible. A little before this, thinking he might be wanted in the front 32 trench, he pushed up HEDGE ROW and found nobody alive in it - they were all killed or buried.

About 5.50 p.m. a mine blew up either in 29 or 30.

Soon after this he saw German infantry jumping over their trenches, which are only 20/30 yards away. He opened a rapid fire with his men, and also threw the bombs from 2 boxes which he had brought up; then being attacked from both sides as well as from the front he retired from 32 to 32 support.

Practically all the Sherwood Forresters in the support trenches pushed forward, as Lieut. Nichols did, to the fire trenches at about the time the Germans attacked. The Battalion bombers, who were in Reserve Wood, also hurried up to the fight, and only one platoon was left in reserve.

The Sherwood Forresters had by this time lost about 330 men and all their best officers, and the remainder were considerably shaken. The strength of the Battalion in the trenches was only about 550.

It is a pity that Col. Banbury who was suffering from the effects of gas at YPRES was on leave in England - Major Keowan was commanding the Battalion.

The Germans at about 6 p.m. put a barrage behind the Sherwood Forresters trenches, and it was very difficult to get along them or from them to Battalion Headquarters; but be that as it may he did not receive information about what had happened until 7 p.m., but previous to this he had informed Brigade Headquarters that a violent bombardment was taking place and had asked for Artillery support.

Battalion Headquarters are about half a mile from the front line.

At about 7 p.m. he reported the situation to the Brigade. At about 7/pm. I sent one of my Staff to Battalion Headquarters to endeavour to find out what was going on and by the time he returned I had organised the counter attack which took place under Col. Norrington.

SECRET

17/3/16.

With reference to the copy of the letter sent by General Fanshawe to the 2nd. Army in answer to several questions I should like to make a few remarks with regard to para. 6 in which it is said that the Division should have issued definite orders stating the spheres of operations for which the 51st. and 52nd. Brigades were each responsible, and the troops placed at their disposal.

Col. Marindin saw General Fell in the morning, and on his return to Divisional Headquarters, and after consultation with me, a telegram was despatched at 2.20 p.m. saying that the Dorsets were placed under Gen. Fell for the purpose of carrying out the counter attack on the BLUFF. This telegram is given on page 15 of the message sent on 14/2/16. General Fell was also told on the telephone that all operations North of the Canal were under him. General Fell has never questioned receiving this order.

Para. 3 of Operation Order No.38 issued on the 15th. and on my file 2 pages after page 15, also deals with this point.

Brigadier General Fell, to whom I have shown the Corps Commander's remarks, says that he knows the ground in question intimately and that in his opinion it was quite possible for the 6th. Dorsets, who should have been ready to march, to have reached the neighbourhood of the BLUFF in time to deliver the attack at 9 p.m., with an hour to spare. I consider that a Battalion should easily reach the BLUFF from DICKEBUSCH in 3 hours.

The Officer Commanding Dorsets sent a "priority" message from WOODCOTE HOUSE at 4.50 p.m. ordering his battalion down.

I have pointed out to Brigadier General Fell that

I consider that he should have sent a Staff Officer to make certain that the Dorsets would be in position at the hour the attack was ordered. His reply is that he presumed that if the Officer Commanding Dorsets found it impracticable to carry out what he himself considered to be a possible order he should have informed him of the fact. If this had been done it would not have been difficult to have postponed the hour for the counter attack.

XVI (5) VIII

8th South
Staffs
Vol. 9
March 1916

T.9

Army Form C. 2118

WAR DIARY
or
INTELLIGENCE SUMMARY
(Erase heading not required.)

Instructions regarding War Diaries and Intelligence Summaries are contained in F. S. Regs., Part II. and the Staff Manual respectively. Title Pages will be prepared in manuscript.

Place	Date	Hour	Summary of Events and Information	Remarks and references to Appendices
H.31.D	1st March	5 pm	Battn march out of camp at H.31.D to R.E Camp at DICKEBUSCH (A.27.c.50) Major R.G Raper returns from sick leave and assumes duties of 2nd in command.	RGR
	"	7 pm	All settled in to Billets – Dispositions & Orders for an immediate move issued.	RGR
	2nd March			
		4.30 am	Battn stand to. Attack launched by 46th B.S against THE BLUFF and trenches captured by the enemy on 14th Feb. last. Intense artillery bombardment.	RGR
		8 am	News received that attack entirely successful. In addition to regaining all lost trenches we have captured the BEAN (a German trench in front of Trench 31) about 200 prisoners taken. Battn has Breakfast.	RGR
		8.55 am	Bde orders 2 Coys to proceed at once to report to 46430B in KINGSWAY DUGOUTS C & D Coys immediately despatched under Major RAPER – Coys arrive safely and employed as carrying parties striking very active on both sides.	RGR
		2.25 pm	Remaining 2 Coys, A & B, proceed to KINGSWAY DUGOUTS under Major Hall (Brown share position of one more and mine to come down from trenches)	RGR
		6.10 pm	D Coy sent to reinforce 1st Gordons & Rotterdams to take over 33 R A Coy in reserve B & C Coys on carrying fatigues	RGR, RGR

Army Form C. 2118

WAR DIARY
OF
INTELLIGENCE SUMMARY
(Erase heading not required.)

Instructions regarding War Diaries and Intelligence Summaries are contained in F. S. Regs., Part II. and the Staff Manual respectively. Title Pages will be prepared in manuscript.

Place	Date	Hour	Summary of Events and Information	Remarks and references to Appendices
KINGSWAY DUGOUTS		6.50 p.m.	Capt: WOOD "D" Coy reports unfavourable to get thro' barrage without heavy loss. Ordered to take cover & await opportunity of getting thro'.	RGR
		7.30	"A" Coy sent to reinforce KINGS OWN. Capt BURNET reports he has taken over the BEAN. Heavy artillery bombardment continues on both sides. B & C Coys employees carrying up sandbags. Stroke Jackson & Johnson Works ----- mm	RSR
	3 Mar.		Artillery bombardment increases in intensity.	RSR
		12.30 a.m.	25 men dispatches for mg line with water.	RSR
		6.30 a.m.	2 parties of 50 men each from B & C Coys sent with ammunition & water to front line.	RSR
		8 a.m.	Major RAPER proceeds to firing line to visit A & D Coys - Ration parties dispatched to these Coys.	RSR
		11.30	Major RAPER returns & reports Ration parties have reached A & D Coys safely. That A Coy is consolidating the BEAN. That the enemy during the night made some ½ hearted attempts to come across in front of the BEAN but were easily repulsed by our rapid fire.	RSR
		2 p.m.	B & C Coys continue work on carrying parties.	RGR
		4 p.m.	Orders received that Battn will be relieved to-night.	RGR
			B & C Coys relieved by K.O.S.L.I. in KINGSWAY DUGOUTS & proceed to Camp H. 31. D.	RSR
			CASUALTIES. WOUNDED - 2nd Lieut Pann, Jackson & Johnson 19 men MISSING (wherein killed) 3 men	RGR

1875. Wt. W593/826 1,000,000 4/15 J.B.C. & A. A.D.S.S./Forms/C. 2118.

Army Form C. 2118

WAR DIARY
or
INTELLIGENCE SUMMARY
(Erase heading not required.)

Instructions regarding War Diaries and Intelligence Summaries are contained in F. S. Regs., Part II. and the Staff Manual respectively. Title Pages will be prepared in manuscript.

Place	Date	Hour	Summary of Events and Information	Remarks and references to Appendices
H. 31. D	4 Mar		A & D Coys returned in the early hours of the morning to Bgd Coy & proceeded to Camp H 31 D	R.G.L.
	5 "		Battn: resting	R.G.L.
			Orders received to move to rest camps near BAILLEUL on 6th inst	R.G.L.
			Draft of 1 Officer & 1 other rank received	
	6 "	9.45	Batt: marched out of Camp H 31 D & proceeded via RENINGHELST WESTOUTRE CROIX DE POPERINGHE & BAILLEUL to Billets near LA CRECHE arriving about 2 p.m.	R.G.L.
			Remainder of day spent in settling into billets.	
			Draft of 50 received	R.G.L.
STEENTJE near LA CRECHE	7 "		BATTN employed in clearing up & interior economy	R.G.L.
			Orders received that Batt: must be prepared to move at short notice within 2 hrs of receiving instructions. Capt G. S. sent to reconnoitre route to LA CRECHE	R.G.L.
	8		Major General Pulteney called & expressed to the Comdg Officer his appreciation of the behaviour of the Batt:n on the 14th Feb. He stated that from plans found in the German trench captured on 2nd March it appeared that the Germans intended to take a good deal more of the line than they actually succeeded in doing. That they intended not only to take the trenches held by the Batt:n but also the support line as well. That owing to the way this Batt:n held on to its trenches the enemy's plans were frustrated and that no Battn in the Div:n had done better than the 8th S. Staffords. The Major Gen: also stated that the G.O.C. 17th Bde had expressed to him his	

1875 Wt. W593/826 1,000,000 4/15 J.B.C. & A. A.D.S.S./Forms/C.2118.

WAR DIARY or **INTELLIGENCE SUMMARY**

Army Form C. 2118

Instructions regarding War Diaries and Intelligence Summaries are contained in F. S. Regs., Part II. and the Staff Manual respectively. Title Pages will be prepared in manuscript.

(Erase heading not required.)

Place	Date	Hour	Summary of Events and Information	Remarks and references to Appendices
			great appreciation of the work of the Batt" in the action on the 2nd & 3rd of March	R.G.R.
	11 March		Major W.A.J. BARKER returned from Hospital & resumed command of the Batt"	R.G.R.
	13 "		Major HALL BROWN 10th Sherwood Foresters returned to his own Batt"	R.G.R.
	14 "		Batt" inspected by Corps Commander	R.G.R.
	16 "		Party of Officers & NCOs proceeded to ARMENTIERES to inspect trenches 40, 41, 42 & 43. S.E of ARMENTIERES which the Batt" will take over from the 8th Lincolnshire Regt. on 19th inst	R.G.R.
	17 "		Another party of Officers + NCOs visited the above trenches	R.G.R.
	18 "		Batt" marched out of STEENTJE at 6.45 a.m arriving at ARMENTIERES at 9.30 a.m where it went into billets – Batt" H.dqrs 35 RUE NATIONALE. Batt" in Div: Reserve and temporarily attached to 64th Bde 21st Div"	R.G.R.
	19	6.45 a.m	Orders received from 64th Bde to stand by & be ready to move at moments notice. Bombardment of trenches N of ARMENTIERES by enemy artillery.	R.G.R.
		8.30 a.m	orders cancelled	R.G.R.
		6.30 p.m	2nd Coy stands for trenches tomorrow at intervals by the remaining Coys. Disposition of Batt" as tomorrow - "B" Coy holds trenches 40 & 71 including MUSHROOM. "C" Coy holds trenches 72 & 73 + immediate support line. "A" Coy holds right of subsid? line with 1 platoon in FIVE DUGOUTS. D Coy HdQrs left of subs? line with two 1 officer + 40 men in PORT EGAL REDOUBT. Relief complete at 9.25 p.m	R.G.R.
	20	10 a.m	Major Genl Pilcher + Brig: Genl Bell go round trenches. Whilst in trench 70, Capt Graham, acting Bde Bombing officer, who accompanied the Generals was shot thro' the head by enemy sniper & dies immediately	R.G.R.

WAR DIARY or INTELLIGENCE SUMMARY

Army Form C. 2118

(Erase heading not required.)

Place	Date	Hour	Summary of Events and Information	Remarks and references to Appendices
ARMENTIERES	20 Mar		Returned into new Batt. H.dqrs at bottom of Rue EGAL AVENUE	RGR
	21 "		2 Officers represented Batt. at funeral of Capt. Graham in Cemetery at ARMENTIERES	RGR
	22 "	10 a.m	Enemy whizz bangs behind right of 42 & 40. Sent Fell inspected subord'y line	RGR
	23		Section "B" Coy relieved by "A" Coy. "C" Coy by "D" Coy.	RGR
	24		Heavy shower. Sent Fell inspected front line trenches in morning. CASUALTIES 1 man killed & 1 wounded	RGR
	25		Lt Col Morrington & Lt Borders went round trenches with Major Barker	RGR
	26	3 pm	Enemy sent 6 crumps into left of subord'y line & inflicted 13 casualties in C Coy all wounded	RGR
			Relieved by 4th Borders. Relief complete 9.25 p.m.	RGR
			Batt. went into billets in ARMENTIERES - B.ttdqrs 66 Rue SADI CARNOT	RGR
	27		Authority received from Brigade for Majr W A J Barker to wear the badges of Lt Col & 2nd G.R.	RGR
			Corbridge (Adj.) throws of captain	RGR
			Batt. employed in cleaning up & internal economy	RGR
	28 & 29 & 31		Batt. furnishing working parties by day & night for work in trenches	RGR
	30/31		CASUALTIES 1 killed 14 wounded	RGR

Lieut. Colonel.
Comdg. 8th Service Bn. So. Staffs. Regt.

8 S Staffs

Army Form C. 2118
Vol. 10

WAR DIARY or INTELLIGENCE SUMMARY

XVII

(Erase heading not required.)

Instructions regarding War Diaries and Intelligence Summaries are contained in F.S. Regs., Part II. and the Staff Manual respectively. Title Pages will be prepared in manuscript.

Place	Date	Hour	Summary of Events and Information	Remarks and references to Appendices
ARMENTIERES	1st April 1916		Batt: in billets - furnishing working parties for trenches by day & night. Party of officers reconnoitred mar country route to trenches	R.Y.R.
			The following are extracts from "London Gazette" of 30th ult:-	
			Ddg Temp Major W. A. J. BARKER 8th Batt. South Staffs Regt. Whilst organising a counter attack he was wounded in four places by a bomb, but continued to command his Batt: throughout the 3 following days till it was relieved." — Companion of Distinguished Service Order	R.Y.R.
			Award of Military Cross	
			"Temp. Lieut: J.E. DIXON 8th Batt. South Staffs Regt. When his trench had been very heavily shelled for 2 hours, and he heard that the enemy were advancing on his right, he went over the parapet and drew us forward, under heavy rifle fire, to see if they were preparing for an attack on his own trench. He was badly wounded."	R.Y.R. T.O
			Award of Distinguished Conduct Medal	
			8/13211 Act⁰. Co. Sgt. Major. H. S. BIRD 8th Batt. S. Staffs Regt. - When the enemy makes an isolated trench he saves the situation by collecting bombs and supervising the erection of stops and barbed wire. During the whole operation he set a splendid example to his Company.	R.Y.R.
			8/13804 L. Cpl. S. NEAL 8th Batt. S. Staffs Regt. He continued to throw bombs during 2 nights after being wounded and refused to leave the trenches till his Batt: was relieved. Though only 19 years of age, this young N.C.O has set a splendid example to his men.	R.Y.R

Army Form C. 2118

WAR DIARY
or
INTELLIGENCE SUMMARY
(Erase heading not required.)

Instructions regarding War Diaries and Intelligence Summaries are contained in F. S. Regs., Part II. and the Staff Manual respectively. Title Pages will be prepared in manuscript.

Place	Date	Hour	Summary of Events and Information	Remarks and references to Appendices
ARMENTIERES	1st April 1916		"S/14689 L. Cpl W. RAWLEY 8 Batt. S. Staff Regt. On return from a reconnaissance he found that one man of his party was missing. He at once went out again, found the man badly wounded, and carried him back under direct machine gun fire. On this occasion he displayed great bravery."	Ry R
	2nd Apl	10.30 am	Batt. attended Flammenwerfer Demonstration at Brit Grenade School.	Ry R
		4 pm	2nd Lt "BAKER" "B" coy wounded whilst going up with Ry. with working party - wound caused by the discharge of rifle of Pte Milne.	
TRENCHES 70.41.72.73.	3rd Apl		Relieved 7th Border Regt in trenches 70.71.72.73. Lead	
		9.12 pm	Relief complete	
	4 "	10.30 am	Major Genl. Pinchin went round front line. Work continued on strengthening 'defended localities' & clearing undefended localities. Considerable enemy sniping but his M.G fire at night.	RSR
	5		Boards placed in front line to indicate exact positions of undefended trenches for guidance of artillery.	RSR
	6	4 to 5 pm	16 Prs registered on undefended localities. No damage done to trenches. Quiet day. Patrols out at night - located enemy listening post. Enemy shelled Regimental Dumps & subsidy line with thirty bombs - no damage - work proceeding on front line. Patrols out at night. CASUALTY - 2-Lt B Konga wounded slightly	Ry R Ry R Ry R Ry R

WAR DIARY or INTELLIGENCE SUMMARY

Army Form C. 2118

Place	Date	Hour	Summary of Events and Information	Remarks and references to Appendices
ARMENTIERES	7th Apl	1.5 pm	Enemy shelled subsid line near Bratidage + Bn Dumps. so much any damage. Information received that 2 Germans had got thro' the line held by the Bde on our immediate right - chain of sentries posted behind front line + patrols put on + all precautionary measures taken. Lt Comm: Burnett & Lt E Brown, R N R attached to Bratidage for 24 hours. Sniping rather less - Our own snipers appear to have got the situation well in hand. 4 Australian Regt relieve on our Bde Right. CASUALTIES - 2nd Lt J. E Brown wounded. Other ranks - 1 killed 1 wounded	RyR RyR RyR RyR RyR RyR RyR
	8 Apl		Work on front line continued. Quiet day. Lt "Com" Burnett departed. Additional working parties put on to demolish Saps D + 30 work on strenger breastworks on either side - Quiet day. Our patrols + wiring parties out at night as usual. CASUALTIES - 2 wounded	RyR
	9 "			
	10 "		Additional work parties on Sap D. Enemy whizz bangz supports behind that front + knocked in Officers Kitchen - also knocked in part of Pot Egal Ave near support line. Put some booby bears on left subsids. Enemy whizz banged in front of gap in afternoon - no damage. line but did no damage. CASUALTIES - 1 wounded	RyR RyR

WAR DIARY
or
INTELLIGENCE SUMMARY
(Erase heading not required.)

Army Form C. 2118

Place	Date	Hour	Summary of Events and Information	Remarks and references to Appendices
ARMENTIERES	11 Apr.	12.20 p.m.	Corps Commander inspected front line & appears satisfied with the work done.	Appx
			2 Australian Officers with 4 N.C.Os attached for instruction	Appx
			Quiet day - rain interfered with work	Appx
		5.55 p.m.	Relieved by 7 Border Regt. Relief Complete	
	12 Apl.		Battn in Rest billets - occupied in cleaning up	P & R
		8 p.m.	2nd Corps wire received stopping all leave after 17th inst.	Appx B
		9 p.m.	Bde wire received with instructions to recall all officers from leave by 18th inst.	Appx B
	13 Apl.	10.15 a.m.	Battn furnishing working parties by day & night to work in trenches	Appx B
			Brig. Gen! Ball wounded & stopped with measles - CASUALTIES WOUNDED 2	Appx B
	16 "		2i/c in command & 2 Coy Commanders visit trenches " 1	Appx B
	18 "		Major Porter & Capt	Appx B
	X 17		1st Lt Blomfield returned to Battn from Hospital	Appx B

TOTAL CASUALTIES for tour – WOUNDED 2 officers
Other Ranks KILLED 2
WOUNDED 6
___
10

6th N. Staffs all? for experience

WAR DIARY
or
INTELLIGENCE SUMMARY
(Erase heading not required.)

Army Form C. 2118

Place	Date	Hour	Summary of Events and Information	Remarks and references to Appendices
ARMENTIERES	19 April		Relieved 7th Border Regt in trenches 70, 71, 72 & 73 Relief complete 9.10 p.m.	P4R
	20 "		Quiet day. Some shelling of FIVE DUGOUTS & PETIT PORT EGAL — CASUALTIES	R4R
	21 "		GOOD FRIDAY — Enemy shells 93.5. & put some shrapnel over entrench'd line — Major Porter and Capt Slocock of 6th Staffs on completion of tour with Batt Scouts	24R
	22		2d Lt Tunney joins Batt — Work continuing on Defences localisation & clearing fields of fire. Quiet throughout day. CASUALTIES WOUNDED . 4	P4R P4R
	23	EASTER DAY	Intermittent shelling all day on Supports & subsid'y line CASUALTIES KILLED 1 WOUNDED 1	24R
	24		Enemy aeroplane brought down by anti-aircraft gun at back of our lines — it fell in NIEPPE — Pilot & observer both killed. Intermittent shelling all day but very little damage done. Major Gen'l Pilcher visited round trenches and expressed himself very satisfied with work done. Moved into new HQrs in ENGLISH ST. CASUALTIES WOUNDED 1	R4R
	25		Considerable shelling at intermediate Brewing Day " "	
	26	2.15 a.m	2 Coys in subsid'y line practise reinforcing support line over the open. Arti'y & Corps Arti'y opened on enemy at 3 p.m. Enemy retaliated principally on S.E. Bt on our left. Hd put shr'p bursts on our supports & also got a direct hit on A Coy HQrs in Trench 70. Enemy opened heavy bombardment on 52 Bde trenches at 7.30 p.m. A small enemy raid was partly penetrated into West Yorks trenches but were driven out leaving 1 killed CASUALTIES WOUNDED 3 ACCIDENTALLY KILLED 1	24R

WAR DIARY or INTELLIGENCE SUMMARY

Army Form C. 2118

Place	Date	Hour	Summary of Events and Information	Remarks and references to Appendices
TRENCHES 40-71-72-73	27 Apl	10am	Enemy shelled subsid^y line but did little damage. Machine guns very active in evening from enemy. Relieved by 4 Bedfd^s Reg^t - Relief complete 9.36 p.m. CASUALTIES. WOUNDED. 4.	AAR
			KILLED 1	AAR
			WOUNDED 25	
			ACCIDENTALLY KILLED 1	
			TOTAL CASUALTIES for tour 27	
ARMENTIERES	28 Apl		Battⁿ in Rest Billets - occupied in cleaning + interior economy	AAR
	29.30		Battⁿ occupied in furnishing working parties by day + night for the trenches	AAR

Hugh Sadler
Lieut. Colonel,
Comdg. 8th Service Bn. So. Staff^s Reg^t.

WAR DIARY or INTELLIGENCE SUMMARY

Army Form C. 2118

XVII S. Staffs
Vol III

Place	Date	Hour	Summary of Events and Information	Remarks and references to Appendices
ARMENTIERES	1st MAY to 5 MAY		Batt'n in red billets. Furnishing working parties for trenches by day & night	R&R
			CASUALTIES WOUNDED 3 ※ 5 off.	R&R / R&R
Trenches 71, 72, 73, 74	5th		Relieve 7th Border Regt in trenches – Relief complete 12 a.m. Just before starting from Armentières report received that enemy heavily bombarding our front line at 9.10 p.m. Gas alarm sounded – 9.30 pm received orders to carry on relief as arranged. Coys proceeded to trenches. Enemy bombarded Railway & Brickery C.T. – No gas encountered but gas shells. Bombardment lifted from our trenches & heavy bombardment started on Australian Brig.R on our right when enemy carried out Bangalore raid. All quiet on our front at 11 p.m.	R&R
	6th		Lt Col W.A.J. BARKER proceed to ENGLAND on leave. Major R.G. RAPER assumed command of Bat'n.	R&R
			C.O. & 2 Coy Commanders N.Z. Rifle Brigade (Canterbury Bn) attached for 24 hrs for experience. Quiet day. Work proceeding on Defended localities & Sakes E & C. CASUALTIES WOUNDED 6	R&R
	7th		Enemy shelled head of PORT EGAL AVE causing 5 casualties. In afternoon enemy shell made breach in D Gap. Work proceeding on defended localities &c – Wiring parties from both Coys wiring at night. Attached officers left in morning. CASUALTIES WOUNDED 10	R&/12
	8th		Enemy whizz banged right subsid'y line in morning. Right subsid'y line in afternoon. Gen'l FELL & Maj. BEN PILCHER both trenches in morning. Garrison of PORT EGAL REDOUBT working on PORT EGAL AVE at night, other work proceeding as above. CASUALTIES WOUNDED 1	R&/11
				T.11

Army Form C. 2118

WAR DIARY
or
INTELLIGENCE SUMMARY
(Erase heading not required.)

Instructions regarding War Diaries and Intelligence Summaries are contained in F. S. Regs., Part II. and the Staff Manual respectively. Title Pages will be prepared in manuscript.

Place	Date	Hour	Summary of Events and Information	Remarks and references to Appendices
TRENCHES T.17.3.74	9th		Quiet day - B Coy relieves A & C Coy relieved D in firing line - work in front line continuing. Wiring parties out at night - Patrol sent out from C Coy discovered enemy working party opposite left of E Gap - M.G. turned on inflicted 3 certain casualties. CASUALTIES Nil	R.y.R
	10th		C.O. & officer 1st Auckland Bn (NZ) attaches for experience. Quiet day - work proceeding as usual. Increase in M.G. & Rifle fire at night - Patrol suspected. Patrol sent out from B Coy reported all quiet in enemy trenches. CASUALTIES Nil	R.y.R
	11th		Enemy Shugs bursed 43.S. causing casualties. Attd NZ officers left in morning. Enemy shot down one of our aeroplanes with M.G. fire in afternoon - machine came down near LILLE POST. Pilot killed observer wounded. Patrol sent out from C Coy up to 15 enemy wire & discovered new M.G. emplacement completed opposite Lft of E Gap. Work proceeding as usual. Wiring parties out at night. CASUALTIES KILLED 1.	R.y.R
	12th		Enemy put 4 salvoes of "coal boxes" on left of redoubt line but did no damage. Officers from 1st Auck: Bn came to inspect trenches - Wind blowing from E. special precaution taken against gas attack. Bn relieved by 3rd N.Z. & Rifle Bn activity at night. CASUALTIES KILLED 1 WOUNDED 3	R.y.R
	13th		2 i/c command of 1st Auck Bn & other officers from came to inspect trenches & to commence taking over. Returned at night by 1st Auckland Bn N.Z. Relief complete 10.15 S.m CASUALTIES WOUNDED 3	R.y.R

1875 Wt. W593/826 1,000,000 4/15 J.B.C. & A. A.D.S.S./Forms/C. 2118.

WAR DIARY
or
INTELLIGENCE SUMMARY

Army Form C. 2118

Instructions regarding War Diaries and Intelligence Summaries are contained in F.S. Regs., Part II. and the Staff Manual respectively. Title Pages will be prepared in manuscript.

Place	Date	Hour	Summary of Events and Information	Remarks and references to Appendices
ARMENTIERES	May 14		Batt:n in Rest billets	
		10.55 p.m.	Batt:n started march to training area. Arrived ESTAIRES 2.30 a.m. & went into billets	
	15	2.15 p.m.	Batt:n marched to MORBECQUE (near HAZEBROUCK) arriving 7.30 p.m. & went into billets - one man fell out on march	
	16	10.25 a.m.	Marched to WARDRECQUES arriving about 5.p.m. Joined here by Capt: IRWIN from 10th Bn who has been posted to this Batt:	
	17	10.20 a.m.	Marches via ARQUES & STONER to NORTBECOURT where Batt: went into billets for course of training	
	18		Batt:n resting. C.O. & Coy Commanders reconnoitred training area. Brig. Gen:l Zell ordered & handed C.O. following special order to publication. "The Brigadier congratulates the 8th South Stafford's Regt on their excellent marching - only one man with the Batt: fell out and as the Batt: marched straight from the trenches without any real rest or dinner, the Brigadier considers the Batt:n has every right to be proud of themselves"	
	19		Company training under Coy Commanders - Lt Col W.A.J. BARKER returned from leave & resumed command of the Batt:	
	20		Company training. Musketry on Ranges	

1875 Wt. W593/826 1,000,000 4/15 J.B.C. & A. A.D.S.S./Forms/C. 2118.

Army Form C. 2118

WAR DIARY
or
INTELLIGENCE SUMMARY

(Erase heading not required.)

Instructions regarding War Diaries and Intelligence Summaries are contained in F.S. Regs., Part II. and the Staff Manual respectively. Title Pages will be prepared in manuscript.

Place	Date	Hour	Summary of Events and Information	Remarks and references to Appendices
NORTBECOURT	May 21	10 A.M.	Batt: Church Parade	R&R
		2.30 pm	C.O. 2nd i/c & Adjt attended Bde Staff ride under Genl FELL	R&R
	22		Company training & night operations	R&R
	23	3 p.m.	Batt: Practised attack on GRAND DIFQUES	R.3.12
	24	3 a.m.	Batt: Practised attack from trenches against trenches (Capt P.P.Burnell sick & struck off strength)	R&R
	25	7.30 a.m.	Batt: training	R&R
	26		Brigade training – practice attack on GRAND DIFQUES.	R&R
	27		Coys at musketry on Ranges - Batt: inoculates.	R&R
	28		(Sunday) Batt: resting	
	29		Coy training	
	30	3.30 pm	Divisional training	
			In the London Gazette of 29th inst: the 2nd Dispatch by Sir Douglas Haig as Commander in Chief is published. In para 8 the following appears:- "While many other units have done excellent work during the period under review (from 19 Dec 1915 to 19th inst), the following have been "specially brought to my notice for good work in carrying out or resisting local attacks, &c &c — namely:-" (inter alia) "8th Service Bn. South Staffordshire Regt"	R&R

M.P. Dunphie

SS 76

A.G. Base

Herewith War Diary
of 8th So. Staffs. Regt
from June 1st to 30th
1916.

W.J. Barker Lt. Col
30/6/16. Comdg 8th So Staffs Regt

8 S Staffs
XVI

WAR DIARY
INTELLIGENCE SUMMARY

Army Form C. 2118
Vol 12

Place	Date	Hour	Summary of Events and Information	Remarks and references to Appendices
NORTBECOURT	June 1		Divisional Route March	R4R
	2		Battⁿ Training	R4R
	3		Divisional practice attack – On the King's Birthday list of Honors & Awards CAPTAIN E W WOOD is awarded the Military Cross. Also the following N.C.O's & men are awarded the Military Medal for services rendered in the field:- 8/13819 L/Cpl EDWARDS A 14 "A" Coy 8/13112 Pte LESTER H 8 "A" Coy	R4R
	4		(Sunday) Church Parade morn. The following para appears in today's "B" Orders :- "The Major Genl. Commd^g 17th Divⁿ is proud to be able to congratulate the Battⁿ on the well merited praise bestowed upon it by Sir Douglas Haig, the Commander in Chief of the Expedi^y Force, in his Last Despatch"	R4R
	5		Battⁿ training	R4R
	6		Brigade Field Day, abandoned owing to rain.	R4R
	7		Brigade Field Day – abandoned owing to rain. News received of the Death of Lord Kitchener	R4R
	8		Battⁿ training	R4R
	9		Brigade Field Day	R4R

Army Form C. 2118

WAR DIARY
or
INTELLIGENCE SUMMARY

(Erase heading not required.)

Instructions regarding War Diaries and Intelligence Summaries are contained in F. S. Regs., Part II. and the Staff Manual respectively. Title Pages will be prepared in manuscript.

Place	Date	Hour	Summary of Events and Information	Remarks and references to Appendices
MORTBECOURT	June 10th		Batt: cleaning up preparatory to move	RyR
	11th	11.30 a.m.	Church parade	RyR
	12th	2.15	Batt: marched out of MORTBECOURT and entrained at AUBIGNY arrived at LONGUEAU (Pas de Somme) not far from AMIENS 5 p.m. marched to billets CARDONNETTE for for kilometres	RyR
CARDONNETTE	13th		Cleaning up in billets - Memorial service for for kilchener	RyR
	14th		Company training	
	15th		-Do-	RyR
	16		C.O. & 2nd i/c & Coy Commdrs went to trenches held by 21st Div. opposite FRICOURT & examined ground behind enemy lines. reconnoitred ground behind our own lines & route to MORLANCOURT	RyR
	17		Coys training	
	18		Church parade 11 a.m. Division Commander went to trenches (see entry 16th) Return at Div. ad 6.30 p.	RyR
	19	3.30 pm	Experimental signalling by ground sheets to with Aeroplanes	RyR
			Extract from London Gazette	
			The undermentioned officers have been mentioned in despatches for gallant & distinguished service in the field	RyR

Lt Col W.A.J.BARKER DSO
Capt & Adj G.R.COLFRIDGE
LIEUT. G.F. ELLIOTT

Army Form C. 2118

WAR DIARY
or
INTELLIGENCE SUMMARY
(Erase heading not required.)

Instructions regarding War Diaries and Intelligence Summaries are contained in F. S. Regs., Part II. and the Staff Manual respectively. Title Pages will be prepared in manuscript.

Place	Date	Hour	Summary of Events and Information	Remarks and references to Appendices
CARDONETTE	June 20		Company training - Staff ride for COs & 2nd in command will Genl Pilcher, 3pm	R4R
	21		Do	R4R
	22		Company training in morning - Batt" training afternoon (wood fighting) 5pm	R4R
	23		Company training	R4R
	24		Lt Col Barker & other officers went up to trenches opposite FRICOURT	R4R
		3.15 p.t.	The Bn & 9th Lincolns practised marching thro' wood in Company training	R4R
		5pm	Preliminary bombardment started	R4R
	25	10am	Church parade	R4R
		12p.m.	Maj Gen. Pilcher addressed Bn on following operations	R4R
	26		General cleaning up in billets preparing to move forward	R4R
	27	8.15 a.m.	Batt" moved out of CARDONETTE & marched to HEILLY - Went into camp near HEILLY	R4R
	28		C.O. (commanding officer) went up to trenches in front of MORLANCOURT. One officer + 1 NCO from each Coy + Bn went up to Morlancourt to reconnoitre ground from then to existing Bde dump + to escort Batt" at Morlancourt	R4R
	29		Company training in camp	
HEILLY	30		Do	
			Other officers went to Morlancourt to reconnoitre	R4R

51st Inf.Bde.
17th Div.

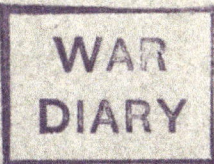

8th BATTN. THE SOUTH STAFFORDSHIRE REGIMENT.

J U L Y

1 9 1 6

WAR DIARY or INTELLIGENCE SUMMARY

Army Form C. 2118

S.S.S (Staff)

Vol 13

Place	Date	Hour	Summary of Events and Information	Remarks and references to Appendices
Morlan-court	July 1	12.35 am	Bn arrived in billets. Rewalk & breakfast at 4.45 am. At 5.30 am stores & bombs issued. Bn were drawn from dump. Packs till dinner. Regt ready to move at a moment's notice. At 4.30 am arrival's were commenced by Troops in front line. Prisoners commenced to arrive. Sudden orders received at 8 pm to move to Meaulte. On arrival, orders received to proceed to 50th Bde HQ, thence in vicinity of Becourt Wood. New instructions were issued. Bn even to relieve 8/7th East Yorks in the front line.	
Treuches Fricourt	2	11 am 12.30 am	Relief commenced at 3 a.m. & completed by 5.30 am. Many wounded lying outside our trenches. The attack by the 50th having failed, shelter given, collected wounded & as they were not fired on, an investigation of trench taken by patrols. German trenches in French numbering found. About 150 were taken & sent down to Bn HQ. Major R.J. Raper organized parties to bomb remaining dug-outs. Our second l.t attack Fricourt. Advance commenced. Fricourt Village captured without opposition. 2nd objective viz edge of Fricourt Wood taken under MG fire. At 12.20 attack by 15 + 17 (Lt Pennick) on 3rd objective viz Lonzenge Alley under supervision of Major Raper. Strong rifle & M.G. fire met with but French carried. Major Raper killed, Lt Curtis + Lloyd wounded. 2 Lieut Brown killed. Impossible to advance further as Lincoln Regt on the right has not kept pace & has not yet occupied northern edge of Fricourt Wood.	

Army Form C. 2118.

WAR DIARY
or
INTELLIGENCE SUMMARY

(Erase heading not required.)

Instructions regarding War Diaries and Intelligence Summaries are contained in F.S. Regs., Part II. and the Staff Manual respectively. Title Pages will be prepared in manuscript.

Place	Date	Hour	Summary of Events and Information	Remarks and references to Appendices
Nr Fricourt Battle of the Somme	July 2nd		Throughout the day, Lieut. W. Tutney had gallantly led battle patrols & had located the enemy in various trenches. At 12 mn. the division still having failed to take Railway Alley which is a continuation of Lozenge Trench already occupied by the 8th S. Staffords, the Sherwood Foresters (W?) made an attempt. Without much success.	
"	3rd		At 4.30 am by a simultaneous assault, the S. Staffords, Sherwoods & Lincolns carried Railway Alley (Crucifix Trench beyond Take the whole of the 185th R.I.R. (Prussian) Prisoners numbers about 20 Officers & 400 other ranks. Position consolidated	
		6 pm	At 6 pm orders received to consolidate a new line 1200 yards further forward. Bn. reached this new line (Lrts known as Horse Trench) a/c.i. dark & chey in all night.	
		3 am	At 3 am 2nd Lieut. Tomlinson sent to reconn. the Quadruple T. point, & at 4 am returned reporting it to be very lightly held.	
"	4th	1.30 pm	Very heavy 2mn Thunder & Lightning	
		3.30 pm	Enemy put up heavy barrage on Crucifix Trench & other continuous throughout afternoon.	
		10.30 pm	Relief commenced by Northumberland Fusiliers who have been ordered to take Quadrangle Trench. Relief completed by 12 mn. The Bn. had then to relieve the Linith. Regt. in the Crucifix Trenches as the Bn. Was the 5th in front ws by heavy at the Noon to rest.	
	5th	1 am	Relief complete	

WAR DIARY or INTELLIGENCE SUMMARY

Army Form C. 2118.

(Erase heading not required.)

Instructions regarding War Diaries and Intelligence Summaries are contained in F.S. Regs., Part II. and the Staff Manual respectively. Title Pages will be prepared in manuscript.

Place	Date	Hour	Summary of Events and Information	Remarks and references to Appendices
Battle of the Somme	July 5th	2 a.m.	52nd Bde in conjunction with hoops of 4th Div on right assault & capture Quadrangle Trench.	
		3.30 a.m.	A & B Coys sent forward to reinforce NF in Wood S line. Heavy bombing by enemy on R.H.Q. & Railway 17.10 continuous shelling throughout the day. Capt Jones wounded.	wpl
		6 a.m.		
		11.30 a.m.	Y & East York relieved Bn. first on B Coy was heavy. Railway Copse I shell wounded out 20 men. Bn marched back to hills carrying 5 officers 105 O.R.	
	6th	at 3.30 a.m.	Total estimated casualties the Bn the far Bellen CT	
			Before Trotter on route over Contarmaison	wpl
	7th	8.30 a.m.	Bn moves off & is held in reserve at Fricourt.	
		12.30 p.m.	Moved to Lonely Copse. Received that attack on Quadrangle Support Trench by Another Bde had failed. Very heavy & incessant shell. Shrapnel & hostile attack on Quadrangle Support. Failed at 3.30 p.m.	wpl
		4.30 p.m.	Bn came up for Shrapnel.	
		7.30 p.m.	Enemy bomb counter up for Shrapnel.	
	8th	6.20 a.m.	Another attack on Quadrangle Support unsuccessful.	wpl
		3 p.m.	Bn also attack on Quadrangle Support fails.	
	9th	10 a.m.	Batt. moves up to relieve Borders in Bottom Wood — Shell Wood Crns.	
		11.30 a.m.	Relief complete. Coy sent up at 11 pm to hold part of Quadrangle Trench awaiting Lincoln Regt.	
		7.30 pm	Relieve 10th S. Staff Bn. will take Quadrangle Support Trench.	wpl

Place	Date	Hour	Summary of Events and Information	Remarks and references to Appendices
Bn H'rs of the Somme.	July 9.		Intention is to attack and trench Artillery preparation 50ᵗʰ Bde to finish Maltzhorn attack on right & another Regt to bomb up Pearl Alley. An sooner trench to taken. C Coy & Pioneers to trench strong point at junction of Pearl Alley & Quadruple Support Trench.	
		8 pm	Gp comms reconnoitred by 2nd in Col. Burke. B & D Coys detailed to attack in 3 lines each. R on night, D on left. A Coy to be in reserve. C Coy holding part of Quadruple Trench. Orders were for complete silence. All entrances to equipment removed. Bayonets covered with burnt up lines. The orders shown through Dn clumps. R Coy bombers attached to reach depot. D Coy bombers to reach left. Bn bombers detailed to reach Lindsen Regt. Who have made no headway in Pearl Alley. Wire cutters with first line & one wire may be intact. Telephone lines run up from Bn H.Q. to Quadruple Trench. Capt Simon detailed to have "Menekin" (man B C Coy) with 20th Shewcrood in their centry in the open in front of Quadruple Trench & C on an alignment parallel to & in line of Quadruple Support Trench. by 11 pm. These men are to give in case of hostile attachment.	
		10pm	Officers Will Join.	
		11 pm	Bn in position 20" by to attack. 2 Coys of R. Shewrood here arrived on 16" Hedge Trench ourselves, by Bn.	
	11/3/21		Advance begun under barrage 5 Ens & Sweeping MG fire from Maltz.Hn & Wall Maltz.Hn	

WAR DIARY or INTELLIGENCE SUMMARY

Army Form C. 2118.

Place	Date	Hour	Summary of Events and Information	Remarks and references to Appendices
Battle of the Somme	July 9	11.10pm	Quadrangle Support Trench taken with the Regiment by the 8th South Staffords Regt in place of M.C. with the 7th bomb. Lewis up & Pearl ally made as handrary but the bombers by leaving the trench altogether gave a chance to [?] but they many casualties. So Bn on right B. S. Staffords failed utterly. Bn was then exposed on its right & left. O.C. S. Staffords never realised y/s on our movement. That Regt on night a/k. an initial attempt would be contest to sit down & do nothing for the remainder of the night. Germans of trenches heavy casualties - attack with bomb from the right, there was hurt 2 b. by B Coy under J "Frank Whitehurst" fought 2 Lieut S Baker & 7 H N. Baker Pioneer Coy were to have built Strong point in Quadrangle Support. but at any attempt on there seconds to support Quadrangle Trench & at 3 a.m. 2.30 pm. & advice mere 2.30pm at Wyfers sent & support forward to Quad Trench. Col Holmerson players heroes in the life.		
	10	2.45 a.m.	Bn to further support & info for Right On Dyke Left the Bn would have been left in Quadrangle Gn. 1st Left 2m hopeless & to relieve Gun 16 of Lynx on On the according to guns of 34 Div & 10 Div Brs to Quadrangle Trench. bringing all wounded forced back. Then seen Officers by 2.30 am Wounded: L6 Shenston, Harper, Wilkes, Webb, Boulton Reed, Macy, Seward Baker, Lt Bradnet Tunney Hughes, Tomalin (& Rowsbury) Adsetsholls, Thornton Snowden (?) Capt Woods, Gibson (wounds), Baggott. Killed: Altern Baker & Baker T, Coley, Majors, Parkley, Tomlinson, a 200 O.Rs. Being day a truce obtained by other Brs on our left in Confrontation & remains of the 8th Sherwood Attempts Quadrangle Support Trench which was on Longer held.		
		10pm.		

Army Form C. 2118.

WAR DIARY
or
INTELLIGENCE SUMMARY
(Erase heading not required.)

Instructions regarding War Diaries and Intelligence Summaries are contained in F. S. Regs., Part II. and the Staff Manual respectively. Title Pages will be prepared in manuscript.

Place	Date	Hour	Summary of Events and Information	Remarks and references to Appendices
Battle of the SOMME.	10th/11th	11 pm	Fresh orders re relief. Capt BURNETT sent up to supervise this Relief completed. Batt marches by coys to DERNANCOURT	
		2.15 am	went there for the day. Casualties in above operations 25 officers 320 O.R.	auth.
		5 pm	Entrain for BAILLY-SUR-SOMME.	
		11 pm	Arrived at SALEUX station. Marched to FOURDRINOY went into billets.	
FOURDRINOY	12th		Battn. rested all day.	auth.
		5.30 pm	Capt. A.W. FARWELL reported for duty.	
	13th		Reorganization of Battn. Lt-Col W.A.S. BARKER D.S.O. admitted to hospital sick. Capt. A.W. FARWELL assumed command.	auth.
		10 pm	Orders received to move next day by road.	
	14th	9.45 am	Parade moved 10 a.m.	
		1 pm	Halt of 2 hours for Dinners continued march at 3 pm.	
		5 pm	Halt of 1 hr for tea continued march at 6 pm.	auth.
"		8 pm	Arrived at BUSSUS went into Billets.	

Army Form C. 2118.

WAR DIARY
or
INTELLIGENCE SUMMARY
(Erase heading not required.)

Instructions regarding War Diaries and Intelligence Summaries are contained in F. S. Regs., Part II. and the Staff Manual respectively. Title Pages will be prepared in manuscript.

Place	Date	Hour	Summary of Events and Information	Remarks and references to Appendices
BUSSUS	15th	9am	Batt: training and reorganisation. Lt. T.K. BARLOW reported killed in action is now reported died of wounds on 15.7.16	aust
"	16th	9am	Batt: training.	aust
"	17th	9am	Batt: training. Capt A.H. WHITBY reported for duty. posted to B coy. Capt C.S. MASSY transferred from C.L. Coy. and assumed command of A Coy. 2nd Lt R.T. THOMSON attached to 5th Trench Mortar Battery	aust aust
"	18th	9am	Batt: training. no return of Bus Helmets by Coys.	aust
"			Lt A. RAMSDEN reported for duty. a reinforcement of 83 O.R. arrived from Notts & Derby Regt, Lincolnshire & N. Staff. Regt.	aust
"	19th	9am	Batt: training. (Reinforcement of 223 O.R. chiefly from Notts. Derby (Regt) 55 fifty from Notts. Staffs	
"	20th	9am	Batt: training	
"	21st	9am	Batt: training. Transport except 2 cookers & 2 G.S. wagons prepared and arrangements for exchange	aust
"	22nd	9am	Batt: training. some O.R. & other Regts in B. to end of the reinforcement and in exchange for South & North Staffordshire Regts	aust aust
		10 pm	Warning order received to move next day.	

1875. Wt. W593/826 1,000,000 4/15 J.B.C. & A. A.D.S.S./Forms/C. 2118.

Army Form C. 2118.

WAR DIARY
or
INTELLIGENCE SUMMARY

(Erase heading not required.)

Instructions regarding War Diaries and Intelligence Summaries are contained in F. S. Regs., Part II. and the Staff Manual respectively. Title Pages will be prepared in manuscript.

Place	Date	Hour	Summary of Events and Information	Remarks and references to Appendices
BUSSUS	23rd 7.16	4.30 am	Men had breakfast remaining transport moved under B?e. arrangement.	any
		6.30 am	Received orders to entrain at HANGEST STATION at 7.40 pm	
		3 pm	Batt. paraded 2 pm and moved off.	
		7.1?	Batt. arrived at HANGEST.	
		11 pm	Batt. entrained – travelled all night.	
	24.7.16	5. am	Batt. arrived at MERICOURT & detrained.	aux.
		6.15 am	Batt. arrived at Bivouac near BUIRE.	
		6.15	Capt C.H. MANGER reports and assumed command.	
Bivouac nr BUIRE.	25.7.16	9 am	Batt. training.	
	26.7.16	9 am	Batt. training. 21st W. HACKETT, A.H.B. TYRRELL & R.W.A. GLEED Joined the Batt.	D acd accd
	27.7.16	9 am	Batt. training. the following officers joined the Batt. 21st W. JOHNSON, R. GALE, F. KITE, W.B. DENT, H. JENNINGS, A.J. BROWNE & H. ACTON	and

Army Form C. 2118.

WAR DIARY
or
INTELLIGENCE SUMMARY
(Erase heading not required.)

Instructions regarding War Diaries and Intelligence Summaries are contained in F. S. Regs., Part II. and the Staff Manual respectively. Title Pages will be prepared in manuscript.

Place	Date	Hour	Summary of Events and Information	Remarks and references to Appendices
BIVOUAC nr BUIRE	27th		The following officers joined the Battn. 2/Lt. W. JOHNSON. R. GALE. F. KITE. W.B. DENT. H. JENNINGS. A.J. BROWN & H. ACTON.	aut.
	28th	6.15	Ceremonial Parade. G.O.C. 17th Division presented the following medals. H/C 2 M.S. BRICKNELL.	aut
		9am	Battn. training. Sgt. CARTWRIGHT. R.W. receiving the Military Medal.	
			Capt. E. BACHE joined the Battn.	
"	29th	10am	Church Parade.	aut.
"	30"	9am	Battn. training. The following officers joined the Battn. 2/Lt. T. PINSON	
	3.0		C. A. SCOTT. D. STACEY. W. P. RHODES. A. B. MILLER. J. WRIGHT. G. S. STEPHENS. aut	
"	31st	9am	Battn. training. C.O. & 2nd i/c go up to recce ground.	aut.

C Knight
Capt.
31.7.16. Comdg. 8th Service Bn. So. Staffs. Regt.

51st Brigade.
17th Division.

1/8th BATTALION

SOUTH STAFFORDSHIRE REGIMENT

AUGUST 1 9 1 6 :::

Vol 14

Containing

WAR DIARY

8th South Staffordshire Regt.

August 1916.

T-14

Army Form C. 2118.

WAR DIARY
or
INTELLIGENCE SUMMARY   8th South Staffs Regt
(Erase heading not required.)

Instructions regarding War Diaries and Intelligence Summaries are contained in F. S. Regs., Part II. and the Staff Manual respectively. Title Pages will be prepared in manuscript.

Place	Date	Hour	Summary of Events and Information	Remarks and references to Appendices
BIVOUAC NR. BUIRE	Aug 1st 1916	8 am	Warning received that Bn would move at 6 pm.	
		2.20 pm	Advanced party sent to POMMIERS REDOUBT	
		6.20 pm	Battn moved. Capt MANGER commanding via MEAULT, FRICOURT to POMMIERS REDOUBT and took over from 1st E.SURREYS. 5/Lst in support.	
			about LONGUEVAL — HIGH WOOD. 5/Lst in support.	
		10.30	Relief completed. Rest of night spent collecting stores from various dumps.	
POMMIERS REDOUBT	2.VIII.16	3.15 pm	Heavy barrages about POZIÈRES. HIGH WOOD.	
		6 pm	Brigadier Saw COs & Bn. H.2rs	
		6.53	Slight shelling about POMMIERS REDOUBT.	
"	3. "	2.40 am	Slight shelling.	
		3.40 am	" " "	
		9 pm	Bn sent to trenches in rear of weeks work.	
		10.15 am	Capt SMYLY & 2/Lt LANGTON sent to gather in formation.	
		10.30 am	H.Q. 2rs moved to old German Dug-out.	
		3.45 "	Lt. SPICER of 2nd Batt. arrived u.s. Attd on 2rd Cemetery.	
		2.30 "	C.O. 2/ith 2nd Battn.	
"	4 "	11.30 am	52nd Bde attack S. and cliff WOODLANE & ORCHARD TRE'N & N. Foulien	
		1.25	Operation orders arrive. Capt BURNETT. MASSEY Fr Day. 2/Lt STANLEY GRIFFITHS	
		12 noon	go forward to line MONTAUBAN — DELVILLE WOOD.	
		4.45 pm	C.O. to Bde H.Q.2rs for conference.	
		10 p	Battn orders issued.	
			Battn runners 2/Lt ALLEN Guiding A.C.D.B. A.L.C. LONGUEVAL ALLEY	
			B m MONTAUBAN ALLEY P.R.R.R.R.	

2449 Wt. W14957/M90 750,000 1/16 J.B.C. & A. Forms/C.2118/12.

Army Form C. 2118.

WAR DIARY
or
INTELLIGENCE SUMMARY
(Erase heading not required.)

Instructions regarding War Diaries and Intelligence Summaries are contained in F.S. Regs., Part II. and the Staff Manual respectively. Title Pages will be prepared in manuscript.

Place	Date	Hour	Summary of Events and Information	Remarks and references to Appendices
In Support of DELVILLE WOOD	5.VIII.16	1.30am	1st K.R.R.'s relief completed. C.O.'s usual conf.	
		3.30am	C by shelled.	
		9.30am	B coy moves along to make room for A.C who are too crowded. All coys working hard deepening trenches.	
		9.37am	O.C. A.C coys to do away with intermittent shelling by MONTAUBAN ALLEY by 6.p.m.	
		11am		
		4pm	A coy wk shelled by 77 mm.	
		7.30pm	Rations march down.	
		8.45pm	Rations taken up by D coy to BORDER Regt in DELVILLE WOOD	
	6.VIII.16	3am	Estimated casualties 20. O.R.	
		1.30am	WIRE received that Capt ELWOOD has been awarded M.C. 2nd Lieut W. GIBSON awarded M.C. No 81/2858 Pte LEE S award D.C.M. for operations July 1st - 11.VII.16.	
		3.a.m.	O.C. A.B.C. move into present positions in DELVILLE WOOD	
		2p.m.	C.O. + M.O. visit BORDER Regt re relief.	
		1.25p.m	Operation orders received in relief of BORDER Regt from Bde.	
		1.45p.m	Both operation orders issued. Ration arrive.	
		8.50p.m	Relief cancelled.	
		9.50p.m	3 concentrated bombs on A coy in LONGUEVAL ALLEY	
		11.pm	Ration taken up to BORDER Regt by D coy.	

Army Form C. 2118

WAR DIARY
or
INTELLIGENCE SUMMARY
(Erase heading not required.)

Instructions regarding War Diaries and Intelligence Summaries are contained in F.S. Regs., Part II. and the Staff Manual respectively. Title Pages will be prepared in manuscript.

Place	Date	Hour	Summary of Events and Information	Remarks and references to Appendices
Support to DELVILLE WOOD	7.VIII.16	2.40 a.m.	Batt. received orders to be in immediate support to BORDER Regt and had orders to attack.	
		3.30 p.m.	A & C coys ordered to "stand to".	
		5.45	A & C coys carrying party sent up to BORDERs with wire & sand bags.	
		2.40 pm	Operation orders received from BORDER Regt. H coy ordered to move up in support Capt BURNETT under orders of O.C. DELVILLE WOOD.	
		5.30 pm	B coy sent to take up C coys position & C to A's old position	
		6 pm	Casualties O.R. 2 Missing 9 Wounded 2 Killed	
		8 pm	Enemy artillery very active near BERNAFAY WOOD	
		10.12 pm	Situation report from BORDER Regt. Their attack failed owing to M.G. fire	
"	8.VIII.16	12.25am	Rations sent up to BORDER Regt. delayed by shelling.	
		3.50	Enemy heavily shelled whole Batt. area.	
		6.20.	Rations went up.	
		3 pm	O.C. DELVILLE WOOD report attack will recommence. A coy goes up.	
		5.40 pm	Casualties 2/Lt A.H.B. TYRRELL wounded at 3 July O.R. 3 killed 18 wounded	
		7:30 p	Bn cancels proposed attack.	
			orders re relief of BORDER Regt. sent to coys. 2/Lt GRIFFITHS sent close with	
"	9.8.16	2.30 am	B coy report 2 platoons buried in trench destroyed by Minnie werfer.	
		4 pm	All coys report relief completed.	

Army Form C. 2118

Instructions regarding War Diaries and Intelligence Summaries are contained in F. S. Regs., Part II. and the Staff Manual respectively. Title Pages will be prepared in manuscript.

WAR DIARY
or
INTELLIGENCE SUMMARY
(Erase heading not required.)

Place	Date	Hour	Summary of Events and Information	Remarks and references to Appendices
DELVILLE WOOD	9/VIII/16	4 am	Dispositions. A Coy. N of wood. C. NE corner & support in wood. B E side of wood. D. in LONGUEVAL ALLEY.	B.E.&D
		7.10am	C.O. visits wood	
		11.25am	Report to Bde. enemy treated at N point of wood. 2/Lt TYRRELL + 14 O.DAY sent down sick	
		6pm	Casualties O.R. 13 K: M.O. 47 wounded & missing	
		6.20pm	Bde. wire essential to locate enemys flank in DELVILLE wood	My.
		7am	Rations arrive	
		9.9 P.M	2/Lt Langton and Hales called to Hd. Qrs. The C.O. explains situation and orders 2 posts to be established in trench	
		9.40 P.M	A and C. Coys ordered to collect their bombing squads immediately at junction of Coys to assist B.O.	
		10.30 Rm	2/Lt. Langton and Hales leave Head Qrs to	
		10.50 P.M	D Coy. send 40 men to assist B Coy. Hrs wiring and digging up	
10.8.16	12.45am	Verbal report received to the effect that B.O. has advanced some considerable distance without encountering the enemy	
		3.0	Full report from C. Coy called Hrs 2nd Lt. Pottery and Burges report Hrs duty failed to B.C. and ordered to take out bombing party to certain sight of Edge of wood opposite new Boch Trench	

WAR DIARY or INTELLIGENCE SUMMARY

Army Form C. 2118

Place	Date	Hour	Summary of Events and Information	Remarks and references to Appendices
DELVILLE WOOD	10.8.16	4.30 a.m.	C Coy report that enemy's trench had been cleared full of dead and wounded. Two impossible to establish bombing post.	
		6 a.m.	2nd Lt Allen sent out to reconnoitre German trench E. of Delville Wood. He advanced twice with the open and reported that the trench was occupied (a fact hitherto not ascertained). This trench runs from the wood towards GINCHY. Lt Allen discovered that trench was well wired in places. One German on sentry duty had half his body exposed.	
		7 a.m.	The C.O. and O.C. Coy of 10th Lancashire Fusiliers arrive to gain information about [to Delville Wood O.P. B no visible wood arrived to establish position]. The Brigadier G.S.I. (Div.) (Col. Allen) arrive & decide that it is absolutely essential to establish posts at all costs in German trench in wood.	
		7.30 a.m.		
		10.30 a.m.	2 north Pathway sent to O.C. to assist 2nd Lt Langton who started out with bombers to establish post in German line N.E. corner of wood.	
		12.15 p.m.	Capt Barrett reports having sent parties of men across in coys and others leaving with parties on the left.	
		2 p.m.	2 bombing squads from 10th Lanc. Fusiliers arrive to relieve our posts in German trench, but relief is impossible.	
		5 p.m.	Wire from Brigade "C in C and Corps Commander send congratulations. Conveyed to those engaged on information obtained last night."	C.B

WAR DIARY or INTELLIGENCE SUMMARY

Army Form C. 2118

(Erase heading not required.)

Instructions regarding War Diaries and Intelligence Summaries are contained in F.S. Regs., Part II. and the Staff Manual respectively. Title Pages will be prepared in manuscript.

Place	Date	Hour	Summary of Events and Information	Remarks and references to Appendices
DELVILLE WOOD	10.8.16	5.40 p	Orders received to reoccupy southern half of ANGLE TRENCH and hand it over to Lond. Territorials.	
		6.45 pm	2nd Lt Langton has advanced 140 yards to within 60 yards of Beek trench fired at from 3 sides. An attempt to establish post further east fails. Casualties: Officers nil O.R. 1 killed, 11 wounded	
FRICOURT	11.8.16	2.40 am	Relief complete. 100 Lane. Leaving. Battn marches back by Companies to bivouac about a mile and a half S.W. of Fricourt all men in bivouac by 5.30 a.m. Day spent in resting and bathing in river Ancre near Buire.	
		5 P.M.	Court of enquiry at Bde. H.Qrs. Bois d'Elage Fricourt to enquire into why posts were not established on German line in Delville Wood.	
BUIRE	12.8.16		Battn. is relieved by the 42nd R. Infy. Bde. about 9.30 a.m. March via BECORDEL noT of MEAULTE down bridge S. of Vaux Mill to old bivouac N.E. of BUIRE. Time of arrival about 12.40 P.M.	
	13.8.16		Lt. Banks returns and resumes command of the Battalion. Bde Church Parade in field near bivouac.	
	14.8.16	6 am	All Bde transport moves to rest area 2nd Lt Allen sent on unit transport to held P.O. note regarding Cadet Inspection and not inspector.	

Army Form C. 2118

WAR DIARY or INTELLIGENCE SUMMARY

(Erase heading not required.)

Instructions regarding War Diaries and Intelligence Summaries are contained in F. S. Regs., Part II. and the Staff Manual respectively. Title Pages will be prepared in manuscript.

Place	Date	Hour	Summary of Events and Information	Remarks and references to Appendices
BOIRE	14.8.16	8.50 p.m.	Capt. C. M. Spears appointed S.A.A. & Q.M.G. 3rd Corps. Leaves the Battalion to take up his duties.	
			Batt. has orders to move following day.	
EZAINCOURT	15.8.16	3. a.m.	Reveille.	
		4.30 a.m.	Leave Bivouac for Prescourt Station.	
		10.30 a.m.	Entrain and leave with 7th Lincolns 61st F.A. and 2 Coys Borders.	
		3.30 p.m.	Detrain at Candas.	
	16.8.16		March to Gezaincourt to billets, arriving at 6-15 p.m.	
BUQUEMAISON			Leave billets 1.15 p.m. moved via HEM & HAUTE VISEE to BUQUEMAISON 2nd Lt. ALLEN and N.R.O. per Coy went in advance leaving GEZAINCOURT at 8.30 a.m. for billeting.	
			Capt. Athelby O.C. Div Pierrot Troupe, and Revn Major SOUASTRE leaves for SOUASTRE.	
	17.8.16		BATT. training.	
	18.8.16		4 am reveille	
BIENVILLERS		6 a.m.	Capt. Saswell leads Batt. on march to BIENVILLERS.	
			Route via LUCHEUX – HUMBERCOURT – LA BELLEVUE – GAUDIEMPRE – ST AMAND – SOUASTRE.	
		10-30 to 2-30	Halt for dinner in valley ¾ miles N of GAUDIEMPRE	
		3-40 to 7 p.m.	Halt at St AMAND orders having been received not to proceed further before 7 p.m. so as not to reach BIENVILLERS before 8.30 p.m.	

Army Form C. 2118

WAR DIARY or INTELLIGENCE SUMMARY
(Erase heading not required.)

Instructions regarding War Diaries and Intelligence Summaries are contained in F.S. Regs., Part II. and the Staff Manual respectively. Title Pages will be prepared in manuscript.

Place	Date	Hour	Summary of Events and Information	Remarks and references to Appendices
HEMVILLERS	18.8.16		The Batt ooccupy billets vacated by Lucan Western to Rifles Bun marched steadily, 16 miles covered and no men falling out.	APS
"	19.8.16		Col. Bates goes on ahead with Brigadier to inspect trenches 2nd Lt Allen goes in advance billeting at BIENVILLERS Capt. Larwell O.C. Coy 2 other officers & Coy Sergt Major C.S.M.'s R.S.M. 16 Platoon N.C.O.'s and Loyt inspect trenches.	
"	20.8.16		Relieve 1st & 2nd R.B. in trenches E of Hannescamps. Bas from billets 2 P.M. 500 yds between Coys and 100 yds between platoons. 'B' Coy on right A Coy on centre C on left flank D Coy in support. Relief completed by 6-5 P.M.	
"	21.8.16		General work in trenches i.e. repairing wiring, and wiring. 2nd Lt Kenyon and T.H.Bates take out party at night to reconnoitre German trench shown on aeroplane photograph in front main land April C. Coy party discover French statue and erected and no wire in front.	
"	22.8.16		General trench work.	
"	23.8.16		Fast and fog of inspection of trench by Major Fleming 7/Lo. R.P.L. Details of work necessary given.	
"	24.8.16		Brigadier goes on leave. Col. Bates assumes command of Brigade Capt. Larwell " " Battalion	

1875 Wt. W593/826 1,000,000 4/15 J.B.C. & A. A.D.S.S./Forms/C. 2118.

WAR DIARY or INTELLIGENCE SUMMARY

Army Form C. 2118

Place	Date	Hour	Summary of Events and Information	Remarks and references to Appendices
IENVILLERS	25.8.16		General trench work.	
	26.8.16		G.O.C. makes a tour of the trenches. 2nd Lt Holborn takes out a patrol to ascertain if Boche trench is occupied. Reports nothing seen or heard. Boche wire about 30 feet thick and good.	
	27.8.16		Relieved by 7th Borders. Relief completed by 5.5.P.M. Batt marched out by Plateau back to BIENVILLERS. Everybody settled in by 7.P.M. 100 men of C Coy sent to FONQUEVILLERS.	
	28.8.16		Evening rest. Working parties from 2–6 P.M. working parties for R.E's supplied by B and D Coys.	
	29.8.16		Baths for 13 Coy in the morning. Working parties for R.E's supplied by A and D Coys (8-30am – 2-30pm) and Lts Langton and Stanley with 50 men went up to support and recover being Pegnes in trenches & relief. Langton led a reconnaissance party by Bonclin to poplars the "OSIER ROB" which was found to be clear.	
	30.8.16		Baths allotted for all specialists. Working parties supplied to R.E's from A and B Coys.	
	31.8.16		Working parties employed by A and D Coys under Capt Bennett.	
	1.9.16		Working parties from A and D Coys employed on protection of trenches.	

J.B. Farewell Capt
Comdg. 6th South Staffords Regt

WAR DIARY
or
INTELLIGENCE SUMMARY

Army Form C. 2118

8 S Stafford Regt
1 of 15

(Erase heading not required.)

Instructions regarding War Diaries and Intelligence Summaries are contained in F.S. Regs, Part II. and the Staff Manual respectively. Title Pages will be prepared in manuscript.

Place	Date	Hour	Summary of Events and Information	Remarks and references to Appendices
BIENVILLERS	Sept 1. 1916		Two Companies at work under R.E.'s in the Trenches. One Company working under Tunnel Coy at FONQUEVILLERS	
	2. 1916		Ditto.	
	3rd		Colonel Barker inspected the Battalion. Church Parade. Two Companies at work under R.E's at HANNES CAMP.	
	4th		The C.O. and Second in Command visited the Boches H.Qrs and inspected Trenches, arranging details of relief. The Batt. relieved 7th Borders Regt in trenches. Relief completed by 1 P.M.	
	5th		Col. Barker attended conference at Bde H.Q. 9th at 4 P.M. Battalion in Trenches. Ordinary Trench routine. Patrol from A Company sent out to inspect German wire. Lower Gap off D Company	
	6th		Ordinary trench routine. A framing and sniping carried out under 2nd Lieut. T.H. Battes & Lieut. J.B. Wilson. Enemy wire not as resume. View to a raid.	T.15
	7th 8th		Ordinary Trench routine.	
	9th		Artillery active to 9:30 PM more.	
	10th		Ditto.	
	11		Patrols sent out by each Company in the hopes of catching a Boche but all to no purpose.	M/B.

1875. Wt. W593/826 1,000,000 4/15 J.B.C. & A. A.D.S.S./Forms/C. 2118.

WAR DIARY or INTELLIGENCE SUMMARY

Army Form C. 2118

Place	Date	Hour	Summary of Events and Information	Remarks and references to Appendices
HANNESCAMP	Sept 12/16		Battalion relieved in the trenches by the 20th Royal Fusiliers. Battalion marched to billets at HANNESCAMP arriving there at 3-15 am.	
	13th		2nd Lieut. H. Arts joined the Battalion.	
	14		97 O.R's reinforcements join the Battalion.	
	15th		Battalion marches to billets at SAILLY-AU-BOIS relieving the 6th Dorsets there. All in billets by 6-40 P.M. Captain Farwell admitted to hospital.	
	16		Battalion relieved 19 West Yorks in the line at HEBUTERNE. Relief complete by 10 P.M.	
	16 & 17		"B" and "D" Coys relieved working party of 10th West Yorks in the line at 11-30 P.M. "D" party worked until 3-30 am in the 7th.	
	17		1 Officer and 100 O.R. reinforcements arrive. Capt Hanson returned from leave.	
	18-19		Battalion at work on trenches. "C" and "B" Coys relieved in line by 3rd Rifle Brigade. "D" marching	
	20-21		Battalion to billets at HUMBERCAMP. "B" billets by 3-30 am 21st.	

WAR DIARY
or
INTELLIGENCE SUMMARY
(Erase heading not required.)

Army Form C. 2118

Place	Date	Hour	Summary of Events and Information	Remarks and references to Appendices
MONDICOURT	22		Battalion marched to billets at MONDICOURT arriving at 11-15 a.m.	
REMAISNIL	23		Battalion left MONDICOURT and marched to REMAISNIL arriving at billets at 11-30 a.m.	
YVRENCHEUX	24		Marched to billets at YVRENCHEUX arriving at 3. P.M.	
"	25		Resting in billets and generally reorganizing and cleaning up	
"	26		Battalion in training from 9 a.m. till 5 P.M. "A" Coy. on range	
"	27		Battalion training, "B" Company on the range from 9 a.m. till 6 P.M.	
"	28		A. C. D. Companies training. "C" Company on range.	
"	29		Het [a]. Battalion training in billets (Companies training, practising (creeping up under barrage) etc.	
"	30		A Coy. on range. Lecture at 1.30: Head Quarters by Col. Cloire on "Co-operation of Artillery and Infantry." Commanding Officer, Company Commanders attended	

APB

Confidential
Vol 6

8TH SOUTH STAFFS REGT
WAR DIARY
OCTOBER 1916.

T.16

WAR DIARY
or
INTELLIGENCE SUMMARY

Army Form C. 2118

(Erase heading not required.)

8 Kings Royal Rifles

Place	Date	Hour	Summary of Events and Information	Remarks and references to Appendices
VRENCHEUX	1.10.16		Reveille 7 a.m. (Holiday) 2nd Lt. Giles reports - "The Duds" entertainment 2-45 P.M. (Clocks put back 1 hour) (Winter time)	
	2.10.16	2.10.a.m.	Orders for move arrive.	
		9 a.m.	Batt. leaves VRENCHEUX and marches to FROHEN-LE-GRAND via HIERMONT, AUXI-LE-CHATEAU. Arrived 1-20 P.M. (Raining hard)	
		2-35 P.M	2nd Lt ARTER sick and admitted to hospital.	
FROHEN-LE-GRAND	3-10-16	8-10 a.m.	Orders for move next day. (Rain)	
	4-10-16		Move cancelled for the day. (Rain)	
	5-10-16		Move again cancelled. (Rain)	
			Batt. marches to HALLOY via route DOULLENS cross roads L'ESPERANCE. Started 8-40.a.m. Route Arrive 1-15 P.M.	
	6-10-16	1 a.m.	2nd Lt BURGESS transferred to R.F.C. as observer.	
			Orders to move to BAYEN COURT (arrive) 4-10 P.M. supplied to R.E.'s at HEBUTERNE (6 Off: 210 OR's) for Corps Signals 8 Off: 460 men.	
	7-10-16		" " 7 Off: 152 men	
			" " for detonating bombs 3 Off: 100 men	
			" " for carrying T.M. ammunition	
	9-10-16		" " for coaching bombs 1 Off: 20 men.	
		7-40 P.M	Major N.C. TWEEDIE arrives.	
			"D" Coy. moves to SAILLY-AU-BOIS. 2nd Lt. HACKETT & Sapping platoon to HEBUTERNE	MPB

1875 Wt. W293/826 1,000,000 4/15 J.B.C. & A. A.D.S.S./Forms/C. 2118.

Army Form C. 2118

WAR DIARY
or
INTELLIGENCE SUMMARY
(Erase heading not required.)

Instructions regarding War Diaries and Intelligence
Summaries are contained in F. S. Regs., Part II.
and the Staff Manual respectively. Title Pages
will be prepared in manuscript.

Place	Date	Hour	Summary of Events and Information	Remarks and references to Appendices
HEBUTERNE	9.10.15	a	Battalion relieved the Shrewsburys in the trenches. The relief was completed at 3.30 p.m. Brimmer trench routine. 2 Lt. L.J. Kelley and 2 Lt. W.B. Willing out for duty. Artillery cut gaps in wire. q. 20 o.r. L.Y. 3 interviews Patrol officers at our head- Staffords at our head- Quarters. Working parties provided. 3 officers 120 oth ranks for 181st Tunnelling Company R.E. Continuous working parties 15 men every 4 hours to report to O.C. Sapping Platoon. 10 men every four hours to report to & Cpy R.E. for survival head quarters dug out.	
"	10.10.15	1 a.m.	Heavy Bosch shelling with lachrymatous shells to West of HEBUTERNE. a few escaped in the village. One Lewis gun and headcarts its damaged.	
		4.30 a.m.	Patrols. 3 officers and 30 oth ranks, patrol German wire, object of the patrol to ascertain whether German 1st line trenches are occupied and whether gaps in the wire had been cut by its our artillery on the 8th inst. Also to bring back samples of the German wire. The patrol was successfully carried out, and information was obtained. Casualties O.R. 1.	
	11.10.15	2 p.m.	Moderate Bosh shelling during the 24 hours. Trench mortars active at 2 p.m. & 2 p.m. and intermittent up to 4 p.m. O.C. Brigadier met O.C. battalion
		4 p.m.	and O.C. 7th Lincolns at Battalion H.Q.s
		11.30 a.m.	

Army Form C. 2118.

WAR DIARY
or
INTELLIGENCE SUMMARY

(Erase heading not required.)

Instructions regarding War Diaries and Intelligence Summaries are contained in F. S. Regs., Part II. and the Staff Manual respectively. Title Pages will be prepared in manuscript.

Place	Date	Hour	Summary of Events and Information	Remarks and references to Appendices
HEBUTERNE	11.10.16	11.30 AM	O.C. consulted with C.O.'s on questions concerning future operations. The Battalion	
		5. P.M.	relieved the Lincolns. The wet was completed at 5 P.M. Working parties	
			ten men working continuously making dump for the iron rations	
			& one Lewisgun.	
"	12.10.16	1 A.M.	Patrol 3 officers S.R. 13th Batt. Lincolns & 1 off & trenches at 1 A.M. with object of examination	
		3.30 AM	of gaps in wire entrain. This patrol found works working on the wire and	
		2.30 AM	drove them in, a 2nd Patrol 1 Officer 13 O.R. left at 2.30 a.m. with same object	
		5. AM	as 1st patrol, this patrol was heavily fired on. 3 Bosche shelling	
			intermittent during the day. Casualties rank & file 3 killed 1 wounded & missing	
	13.10.16	1.AM	Bosche working in connection with two Lewis guns found lying near some 150 yds	
		6 AM	from the Bosche trenches enabled fire to be directed upon Bosche working	
			parties mending wire in afps. Trench mortar fire from 1 A.M. & 2 a.m. heavy	
		9.30 AM to 10.30 AM	Shelling from 9.30 a.m. & 10.30 A.M. Trenches knocked to about in several	
			places.	
	14.10.16	9 AM 11 AM	Intermittent shelling between 9 A.M. and 11 A.M. at 4 P.M.	
		4 PM	the Yorks & East Yorks relieved the Battalion in the trenches the	

Army Form C. 2113.

WAR DIARY
or
INTELLIGENCE SUMMARY

(Erase heading not required.)

Oct 1916

Instructions regarding War Diaries and Intelligence Summaries are contained in F. S. Regs., Part II. and the Staff Manual respectively. Title Pages will be prepared in manuscript.

Place	Date	Hour	Summary of Events and Information	Remarks and references to Appendices
Aboulaine	14/10	4 to 6 PM	relief was completed by 6 P.M. The Battalion went into billets in Sailly-au-Bois. 2/Lt. J. L. Whitcher rejoined the Battalion. Casualties 2 O.R. wounded.	
Sailly au Bois	15/10	3 pm	Lecture held officers at Souastre on use of "Tanks in action".	
"	16/10		Battalion training	
"	17/10	2 PM	Battalion moved into billets at Souastre.	
"		3 pm.	to Companies bathed and training in the training area.	
		3.30 PM.	3.30 P.M. Battalion interviewed a demonstration of push-pipes.	
Doullens	19/10	12.30 PM	Battalion marched to Doullens and on arrival went into billets. The Commanding officer took over the duties of acting Brigadier. Lieuts F.H. Cotterill. J. Foster. J.W. Phillips & 2" Lt R.V. Cotterill joined the Battalion	
	20/10		Battalion remained in billets	

WAR DIARY
or
INTELLIGENCE SUMMARY

Army Form C. 2118.

OCT 1916

Place	Date	Hour	Summary of Events and Information	Remarks and references to Appendices
Doullens	21st	2 p.m.	Regimental transport moved by march route to TALMAS.	
VILLE sur AUCRE	22nd	1.30	Battalion marched to Le BON AIR sidings 1½ miles and embarked. On arrival at MERICOURT proceeding via AMIENS. The battalion subsequently marched to VILLE sur ANCRE and went into billets.	
		9 P.M.	Time of arrival 9 P.M.	
	23		Battalion remained in billets. Lt. C.O. attended a conference at Hn/z H.Q.3. Lt Col Walker + pte. Munyon were awarded the military medal for gallant work when at HEBUTERNE.	
	24		Remained in billets. Battalion training.	
	25		Remained in billets. Surplus kit was dispatched to Div'l dump at CORBIE. 2/Lt. Hackett went sick into hospital.	
	26		Battalion remained in billets.	
	27	8.50 AM	Battalion leaves by march route for the CITADEL. arrived in camp	
CITADEL		12-30 P.M.		
"	28		Rain all day. Physical drill, enterprise etc. 2 x 2 Lt. Hicks	
"	29		Company training. Leave.	
"	30		Col. Berkes came up to take command of 12th Divisional School of Instruction.	

MPB.

… Army Form C. 2118.

WAR DIARY
or
INTELLIGENCE SUMMARY

OCT 1916.

(Erase heading not required.)

Place	Date	Hour	Summary of Events and Information	Remarks and references to Appendices
CITADEL	30th		Major H.C Tweedie D.S.O. assumes command of the Battalion.	
	31st	8.20	Moved to MANSEL camp distance three miles. Location between CARNOY and MANETY. arrived 12.15 pm	

H.C. Tweedie Major

5/17

WAR DIARY
8th South Staffordshire Regt
November 1916

T.17

WAR DIARY or INTELLIGENCE SUMMARY

Army Form C. 2118.

NOV 1916

Place	Date	Hour	Summary of Events and Information	Remarks and references to Appendices
MONTAUBAN	Nov 1-16	2 p.m.	Move from Morval Camp to F Camp near MONTAUBAN	
	2		Remain in F Camp	
	3	1.30 a.m.	Move to SUPPORT line NW of LESDOEUFS (Headquarters GERMAN DUMP) Advance party start 9-45 a.m. Batt. start 1-30 p.m. Major H.E. Tweedie D.S.O. wounded. Capt. R.P. Durrell goes up to take command of Batt.	
	4	7-30 p.m.	Relieved of 1 Platoon in the line 2nd Lts. STANGER and DAVIS join.	
	5		Day in line. Heavy shelling whole day. 5 officers wounded: 2/Lt Phillips, 2/Lt Green, Morey, 2/Lt Wright. Capt Newton slightly wounded set duty 2/Lt I. PINSON reconnoitred old Gun pits in advance of ZENITH Trench and found same unoccupied. 2/Lt. Knight assumes command of B Coy.	
	6	5 p.m.	Relieved in line by 10 Stewards returned to Support line.	
	7	5 p.m.	Relieved in support by 4 Gordons returned to F Camp. Working next day. Total casualties for tour: 7 Officers wounded. 42 O.R. killed wounded.	A Coy

WAR DIARY or INTELLIGENCE SUMMARY

Army Form C. 2118.

Place	Date	Hour	Summary of Events and Information	Remarks and references to Appendices
MONTAUBAN	Nov 8-16		at F Camp. R.E. carrying party of 2 officers & 50 O.R. to Bde H.Q.	
	9		do. do.	
	10		at Irish Guards hut over F Camp Occasional shelling of camp, environs at night.	
	11	5 p.m.	Relieve Bordens in Support (HQ GERMAN DUMP). Enemy shelling fairly heavy from 5 to 9 p.m. Continues throughout night.	
	12		Our own artillery in night programme provoked heavy retaliation about SUNKEN ROAD 2/Lt. H. Jennings killed - shell fire. 2/Lt. W. Johnson wounded by same - died 45 minutes later. 2/Lt. W. Hackett sick. Starting at 4 p.m. A Coy. and Coy B relieve right companies of Lincolns in line rebat support in ZENITH CRUSTY and LARKHILL trenches. A Coy catches barrage near Sunken Road. Bn. HQ remain at GERMAN DUMP. Every night (12th, 13th) several of Lincolns in dugout near trench in front of ZENITH from GUN PIT to bombing stop in ECLIPSE trench. Revd COTTERELL slightly shell shock. Slept in HQ dugout 2/Lt RHODES sick A Coy.	

WAR DIARY
or
INTELLIGENCE SUMMARY

Army Form C. 2118.

Place	Date	Hour	Summary of Events and Information	Remarks and references to Appendices
	Nov 13-14	3 a.m.	Note from Capt. Moony "Gale has collapsed". 2/Lt. Hopken out to A Coy.	
		5.45 - 6.25 a.m.	Ehense attack by Germans on Right Flank. Enemy retaliate on our front. 30 yards of ZENITH blown in.	
			Bn relieved by part of 1st Guards Bde. The Battn relieved by 2½ companies of 1st Irish Guards. Relief complete 9-30 p.m.	
			Bn. goes to D Camp N of BERNAFAY WOOD (bivouacs & dugouts)	
			2/Lt. A.C. ALLEN goes to HANGEST in Your Major.	
	14	6 p.m.	Move to MANSELL CAMP in single file to get thro' traffic	
		9"	Arrive in camp - very cold night.	
	15.	3 a.m.	Transport starts for SANDPITS Camp to join Arrival from to link to Corps Rest Area.	
			Band of 1st Welsh Guards plays in camp. 2/Lt. Phillips rejoins.	
			Rev A. CHERRINGTON attached.	
MEAULTE		12-30 p.m.	Bn marches to MEAULTE; in billets 2-30 p.m. Very cold night.	
	16	9 a.m.	Bn marches to EDGE HILL STATION entrains 10.40	
HANGEST		6 p.m.	Arrive HANGEST. Met by A.A.Q.M.G. who tells us we are to go to RIENCOURT	5.G.
			Move there by Bn. Arrive in billets 9 p.m.	

Army Form C. 2118.

WAR DIARY
or
INTELLIGENCE SUMMARY

(Erase heading not required.)

Instructions regarding War Diaries and Intelligence Summaries are contained in F. S. Regs., Part II. and the Staff Manual respectively. Title Pages will be prepared in manuscript.

Place	Date	Hour	Summary of Events and Information	Remarks and references to Appendices
RIENCOURT	Nov. 17-16		Day of rest. Men bathing. Transport arrive 6 p.m.	
	18.		do. Kit inspection	
	19.		Church parade.	
	20.		Coy. training. Mini canteen opens in Recreation Room.	
	21.		do.	
	22.		do. Draft of 119 O.R. arrive	
	23.		do. Cinema show in Recreation Room, stays for 3 days.	
	24.		do. Batt. team played 1/4" R.E. Result 6-1 (win)	
	25.		do.	
	26.		Church parade	
	27.		Coy. training. Football. Played 51 M. Battery. Result 3-2 (win).	
	28.		do. do. Played 51 M.G. Coy. 4-0 (won)	
	29.		do. 6-0 (won).	
	30.	noon	G.O.C.'s inspection. Football: Played 51 F.A.	
			Lt. Phillips appointed Town Major of RIENCOURT	

M P Burnet Capt
2nd Batt South Staffs Regt
Cmdg
30.11.16

> 8th (S) BATTALION,
> SOUTH STAFFS.
> REGIMENT.
> No. 622
> Date. 1-1-17

D.A.G.
 Base.

Herewith War Diary of 8th South Staffordshire Regt for month of December 1916.

R P Bennett
Lieut. Colonel.
Comdg. 8th Service Bn. So. Staffs.

Army Form C. 2118.

WAR DIARY
or
INTELLIGENCE SUMMARY
(Erase heading not required.)

Instructions regarding War Diaries and Intelligence Summaries are contained in F. S. Regs., Part II. and the Staff Manual respectively. Title Pages will be prepared in manuscript.

18 Staff Regt
Vol 18

Miss Foster

T.18

Place	Date	Hour	Summary of Events and Information	Remarks and references to Appendices
ALDERSHOT	1/12/16		Battalion Route March. Drivil Musketry – Videttes, Sentry, Prisoners.	
		6/30 pm	Company movement by night.	
	2/12/16		Guards - notation in afternoon.	
			Battalion Bathing.	
			Companies turned out Hasties for protection.	
	3/12/16		Church Parade.	
			Football match against Bordon (at Home) Result 1–1.	
	4/12/16		General Instruction in morning.	
			Battalion Training.	
	5/12/16		Battalion Training.	
			Football back against Claymore (Away) Never Staffords 2 Bordon 0.	
			Battalion Route March to match.	
	6/12/16		Coy Route March: K–kings, Long, Surveys, Reconnoi-	
			Special instruction in afternoon.	
			Company Movements by night.	
			Football match against Bde H.Q., Reserve Staffords 3 H.Q. @ 1/54.	

WAR DIARY
or
INTELLIGENCE SUMMARY

Army Form C. 2118.

Place	Date	Hour	Summary of Events and Information	Remarks and references to Appendices
RIENCOURT	7/12/16		Battalion in attack. Brig-Gen Trotter present	
	8/12/16		Battalion training.	
			Gas Helmet Inspection	
			Trench Mortar accident at School of Mortars Lieut H Bottomley of 1/5 Staffords severely wounded	
	9/12/16		Company training.	
			C.O. inspected Boys in two Marching Order	
	10/12/16		Church Parade	
			Re Play football match against Brigade Reserve L/Staffords 3 Staffords won One League. Bombers 0	
	11/12/16		Battalion moved to Buneroit at long last, but Bottomleys wound,	
			C.O. at Dur Conference.	
	12/12/16		Battalion entrain to Bellow at Corbie	
CORBIE	13/12/16		Inspections	
	14/12/16		Battalion training	
	15/12/16		Battalion training	
	16/12/16		Battalion training.	
			Lieut O.T. ad Physician attach'd to D Coy 2 Lt S Townes, 1/6 Gwen in accidentally shot Townes in hospital at Amiens.	

WAR DIARY or INTELLIGENCE SUMMARY

Army Form C. 2118.

Place	Date	Hour	Summary of Events and Information	Remarks and references to Appendices
CORBIE	9/7/16		Arrived Corbie.	
			C.O. Capt E Moody, 2/Lt Hibbert Rev. B.A. Brampton to & went to Lt Bottomley's funeral at Amiens.	
	18/7/16		Battalion training.	
	19/7/16		1/6. Brewis interred at La Neuville. D Coy attended funeral.	
			Battalion Training. Bayonet attack on trenches.	
	20/7/16		2 Lieut's Smith + Broughton rejoined Bn to draft.	
			Battalion Training. Bayonet attack	
	21/7/16		Battalion Training.	
			Lt = Brewis funeral took place, all available off. of Batn.	
	22/7/16		Officers had dinner in Bn. H.Q.	
			7/L/Cpl Barker, Pte Boyles + Burke awarded Military Medal.	
			Battalion Training. Troops warned for trenches.	
	23/7/16		Battalion entrained Kings Day	
	24/7/16		Received Orders.	
			Battalion moved to Ho–? Couch at Sunset by bus.	

Army Form C. 2118.

WAR DIARY
or
INTELLIGENCE SUMMARY
(Erase heading not required.)

Instructions regarding War Diaries and Intelligence Summaries are contained in F. S. Regs., Part II. and the Staff Manual respectively. Title Pages will be prepared in manuscript.

Place	Date	Hour	Summary of Events and Information	Remarks and references to Appendices
Camp Curragh	26/2/16		Battalion training. Staining up Camp etc.	
	27/2/16		Battalion ordered to send an Advance Party en route for trenches. P.B. 1525 and Staff. This Party left at 8:15 p.m. Entrained for training under Brigade arrangements.	
	28/2/16		Battalion moved to trenches, North of Kes Boeufs. Lucky day to get sufficient dug-outs and in bad condition generally.	
	29/2/16		Battalion in line. Very wet & stormy night. 1 man killed & 7 men wounded. 13 Coy, on carrying party.	
	30/2/16		Division on right. put up a lot of shewing in the afternoon & enemy retaliated on our own. no casualties. Battalion relieved by 7. Dorsets, & returned to 21 Camp. 2 Men wounded on / marching coming out.	
	31/2/16		Cleaning up etc.)	

J.P. Beresford, Lieut. Col.
Comdg. 8th Service Bn. So. Staffs.

Army Form C. 2118.

WAR DIARY
or
INTELLIGENCE SUMMARY.
(Erase heading not required.)

8 S Stafford Regt
Oct 17

Place	Date	Hour	Summary of Events and Information	Remarks and references to Appendices
CARNOY	1.1.17		Battalion in Camp 21 Carnoy. (Parade Service 8-30 a.m.) Training Lt. Col. R.P.A.J. Barker D.S.O. 8/Yorks Battalion & Major R.P. Burnet and Capt. G.C.R. Elvidge awarded The Military Cross in New Years Honours	
"	2.1.17		Battalion moves up to Guillemont Camp, arriving at 4 P.M. D Company moves up to FLERS LINE and provide nucleus carrying parties. 2nd Lt. Stanley proceeds on leave.	
GUILLEMONT	3.1.17		Battalion moves from GUILLEMONT to Front Line in front of LES BOEUFS and MORVAL. B Co. occupies (BENNETT and LINCOLN Trenches A and C Coys in support (ANTELOPE and SLUSH) D Co. in Reserve (Ox Trench)	T.19
TRENCHES	4.1.17		Relieve 7th Yorks. Relief complete 9-30 P.M. Trenches in bad state of repair but comparatively dry 60 yards of wire fencing put up during the night. Left half of "B" Coy evacuates BENNETT Trench before dawn in consequence of our artillery bombardment	
"	5.1.17			BPB

WAR DIARY or INTELLIGENCE SUMMARY

Army Form C. 2118.

Place	Date	Hour	Summary of Events and Information	Remarks and references to Appendices
TRENCHES	5.1.19		6 "LANDWEHR" Trench (Offrs and front) Enemy aeroplanes active and flying low over Trenches. Firing M.G's	
		1.20p	Our artillery bombard LANDWEHR and LANDSTURM Trenches. Germans retaliate slightly in vicinity of FLANK AVENUE.	
		1.55p	No casualties. B Coy drams and deepens BENNETT Trench to (6 - 8 ft). A and C Coys deeply wiring	
	6.1.19		Parties 40 yards put up above re-entrant (completed). 2nd Lt HACKETT and 6 O.R's patrol encounters hostile patrol	
		1 am	of 60 observe lay Sergt Majors CURTENEY missing. Signallers lay a double line to front line Trenches.	
			Brigadier General TROTTER calls at Batt Hd Qrs. Battalion relieved by the 6th DORSETS. Relief complete by 7.55 pm.	
			Batt: retiring to Camp 21 Carnoy. 2nd Lt Nelson returns from leave.	
CARNOY	7.1.19		Batt: resting, clothes drying etc. and rifle inspection of all Coys by Armourer Sergeant	10P.B

WAR DIARY or INTELLIGENCE SUMMARY

Army Form C. 2118.

Place	Date	Hour	Summary of Events and Information	Remarks and references to Appendices
CARNOY	8.1.17		Battalion bathing by Companies A.D.C.B. (new underclothes issued) Rifle inspection	
		5.45pm	Lecture in Y.M.C.A. hut by an R.F.C. officer on (Communication between aeroplanes and Infantry) Officers and N.C.O's to attend	
	9.1.17		Battalion moved to Camp at Guillemont. A Coy to Kent Lane. A,B,+D. Coys. carry ordnance from Quarry to Railway Dump	
	10.1.17		Battalion rested 7th Night in hut. D Coy & Kenora 1/2 A Coy in new Kitchener To lunch. 1/2 A Coy to Thurles. B Coy to Antelope. C Coy & Bovril Relief complete 9/10 pm. Previous dark night	
	11.1.17		Battalion in trenches. Very Stormy night. Chadston, Brotherton from D Coy to mount.	
	12.1.17		Battalion in trenches. Very Stormy night, Evenstone & Lt Conoley Stores blown to pieces.	
	13.1.17		Relief 9/t 10am got on here. Heavy snow had to be broken, which before coming for tommy. Casualties of enemy came from Bruden+Lancaster Evenstone + Lt Co

WAR DIARY or INTELLIGENCE SUMMARY

Army Form C. 2118.

(Erase heading not required.)

Place	Date	Hour	Summary of Events and Information	Remarks and references to Appendices
In Line	12/1/17		(Cont). Very good shooting, knowing retaliated. Bomb from her own Stokes guns, No damage done. One gun at 2/45 p.m. posts manoeuvre at dusk. 2/Lt Rigden walking round empty trenches, many adverse flare & L.G. fired on Enemy Patrol, bombing & Lydite Patrol held up, scattered remainder. Relieved by 6 Dorsets, 3 Platoons of Dorsets left in Line. Potences. Relief complete 12/20 A.M. IX III March back to Camp XXI. Men abroad & cleaned up. Weather?	
Camoy Camp	14/1/17		Cleaning up & resting. Foot inspection by M.O. & Lt. 8 O.R's admitted trench foot. 2/Lt Hebert, 70 O.R. Battalion marched to hutts at Morlancourt. Lt Pigeon & Lt Lefranc. Leave from 10/1.5 A.M. Intact Camp for P. & E. Intigues. Arrival Morlancourt 2/45 P.M.	
Morlancourt	16/1/17 17/1/17		Resting, Cleaning, Clothing. Parts to Bois for 3 days. Snow at night. Coy Parades. If there to parade for 3 Brigs. Major Bennett in com Snow of feet.	

Army Form C. 2118.

WAR DIARY
or
INTELLIGENCE SUMMARY.

(Erase heading not required.)

Instructions regarding War Diaries and Intelligence Summaries are contained in F.S. Regs., Part II. and the Staff Manual respectively. Title pages will be prepared in manuscript.

Place	Date	Hour	Summary of Events and Information	Remarks and references to Appendices
Maricourt	18/1/17		Brig. Parker & O.I. O.P. proceed on horseback by Bernafay to Rocquigny. Return thereover 1 op m. Bat' Hrs & Hrs Subsections entraining.	
	19/1/17		C.O. lectures to officers. Brig. Parker & C.O.'s were Brig' Gymnastic displays. C.O. in charge. C.O. lectures to officers at Hardecourt ruins. A.B. & C. Coys bath at Maurepas.	
	20/1/17		Brig. Parker. Church Parade.	
	21/1/17		Brig. Parker. C.O. goes to Hq B for conference.	
	22/1/17		C.O. Parker joins R.H.L.	
	23/1/17		Brig. Parker. C.O. Army Officers & O.R. to H.q. 9 Squadron flying corps for demonstration in contact aeroplanes.	
	24/1/17		Brig. Parker. Preparing for move to B.O. picquets.	
	25/1/17		Battalion marched from Maricourt to Bonfay took 5/C 15/2 hours. Brig. Parker. Start 10/10am. Arrive 2.35pm. Very heavy kit	
Bonfay	26/1/17		Bonfay to Boulenois trench area (west St Pierre) Divisy 6 Reserve Bat. A.Coy Knotter trench, B Coy Maxwell Road supports. Brig Guinchy Post.	

T/134. Wt. W708—776. 50c000. 4/15. Sir J. C. & S.

WAR DIARY
or
INTELLIGENCE SUMMARY.
(Erase heading not required.)

Army Form C. 2118.

Place	Date	Hour	Summary of Events and Information	Remarks and references to Appendices
	26/11/17	4 (p.m.)	Start 3.5 p.m. on arrive 4/30 p.m. 917 Platoon the escort Brigade horses. Guillemont. Very cold N.E. Wind. C.O. & 2/Lt _____ Bn HQ front line	
	27/11/17		Relieve 12th KRR's in line A.B. & 6 Coys in front line, D Coy Support. Relief complete 7/30 p.m. Very quiet – no 9.45	
		4/30 a.m.	Enemy carry out unsuccessful operation, objective games & 6 of A & 350 OTB prisoners.	
			Bde moved to _____ ack – but in heavily shelled.	
		3 p.m.	2/Lt Ahidock & S.O.T.B. from _____ report _____ Pate	
		7 p.m.	Recent news. Enemy been _____ from _____ on Plateau to _____ large numbers.	
			Batn HQ in Quarry.	
	28/11/17		Very Quiet. Ground too heavy for digging – no _____ A Coy arc of Back Areas 5 Bn HQ shelled _____ heavy. _____ B Coy 4 OTB _____ D Coy 1 OTB _____	
	29/11/17	11.30 to 5 AM	Patrol from C 73 went out. Send Enemy wire _____ continued up no gaps. Sent no casualty. Heard my working	

WAR DIARY
or
INTELLIGENCE SUMMARY.
(Erase heading not required.)

Army Form C. 2118.

Place	Date	Hour	Summary of Events and Information	Remarks and references to Appendices
	29/1/19 (cont)		A boy slightly shell. Ball retrieved 4.75 Inches — march to 6. Br.6. Bgd. Barn. Regt. H.Q. 4.15 Bgd. 6 Blackthorn Bank. Relief complete 7/4.15 p.m.	
	30/1/19		Battalion convey out 13 Bay 107 Mules 2 commenced 5 by 107 arrival Battalion marched to tent I.S.C. arrival about 2.30 p.m. Repeat inj.g. Prophylaxis trench feet under A.D.M.S.	
	3/1/19		Officer from H.Q. I. Corps nominated orders to give Snow in forenoon.	

Wyndham ken t/Col
Comg pt So Staffs Regt.

D.A.G.
BASE.

> 8TH (S) BATTALION,
> SOUTH STAFFS.
> REGIMENT.
> No. 860
> Date. 1 3/17

Herewith War Diary of
8th Battn South Stafford
Regt from 1-2-17 —
28-2-17.

W.H. Barker Lieut. Colonel
Comdg. 8th Service Bn. So. Staffs.

WAR DIARY or INTELLIGENCE SUMMARY

Army Form C. 2118.

S S Stafford

Vol 20

Place	Date	Hour	Summary of Events and Information	Remarks and references to Appendices
Bonfay	1/2/17		Battalion marched from Bonfay back to Boulainvillers area. Guard 1/3.30 pm. Relief complete 3/30 pm. D Coy. Intermediate trench. B Coy Moronvillers Comm Dugouts. A Coy. Kniston trench. C Coy Boulainvillers Wood. D Coy on fatigues under 77 F.F.C. in support line. Base relieves of Northumberland Fus in fire & some sectors at last time. D Right & Centre. B Left & Reserve.	T.20
Boulainvillers	2/2/17		Relief complete 3/30 pm. Frost very severe. Patrols on right had been badly damaged by our artillery. Some made at Bec AM Q. & sent forward by 11/15 pm. Boys worry & working to fire up posts. Ground very hard but appreciable progress made.	
Fire	3/2/17	Hrs	About 6-6 shells short in right of D Coy. S.A.A. sudden hostile bombardment to our right. L.O.O. Rifle from retribution. Heavy M.G. & one attempt at Bosch raid beaten off and a front line of 6 Coy caught a working party releasing at	P.H.

WAR DIARY or INTELLIGENCE SUMMARY

Army Form C. 2118.

Place	Date	Hour	Summary of Events and Information	Remarks and references to Appendices
	3/7/17 (cont)		bottom trench connecting posts. Bombers holding off an -20 men to assist D Coy. Coys by now had from D Coy to B Coy on right. C.O. Chas. of O.O. to reinforce D and B Coys from line. 6" shell in A Coy front line C.O. have arrived to arrange relief of	
	4/7/17	Before dawn	A & B Coys Coys started on front line embankment of Potsdam trench effort. Enemy shell D Coy with 8" How. 1 man slightly wounded.	
		11.20 12.30		
		noon	rate that bombs arrived at Potsdam trench	
		3.30 p.m.	Great-coats & blankets were lightly sacked, one pair brought down behind the lines.	
			Battn relieved by 7th hund. Relief complete 7.15 p.m. A & C Coys to Half horn. B.D. Coys to Bois Lore	
	5/7/17		Battn marched to Bourjany camp	
	6/7/17		Coy commanders and others to near Bro Rofucilon Batta Baths. C.O. away. Lt Col Keneston in command	p. W

T2134. Wt. W708 –776. 50C000. 4/15. Sir J. C. & S.

WAR DIARY
or
INTELLIGENCE SUMMARY.
(Erase heading not required.)

Army Form C. 2118.

Place	Date	Hour	Summary of Events and Information	Remarks and references to Appendices
BRONFAY	7/2/17	10 p.m.	Rations for tour in line sent off from PLATEAU station by DECAUVILLE Rly. to HAIE WOOD.	
		10–12 noon	Enemy shell PLATEAU and BILLON farm with 11-inch shells. Lt.-Col. W.A.J. BARKER D.S.O. acts for G.O.C. 57th Infy Bde while he is away on leave. Capt. J.D. HEWETSON in command of Battalion.	
			Battalion moves to BOULEAUX WOOD area: leave BRONFAY 1.30 p.m. Relief complete 5.45 p.m.	
		6 p.m.	100 men from A & D Coys report T.M. Battery COMBLES for carrying duties.	
		8.15 p.m.	B & C Coys work under 77th R.E. till 1 a.m.	
BOULEAUX	8/2/17	7.30 a.m.	7th Yorks attack and capture 300 yards of French on highest ground in SAILLISEL directly on Right of Battalion frontage.	
		4.30 p.m.	Coys move up to Intermediate line. C.O. and Adjutant arrive QUARRY Batt. Hd Qrs.	
		5.30 p.m.	Enemy place very heavy barrage on SAILLY-SAILLISEL village and CHATEAU WOOD. Sgts B, D, & A Coys killed in Intermediate line.	
		5.40 p.m.	Headquarters Coy. arrive in QUARRY.	ASW.

WAR DIARY
or
INTELLIGENCE SUMMARY
(Erase heading not required.)

Army Form C. 2118

Place	Date	Hour	Summary of Events and Information	Remarks and references to Appendices
	8/2/17	6 p.m.	C Coy. pass QUARRY on way to line. Enemy barrage slackens. 2/Lt N.W. GIBBONS wounded.	
		6:20 p.m.	B Coy arrive QUARRY (reserve Coy).	
		6:45 p.m.	D Coy start up from intermediate line and reach front line with 1 man wounded.	
		7 p.m.	30 men from B Coy under L/Sgt Hickman and 19 Northumberland Fusiliers carry up 50 boxes bombs to line captured by 7th Yorks - passing successfully through heavy barrage.	
		7:15 p.m.	A Coy leave intermediate line - 2/Lt D.M. BIRDSEYE and 1 O.R. killed. 2/Lt J.S. WILSON wounded and 10 O.R. in Chateau wood.	
		8:50 p.m.	Enemy put up 3 red rockets followed immediately by heavy barrages. Two green rockets seen in front. S.O.S. sent up by orders of O.C. 9th Northumberland Fusiliers at Batt. H.Q. All telephone wires broken.	
		9:10 p.m.	Situation much quieter.	
		9:42 p.m. 11:1 p.m.	} Heavy hostile barrages - on line and West of SAILLY. 2/Lt E.A. STAINES & C.A. SCOTT go on leave.	
	9/2/17	12:15 A.M.	First news from front line received at Batt. H.Q. Only 40 men of Coy have reached front line. O.C. A Coy reports 2/Lts H.H. ACTON & R.V. COTTERELL with 2 platoons B Coy, 1 Lewis gun, and 1 Batt. Bombing Squad sent to reinforce A (centre) Coy.	
		2:30 A.M.	Relief of 9th Northumberland Fusiliers complete.	
		3 A.M.	C.O. goes round line - brings 2/Lt WILSON back to Batt. H.Q.	AFW

Army Form C. 2118

WAR DIARY
or
INTELLIGENCE SUMMARY
(Erase heading not required.)

Instructions regarding War Diaries and Intelligence Summaries are contained in F.S. Regs., Part II and the Staff Manual respectively. Title Pages will be prepared in manuscript.

Place	Date	Hour	Summary of Events and Information	Remarks and references to Appendices
LINE SAILLY - SAILLISEL	9/2/17	3-30 A.M.	Situation quiet.	
			Enemy keeps up a steady slow fire on SAILLY all day. His aeroplanes busy the whole time.	
		10 A.M.	A few 4.2" shells around the QUARRY.	
			Following received from G.O.C. 50th Bde. – in command of left group – "The Brigade Commander considers that the relief on the night of 8/9th was very well carried out and is pleased that a supply of grenades were got through to SASH" [.7th Yorks].	
		6.45 p.m.	Capt Macey "D" Coy reports enemy shelling ceased.	
		10.13 p.m.	Heavy hostile artillery barrage on Château Wood and valley to North.	
		10.40 p.m.	About 10 4.2" shells into the QUARRY. Shelling ceases on retaliation.	
	10/2/17	1.45 A.M.	Another heavy barrage – connection by phone with all Coys goes. One shell in D Coy trench kills 2 men and wounds 5.	
		2.15 A.M.	Practically all quiet again.	
			Desultory shelling of front Coys all day. Enemy planes busy.	
		2 p.m.	Our Corps artillery bombard BOSNIA trench – 1000 yards to our left – for fifty-five minutes.	
		5 p.m.	Enemy retaliate on our left with howies and trig mortar bombs, especially around Left Coy H.Q.	AAW

Army Form C. 2118

WAR DIARY
or
INTELLIGENCE SUMMARY
(Erase heading not required.)

Instructions regarding War Diaries and Intelligence Summaries are contained in F.S. Regs., Part II. and the Staff Manual respectively. Title Pages will be prepared in manuscript.

Place	Date	Hour	Summary of Events and Information	Remarks and references to Appendices
Line	10/2/17	9.30 p.m.	Relieved by 7th Division. Relief complete. 2/Lt BACON joins. Battalion marches back to MALTZHORN and BOIS DOPE Camps. Att. in by 11 p.m.	
	11/2/17	12 noon	Batt. marches to BRONFAY Camp. All in camp by 2.45 p.m.	
BRONFAY FARM.			2/Lt S. BAKER awarded the CROIX DE GUERRE for effecting single handed the capture of 40 Germans on July 3rd, 1916 near RAILWAY ALLEY – This episode was the prelude to the surrender of the 186th Prussian Regiment.	
	12/2/17	1.30 p.m.	Major R.P. BURNETT M.C. returns from leave to England. Battalion bathing. 2/Lt R.W.A. GLEED returns from hospital. 2/Lt A.L.G. HIDER relieves Lt/Col A. GREEN as Town Major. MALTZHORN Camp. Lt/Col W.A. BARKER D.S.O. assumes command of 51st Infty. Bde. Major BURNETT M.C. O.C. Batt. Battalion undergo trench treatment for bluish light. All in by 6.40 p.m.	
	13/2/17	1.30 p.m. 8.30 p.m.	Battalion moves to BOULEAUX WOOD area. 150 men from B and C Coys work under 77th Field Cy R.E. 100 men from A and D " ditto.	
BOULEAUX WOOD	14/2/17	12.30 A.M.	relieve 9th Northumberland Fusiliers in line. Relief complete 8.40 p.m.	
Line.	15/2/17	11.5 AM 3.30 p.m 3.45 p.m to 3.55 p.m	During morning 3 enemy aeroplanes fly very low over SAILLY and HEBUE. Enemy barrage Chateau Wood. Our artillery reply. 3 enemy balloons visible high and close forward East of SAILLY SAILLISEL. Heavy enemy bombardment of HEBULE and S.W. Corner of SAILLY with 8", 5.9". Machine gun fire heard on our right. No casualties.	APW

WAR DIARY or INTELLIGENCE SUMMARY

Army Form C. 2118

(Erase heading not required.)

Instructions regarding War Diaries and Intelligence Summaries are contained in F.S. Regs., Part II. and the Staff Manual respectively. Title Pages will be prepared in manuscript.

Place	Date	Hour	Summary of Events and Information	Remarks and references to Appendices
line SAILLY-SAILLISEL	15/4/17	4.5–5pm	Our artillery bombards enemy lines opposite very effectively in answer to their bombardment.	
		5.55pm	No shelling on our front line. All quiet.	
		11.30pm	Recon by ("A" Coy) carry up large quantity of revetting material to front line. 4 men wounded (1 died of wounds). 3 Coy sends out patrol.	
	16/4/17	1.30 AM	2/Lt T. Baker patrols enemy wire.	
			Before dawn part of C and D Coys evacuate front line for heavy bombardment by our artillery.	
		10.25 AM	Bombardment cancelled. C and D Coys reoccupy line in small parties.	
			Several hostile balloons up. Artillery active on both sides.	
		3.30 pm	Situation quiet.	
		5.30 AM	Enemy bomb PLATEAU station and destroy ammunition dump.	
MALTZHORN			2/Lts T.H. BAKER and F.S. CREASY rejoin with draft of 61 O.R.	
		10.30 pm	Relief by 7th Lincolns complete. Coys march independently to MALTZHORN and BOIS DORÉ. 4th ACTN & GLEED with 100 O.R. remain for 3 hours work.	
	17/4/17	1.10 AM	Battn. all in.	
			2/Lt S. BAKER receives CROIX de GUERRE medal from Genl. NIVELLE at QUERRIEU (4th Army Headquarters).	
		12 noon	Battalion marches to BRONFAY via CARNOY (to avoid PLATEAU). All in 3.45 PM.	AFW

1875 Wt. W 593/826 1,000,000 4/15 J.B.C. & A. A.D.S.S./Forms/C. 2118.

WAR DIARY or INTELLIGENCE SUMMARY

Army Form C. 2118

Place	Date	Hour	Summary of Events and Information	Remarks and references to Appendices
BRONFAY	17/2/17		Small box respirators issued to Battalion.	
	18/2/17		Batt: entrains PLATEAU station for CORBIE, wait on station 12.30 p.m. till 4.20 p.m. Arrive CORBIE 8.15 p.m. March to billets in LA NEUVILLE. Transport moves by road.	
LA NEUVILLE	19/2/17		Stats 10.30 A.M. arrives LA NEUVILLE 4.50 p.m. Kit inspections.	
	20/2/17	10 A.M.	A Coy goes to ALLONVILLE wood for wood cutting.	
		11.45 A.M.	2/Lt BATON and 40 O.R. to Army Musketry Camp PONT REMY. Return in billets - practise with box respirators. Wet day.	
	21/2/17		Coy route march.	
	22/2/17		Draft of 88 other ranks join Battalion training.	
	23/2/17		Battalion reorganizing according to new scheme.	
	24/2/17		Battalion (less A Coy) bathe in CORBIE.	
	25/2/17		Church Services.	
	26/2/17		B, C, and D Coys have Small Box Respirators fitted in Tear Gas. Training.	
	27/2/17		2/Lt J.A ARMSTRONG joins Battalion. Lt Col W.A.J. BARKER D.S.O. returns from command of Brigade and assumes command of Battalion. Battalion training. 2/Lt R.T. BEARS sick admitted to Hospital.	
	28/2/17		Battalion Training. A Coy returns to Battalion from ALLONVILLE wood. B.SM furnishes Divisional guard of 2 N.C.Os and 6 men.	

> 8TH (S) BATTALION
> SOUTH STAFFS.
> REGIMENT.
>
> No. 1001
> Date 1/4/17

D.A.G.
Base.

Herewith War Diary of 8th Battn South Staffordshire Regiment from 1st to 31st March 1917.

1-4-17

W.A.J. Sankey Lieut. Colonel.
Comdg. 8th Service Bn. So. Staffs. Regt.

WAR DIARY or INTELLIGENCE SUMMARY

Army Form C. 2118.

Vol 21

Place	Date	Hour	Summary of Events and Information	Remarks and references to Appendices
LA NEUVILLE	1.3.17		Battalion training at LA NEUVILLE. Coy. attacks over formation. A Coy. filled with new Bns. registered on "Tat" gas cylinders found 1/2 mile by road to RUBEMPRE	App. B
RUBEMPRE	2.3.17		Battalion leaves LA NEUVILLE at 8-30 a.m. and marches to RUBEMPRE. Time of arrival 1-30 p.m. Afternoon testing R.Q.M.S. Bill J.T. appointed Temp Q.I. Master	App. B
"	3.3.17		Battalion training. Coy. attacks. A Coy. on range. L/Cpl Broadhurst wounded (nil dad) local.	App. B
"	4.3.17		Battalion training 9-1 p.m. Specialists under Specialist officers. Afternoon football versus Brigade "D" Lt. A.W. Gibbons rejoined	App. B
"	5.3.17		Battalion on Bde training ground from 8-10 a.m. Battery 2-4 p.m. in absence of field 3-30 - 4-30 p.m. Lecture to officers by Commanding officer	App. B
"	6.3.17		Companies on range when not training, either in Billets or on training ground. Afternoon rest. Officers and O.R.'s go on Bde. training ground subject: Outposts without troops.	App. B
"	7.3.17		Bde training ground Coys on outposts platoons out out on Patrol Lewis gunners on range. Bombers platoons in throwing Pits 2-30-3-30 Lecture to L.C.O.'s on Lice kill Pte. Biddle 11th Devonshire received live Vickers & Royal Bennet	App. B

WAR DIARY or INTELLIGENCE SUMMARY.

Army Form C. 2118.

Instructions regarding War Diaries and Intelligence Summaries are contained in F. S. Regs., Part II. and the Staff Manual respectively. Title pages will be prepared in manuscript.

(Erase heading not required.)

Place	Date	Hour	Summary of Events and Information	Remarks and references to Appendices
RUBEMPRE	8.3.17		Firing on Range. Musketry. Platoon and Coy. drill. Recoup of Sections preparatory to a right attack. Light operators forming up preparatory to an attack at dawn.	AAB
"	9.3.17	9-10 P.M	Battalion in attack. 3 P.M. Lecture to all officers R.O.B. and C.O.'s by Col. Mills (17th Div)	AAB
"	10.3.17		Firing on range. Musketry. Platoon and Company Drill. Afternoon football. Picnic Bordeux	AAB
"	11.3.17		Service in morning. Afternoon off.	AAB
"	12.3.17		Battalion training. Bivouac party proceed to GEZAINCOURT.	AAB
GEZAINCOURT	13.3.17		Battalion from RUBEMPRE to GEZAINCOURT. Time of arrival 2-30 P.M.	AAB
MAIZICOURT	14.3.17		Battalion leaves GEZAINCOURT for MAIZICOURT. Time of arrival 2-45 P.M.	AAB
REGNAUVILLE	15.3.17		Battalion leaves MAIZICOURT for REGNAUVILLE. Time of arrival 2-15 P.M.	AAB
"	16.3.17		Cleaning up. Inspections etc.	AAB
"	17.3.17		Musketry. Physical training. Platoon and Coy. drill in morning. Inspection of ammunition and equipment etc.	AAB
"	18.3.17		Church Parade. on training Ground.	AAB
"	19.3.17		Training. Musketry. Platoon drill etc. Inspection of officers kits, or soldiers	

T2134. Wt. W708-776. 50(000). 4/15. Sir J. C. & S.

WAR DIARY or INTELLIGENCE SUMMARY

Army Form C. 2118.

Place	Date	Hour	Summary of Events and Information	Remarks and references to Appendices
REGNAUVILLE	19.3.19		without troops.	6/43
"	20.3.19		Physical training, Bayonet fighting, Platoon drill, Sec schemes still in hillies. Training in route by Platoon. Coned Coys & marching order inspection by commanding officer	
"		5-7 pm	Lecture by Col. to Officers and S.N.C.o's (Temp) Capt. R.P. Burnett S.C. & Lt. (Temp) knight and appointed second in command of Battalion.	13/13
"	21.3.19		Training. Demonstration given by a Platoon of "D" Coy + Lewis Gunners and Rifle Grenadiers (forming all enemy strongpoint) showing use of LG covering fire and firing LG on the move. Divisional Staff attend.	14/13
"			Firing on range in afternoon. Lt. J.H. Phillips reported from PONT-REMY	15/13
BUIRE-AU-BOIS	22.3.19		Battalion leaves REGNAUVILLE for BUIRE-AU-BOIS. Time of Arrival 3.40 pm. 2nd Lt. T. HARE sent to hospital.	16/13
BEAUDRICOURT	23.3.19		Battalion leaves BUIRE-AU-BOIS at 8-15 am for Mt BEAUDRICOURT. Time of arrival 3.30 pm. 12 Coys left at BOUQUE MAISON for work on schools. These Coys rejoin Batt'n at night 7 P.M.	2/13
"	24.3.19		Battalion resting, cleaning up etc.	3/13
"	25.3.19		Church parade for B.Q., A.C. & D Coys on working parties at work on schools.	8/13
			BOUQUE MAISON area. Return at 7 P.M. 2nd Lt. Chooks admitted to hospital. Lt Phillips goes to Divisional as S.S.C. Bomber	

Army Form C. 2118.

WAR DIARY
or
INTELLIGENCE SUMMARY.
(Erase heading not required.)

Instructions regarding War Diaries and Intelligence Summaries are contained in F.S. Regs., Part II. and the Staff Manual respectively. Title pages will be prepared in manuscript.

Place	Date	Hour	Summary of Events and Information	Remarks and references to Appendices
BEAUDRICOURT	26.3.19		Battalion training in vicinity of billets, firing on range. Capt J.S. Baker assumes command of "A" Company. Lt S. Newton admitted to hospital.	AAB.
"	27		Three Companies B.O.D. at work on road repairs in vicinity of BOUQUEMAISON	AAB.
"	28		Training in billets. Officers on map reading and sketching by Commanding Officer. C.O. attended Conference at Brigade 5-30 P.M.	AAB.
"	29		Very wet day. Inspects in billets.	AAB.
"	30		Training in vicinity of billets. C.O.'s en route march	AAB.
"	31		3 Companies on working party in neighbourhood of BOUQUEMAISON. Inspection of transport by Divisional Inspector 10-30 a.m. afternoon football	AAB.

W.G. Foulser
Lieut Colonel
Comdg. 8th Service Bn. Sr. Staff Regt

T.134. Wt. W708–776. 500,000. 4/15. Sir J. C. & S.

Army Form C. 2118.

WAR DIARY
or
INTELLIGENCE SUMMARY.
(Erase heading not required.)

8th U.S. Staff

Place	Date	Hour	Summary of Events and Information	Remarks and references to Appendices
OPPY	1.4.19		Battalion bathing.	
BEAUDRICOURT	2.4.19		Left on roads at BOUQUEMAISON abandoned	
"	3.4.19		Brigade field day. Divisional Conference at D.H.Q	
"	4.4.19		Battalion training. Notice to move received.	
MONCHEAUX	5.4.19		Battalion leave at 8 am for MONCHEAUX (7 miles) arrive 12 noon	
"	6.4.19		Battalion resting (Good Friday) Orders received to move to GIVENCHY-LE-NOBLE	
GIVENCHY-LE-NOBLE	7.4.19		Battalion march to GIVENCHY-LE-NOBLE (about 7¼ miles) arrived about 1-30 P.M.	
NOYELLETTE	8.4.19		Battalion arrive here at 12 noon (distance 6¼ miles)	
"	9.4.19	1 am	Battalion under 4 hours notice to move.	
		5-30 am	Zero hour.	
		11 am	Battalion receives news of 1st line being taken.	
		11-30 am	Dinners.	
		3-45 P.M	Battalion has orders to move at 4-20 P.M	
		4.20 P.M	Battalion leave NOYELLETTE.	

T.22

Army Form C. 2118.

WAR DIARY
or
INTELLIGENCE SUMMARY.

(Erase heading not required.)

Instructions regarding War Diaries and Intelligence Summaries are contained in F.S. Regs., Part II. and the Staff Manual respectively. Title pages will be prepared in manuscript.

Place	Date	Hour	Summary of Events and Information	Remarks and references to Appendices
	9.4.17.	5.40 P.m	Battalion hear news of capture of 3700 his, many prisoners, cavalry on the way.	
		8.45 P.m	Heavy hail and snow storms.	
		10.20 P.m	Orders received to bivouac for night on road-side, about 3 Kilometres west of ARRAS. Bitterly cold, snow and sleet fall heavily.	MB
	10.4.17	12.25 am	Orders to send Guide for billets. Cookers to arrive for breakfast at 5.30 am.	
		2.20 am	Order received "Be ready to move at 30 minutes notice from 6 am".	
		5.00 am	Hear that it is impossible to get cookers up for breakfast.	
		7.40 am	2/Lt ARMSTRONG and 5 NCO's sent to ARRAS to billet Battalion.	
		9.30 am	Ordered to march to ARRAS at 10.15 am. 2/Lt. HARE reforms.	
		10.15 am	March to ARRAS.	
		11.30 am	Battalion billeted in cellars.	
		12.55 P.m	"No move probable before 2 p.m. Dinners and cook. 1 days iron rations to be issued before 2 P.m. Guide to be sent for billets. Leaving WARLUS at 12 noon.	

M Bennett Major
2 i/c Command
2/5 S.R.

WAR DIARY or INTELLIGENCE SUMMARY

Army Form C. 2118.

Place	Date	Hour	Summary of Events and Information	Remarks and references to Appendices
ARRAS	10.4.17	4 P.M.	1 day's iron rations drawn and issued	
		4.30 P.M.	Corks arrive. Rum and Groceries to be drawn	
		5.45 P.M.	Tea and Rum issued. Snow storms throughout the day.	R.H.B.
	11.4.17	2.30 am	Orders to send 600 men for working party to 228th R.E's ARRAS Station at 9 am (cancelled at 8am)	
			Reports of attack (1500 prisoners, 250 Officers, 113 guns, 168 m.g's, 50 T.M's, capture of VIMY RIDGE, advance of 5 miles on 12 mile front.)	
	11.4.17	2.30 am	"NEWS" ACHEVILLE abandoned, Boches retiring to DROCOURT and BOIS BERNARD – prisoners 200, and 40-80 guns. Can. Corps. 3,400.	
			Can Corps advancing to 1st Objective 4 P.M. Batt. of 37th Div. along full ORANGE-HILL. 4th Army hold ridge HARGICOURT – LE VERQUIER.	
		8am	Working party cancelled.	
		10.30am	Rumours that we are N.E of MONCHY and that 5th Army forcing towards PUEANT.	
		11.21am	Ordered to detail 400 men for clearing up at ARRAS Station at 12 noon 4th HACKETT to arrange Belt transport Officer.	

H. M. Burgess
2nd Lieut.
2nd Lieut. Staff

Army Form C. 2118.

WAR DIARY
or
INTELLIGENCE SUMMARY.
(Erase heading not required.)

Instructions regarding War Diaries and Intelligence Summaries are contained in F.S. Regs., Part II. and the Staff Manual respectively. Title pages will be prepared in manuscript.

Place	Date	Hour	Summary of Events and Information	Remarks and references to Appendices
ARRAS	11.4.17	11.45am	Guides sent to PLACE-du-THEATRE for Italians.	
		12.45 pm	Situation reported "General attack made by 17th, 6th and 7th Corps and 5th Army. 15th Div N.E. of MONCHY, 37th Div said to be in MONCHY. LA-BERGERE farm captured, heavy barrage W of MONCHY. Fifth Army gained 1st objective BULLECOURT - QUEANT. Italians arrive.	
		2.30 pm		
		3.30 pm	Having relief "7th Div. transferred to VII Corps, ordered to relieve 15th Div. E.N of MONCHY at night	
		4.15 pm	Working party withdrawn.	
		9 pm	91st Bde put at 60 min. to notice from 6 am (12th inst) to move into Reserve in BATTERY-VALLEY and FEUCHY.	12PB
			Snowing all night	
	12.4.17	6 am	Breakfast	
		9.30 am	Ecleter "B" arrives in ARRAS. P.O. visits Bde and Coms Plan of attack of 6th Corps. Explained to O.C. Coys.	
		11 am	Dinners	O/P Beccaed front of 2nd + in Sanct Noffe Ky 3rd in Sanct Noffe Ky

WAR DIARY or INTELLIGENCE SUMMARY

Army Form C. 2118.

Place	Date	Hour	Summary of Events and Information	Remarks and references to Appendices
ARRAS	12.4.17	6.10 pm	Orders to send advance parties to reconnoitre accommodation in RAILWAY-TRIANGLE East of BLANGY (occupied by 46th Bde)	
		6.30 pm	1 officer and 1 N.C.O. per Coy forward then.	
		6.50 pm	Warning order "53rd Bde will probably relieve 50th Bde on night of 13/14th. 51st Bde will relieve 52nd in support. 53rd Bde will probably move to Railway Triangle early on morning of 13th."	
		9.30 pm	Orders received to hand starting point at 6-12 am 13th inst. Advance parties report many dug-outs (several flooded) in Rly TRIANGLE, in embankment 30' high, also large tunnel. Suppose to progress of G.S. and L.W's. A few H.V. shells on ARRAS late in afternoon.	EAB
	13.4.17	5 am	Breakfast.	
		6.5 am	Batt: fall in	
		6.12 am	Batt: marches from ARRAS to RLY. TRIANGLE 1½ Km S.W. of ATHIES (100 yds between Coys) route along railway	
		8.30 am	All in Coy tunnel under embankment or in trenches.	
		1.30 pm	Attack by 29th Div: and 50th Bde postponed 24 hours.	

B.H.Berney
Major
Commanding
8th Batt: Suffolk Rgt

Army Form C. 2118.

WAR DIARY
or
INTELLIGENCE SUMMARY.
(Erase heading not required.)

Instructions regarding War Diaries and Intelligence Summaries are contained in F.S. Regs., Part II. and the Staff Manual respectively. Title pages will be prepared in manuscript.

Place	Date	Hour	Summary of Events and Information	Remarks and references to Appendices
RAILWAY-TRIANGLE	13.4.17	1.55 P.m.	S.O.S. changed.	
		5. P.m.	2/Lt. SCOTT, GREEN, SMITH and WHITAKER reconnoitre route to FEUCHY Chapel.	
		6.30 P.m.	Arrival of rations.	
		8 P.m.	Tractors to arrive for A, B and C Coys.	1293
			Operation Orders. Batt. will relieve 1st ESSEX and part of 50th Bde East of	
	14.4.17	12.5 a.m.	MONCHY, probably after midnight 14/15th	
		7. a.m.	Breakfast.	
		9.30 a.m.	Coys clearing of mud, bury & knees, collect and dump salvage.	
		12 noon	Brigadier interviews Commanding Officers. Batt. will now relieve 2nd HANTS. in Bde reserve W. of MONCHY.	
			29th Div. reported to have attacked and gained objective S.E. of MONCHY in early morning	
		2.30 P.m.	Situation. 29th Div. heavily counter-attacked falls back to original line. Batt. at 30 minutes notice to move.	
		2. P.m.	Coys. send parties for 1 Mills Grenade per man	
		2.45 P.m.	CO interviews O.C. Coys. and explains situation.	
		3.30 P.m.	Q.M. and 2/Lt HARE arrive with rations on Pack animals. Rum issued.	

M.P. Bracewell Major
i/c Comm. 1/5/16 Bn
3rd Essex Regt.

WAR DIARY or INTELLIGENCE SUMMARY

Army Form C. 2118.

Place	Date	Hour	Summary of Events and Information	Remarks and references to Appendices
	14.4.17	3.30 P.m.	Showers and hailstones more forward at about 4 and 6 P.m. respectively.	
		4-4.30 P.m	Heavy Boche barrage from S. of MONCHY to NORTH of river SCARPE.	
		7.45 P.m	Information from Bde Hqrs of probability of standing fast for the night. Coys warned. Bivouacs re-erected.	
		8.15 P.m	Bde Hqrs confirms above information. Greatcoats re-issued to Coys. Batt. to stand fast in present position. 29th Div. believed to have lost assembly trench E. of MONCHY, and intend to retake same.	1270
	15.4.17		2/Lt KELSEY rejoins from hospital (at Echelon "B" transport in ARRAS)	
		12.30 P.m	Brigadier brings in new "Scheme" as indicated by Hours this morning. MONCHY in a narrow salient.	
		12.45 P.m	C.O., 2/ic, Scott and GREEN, and 1 Off. and 1 S.C.O. per Coy reconnoitre route and meet representatives of people to be relieved (1st Lanc. Fus.)	
		1.45 P.m	Bde. B.O. informs "no" no relief to-night.	
		4 P.m	Arrival of rations.	
		8.15 P.m	Batt. sets out to work under 2nd held by A.E. on ORANGE HILL & CHAPEL HILL line. Capt. Foster in charge of party.	R.P.Bennett Major 2nd in Command 10th South Staffs Regt

T2134. Wt. W708-776. 50C090. 4/15. Sir J. C. & S.

WAR DIARY
or
INTELLIGENCE SUMMARY.
(Erase heading not required.)

Army Form C. 2118.

Place	Date	Hour	Summary of Events and Information	Remarks and references to Appendices
	15.4.19	8.53 p.m	Commanding Officer returns.	App 3.
	16.4.19	2 a.m	2/H Green returns, having completed disposition of 1/2nd Lanc. Hus. (62th Batt. 29th Div)	
		3.40 a.m	Bgd. returns from working party, having completed job. Cas. 3 OR's wounded (1 at duty)	
		7.30 p.m	Rain.	
	17.4.19		Same received that the French have captured 11,000 prisoners and are being heavily counter-attacked by fresh Divisions. During the morning A and C and D Coys change positions.	App 3.
		12.25 p.m	A few shells round the TRIANGLE. 2 OR's of A Coy Killed.	
		2 p.m	C.O. visits 52nd Bde HQ. N of MONCHY (Staffs and Borders to attack N of MONCHY and enter SCARPE.	
		6.30 p.m	Send a few orders received that 51st Bde will relieve 52nd Bde on 18th inst. Staffs to relieve 10th Lanc Fus on Left, Borders on right.	
		9.30 p.m	Situation report: 5th and 6th French Armies have taken 12,000 prisoners (15th inst) many counter-attacks. 4th French Army attacked on 15th inst from MAUROY to AUSERIBE, penetrated 1-2 kilos.	

A.M.Bussell Lt Col
o/c J. Staff Rg.

WAR DIARY
or
INTELLIGENCE SUMMARY.

Army Form C. 2118.

Place	Date	Hour	Summary of Events and Information	Remarks and references to Appendices
	18.4.17		Rainy morning, ground terribly muddy.	
		11.30 am	C.O. attended Conference at Bde. HQ.	
		2.20 pm	C.O. explains situation and plans to all Officers and N.C.O's.	
		7. pm	1 Offr. and 1 N.C.O. per Coy. go ahead to locate posts in front in daylight.	
		7.30 pm	Batt: starts from RLY Triangle along railway to front line S. of river SCARPE, N. of MONCHY - LE - PREUX in relief D.C.B.A. Hd. Q.ⁿ Relief complete. Coys in line right to left D.C.B.A. 10ᵗʰ L.F's Lewis party behind for short time to continue C.T. to A Coy. from Rly. 2 Coys. of Yorks and Lancs. at work during night digging assembly trench N. from LONE COPSE (right of Batt: Front) C.Coy. ordered to occupy it with one platoon when complete.	W.P.B.
	19.4.17	10 P.m.	Situation normal. C.Coy. report intermittent shelling 10 P.m. to 11-15 P.m. 1 Platoon of C.Coy. occupy assembly trench N. of LONE COPSE.	
		3-4.30 am	Each Coy. sends out patrol 2/Lt. BARLOW went to ahead of T trench opposite woodland, was fired on twice. Enemy sent up several very lights, much on the alert, occasional sniping.	

A.P.Birnitt Major
2ⁿᵈ in Command
4ᵗʰ South S.W.B.

Army Form C. 2118.

WAR DIARY
or
INTELLIGENCE SUMMARY.
(Erase heading not required.)

Instructions regarding War Diaries and Intelligence Summaries are contained in F.S. Regs., Part II. and the Staff Manual respectively. Title pages will be prepared in manuscript.

Place	Date	Hour	Summary of Events and Information	Remarks and references to Appendices
	19.4.17		Took guard with 9th Borders on right and 5th Gordons on left. Flat during night. Obtaining C.T. from R.E. to find tire, deepening and widening trench where necessary, extending trenches to make one continuous line.	
		4.40am	C.O. makes tour of line.	
		9.am	Situation quiet.	
		2.pm	Situation normal, intermittent shelling on posts and line. Poor visibility. Casualties for previous 24 hours 6 O.R.'s wounded.	
		4.45pm	Orders received that York. Rgt. (50th Bde) will relieve us to-night.	
		6.pm	Billeting party sent to BROWN LINE.	
		9.10pm	F.O.O. reports an S.O.S. sent up on our front. False alarm. Heavy shelling N.T of river SCARPE. Promiscuous shelling of Rly., FEUCHY etc.	
			Enemy put a barrage 200 yds W of his T.head – in front of me, evidently tried to frattico spritted down. 24th Barlow behind N.E. of LONE COPSE to discuss.	
		9.40pm	Stopped enemy put trick all over	
		11.50pm	Relief by York. complete. Coys. move independently to BROWN LINE. Putt up salvos from Dow Colour FEUCHY.	

A.P. Burnett Major
in "G" Command
2 i/c. 7. 365/R Rgt

WAR DIARY
or
INTELLIGENCE SUMMARY.
(Erase heading not required.)

Army Form C. 2118.

Place	Date	Hour	Summary of Events and Information	Remarks and references to Appendices
	20.4.17	1 am	Batt. sell in BROWN LINE.	
		3.10 am	Enemy shells neighbourhood of Batt. bivouacs for 15 minutes. No casualties. Shrapnel shelling of area around gun emplacements close to BROWN LINE and W. of it, about a dozen gas shells fell over during morning.	
		4.10 pm	Batt. relieved by 9th N.F's. Horses across country to ESTAMINET corner then via CAMBRAI rd. to ARRAS. Batt. in caves, all in by 6.45 pm	RPB
	21/4/17		Batt. bathes in Grande Place. ADS in the morning. CO (Lt. Col. Digglehurst?) goes to HQs 51st Div/ 13th Bde Rly Triangle for CO's conference & returns at 2.15 pm	
		11 am		
		2.30 pm	Orders to move receivd to Coys.	
		4 pm	CO sees all offrs & explains plan of attack. Bde dept in order.	
			Bonaville to near Citadel ATRAS	
		6.15 p	Batt. Move to fm. line Philoma in the Rock Cambrai Road Ce. Plomont Comer thence across country to junction of Rookery & the Brown Line	
		7.45 pm	CO received order from 50th Div. O.O. to cross Brown Line before starting party to work parties busy on front line	

Army Form C. 2118.

WAR DIARY
or
INTELLIGENCE SUMMARY.
(Erase heading not required.)

Instructions regarding War Diaries and Intelligence Summaries are contained in F.S. Regs., Part II. and the Staff Manual respectively. Title pages will be prepared in manuscript.

Place	Date	Hour	Summary of Events and Information	Remarks and references to Appendices
Vierres S	27/4/17	12h	Bn. leave Brown line to relieve 1st Yorks in front line south of River Scarpe. 1st Yorks have one company out on covering party to a working party of 3 yrks & leics. Digging assembly trench about 600 yds in front of front line. Working party did not return & the relief was not complete till daylight.	
			Yorks have patrols along southern side of railway Jouvais & Roeux. Patrol fires on & shelters enemy post in water tower on side of lake.	
Attri	28/4/17	10:30am	Relief complete with exception of covering party of about 100. Patrol mentions above returns & covering party sent to support side of Roeux.	
		2am		
		4 am	CO with front line & front troops.	
			Roeux & trenches & high bank.	
		3:30pm	Officer Other ranks from BHr.	
		4:30pm	CO returns & dictates operation orders to carry copy to Bn H.Q.?	
		5:15	Op's issued to Coys.	
		9pm	BC Roger calls at BnHQ.	

WAR DIARY or INTELLIGENCE SUMMARY

Place	Date	Hour	Summary of Events and Information	Remarks and references to Appendices
	22/4/17	7.26 A	Artillery Programme received	
		7.30 "	Brigadier calls to see C.O.	
		8 "	Artillery Programme sent to Coys.	
		8.27 "	Bn H.Q. moves to C Coy H.Q. in front line	
		8.30 "	Working parties B Coy sent out to cover working parties front x	
			Bn. Co digging Assembly trenches	
		10 "	Women A Coy carrying forward from the bomb store specified by R.E.	
		9.45 "	Gas projectors into the wood sent out by J. Reeve	
		10.30 "	C.O. goes to Bde H.Q. for final arrangements as to liaison W.B.	
		11.20 "	Bde O. Bn. C/F. Returns to Bn H.Q. at 11.30 pm	
		12 m.n	H.Q. Men hurt to all men	
	23/4/17	2 am	Coys commence moving to Assembly trenches. 2 " Lieut Scott & Lieut Hughes had from Bn H.Q. to Assembly trench to guide & report completion at 2.50 am.	
		3.30 am	Capt Foster reports that all Coys are in position in Assembly trenches. C.O. report same to Bde.	
		4 am	C.O. & H.Q. on move forward to Assembly trench leaving telephone Serjeant & Staff to forward messages from H.Q. to Bde H.Q.	

WAR DIARY or INTELLIGENCE SUMMARY

Army Form C. 2118.

Place	Date	Hour	Summary of Events and Information	Remarks and references to Appendices
Vimy S Att[ac]k	29/4/19	4.35am	CO myself on my knees who are all in position. Guns down & ready to storm. Men in excellent spirits	
		4.45am	Artillery barrage opened on the line 200 yards ahead of enemy trench. Went at pace.	
		4.47am	Lost touch with A Co on left.	
		4.49	A Coy barrage lifts onwards.	
			When A Coy barrage lifts on to enemy trench, lost touch after	
			Artillery barrage lifts on to enemy at enemy trench & reached gallery B.C.	
			When I arrived all front left trench	
	4.51	Jn. from B/l Hewitt	
		4.55	A large indent found that went about 9ft over & about	
			3 bays. Several killed & wounded men lying on enemy wire	
		5am	when they were heavily hosing in. Orders	
			Co pushes forward + a front to guide & engineer	
			Co pushes forward. Coys which are much more bent.	
			Also asks Artillery from Officer to be drawn back on our enemy	
			has now gone in.	
			Front trench.	
		5.10y	A shout on second front enemy on enemy berry	

Place	Date	Hour	Summary of Events and Information	Remarks and references to Appendices
Trenches ATTACK	27/4/17	5.15a	Our 1st Wave Rifle section S/Noward to Enemy trench again. In a second line Any came under galley MG fire from Our left flank & many more casualties were [illegible] suffered. Co. & two Offrs. becoming Casualties. H When 3rd & 4th waves crippled at a standard point any Artillery barrage on Our Enemy 1st trench.	
		3.30am	A General advance & Enemy break through this time with Bn given. Out line being driven from Our right slope Our attack came to a Standstill from Our left. And our Enemy wire.	
		5.40	Bn stand by with Dawn. Remaining Offrs & 2 Cos. ordered to make up deficiency in 3 Cos. to occupy Our assembly trench & L. HQ. About this time Bn Y2 Lincolns Regt. (12th Suffolks too) arrives & about 7:30 am received order from Bde to make another attempt. This was also not however successful.	

Army Form C. 2118.

WAR DIARY
or
INTELLIGENCE SUMMARY.
(Erase heading not required.)

Place	Date	Hour	Summary of Events and Information	Remarks and references to Appendices
Vimy Area	23/4/18		Heavy bombardment of this day. Staffords & Lancasters Regiments & Bttys in what the Enemy put down & very heavy barrage on the position chiefly of 5.9's. Our artillery burst a tremendous bombardment over position occupied by Stafford & Lancasters as soon as the enemy were seen. They had to withdraw also.	
		6 pm	Co. received mobilisation Rial Survey were [illegible] their counter attack down the Palos Valley, [illegible] D by 2 actions & across the valley going up good end of high bank to the Lake & dig small strong posts. They were stored in Y.L.L.C. 'B' [illegible] inflicted by Enemy on Lancashires Trench keeping cleared	
		9 pm	Baths with D. Down.	
	24/4/18	4 am	by Y's [illegible]	
		1 pm	Bryans Buncett Q.S.	
		3 pm	to personnel from the depot by own no. water No. 2. Coy.	
	25/4/18	1 am	on. No relief would be [illegible]	

Army Form C. 2118.

WAR DIARY
or
INTELLIGENCE SUMMARY.
(Erase heading not required.)

Instructions regarding War Diaries and Intelligence
Summaries are contained in F. S. Regs., Part II.
and the Staff Manual respectively. Title pages
will be prepared in manuscript.

Place	Date	Hour	Summary of Events and Information	Remarks and references to Appendices
Hamel	25.9.	6 am	Bn. relieved in Bg Firing by 7' Suffolks & go to ATTN.	
ATTN.		7.45 am	Breakfast.	
		8.15 am	March to Station.	
		11.30 am	En'd'rained at ATTN. Unload & detrained at SAULS LARGUEAN	
		1.20 pm	March to billets at Beauval, Coy's arriving 4.30 pm	
Beauval/Court.		6.45 pm	Fire occurred in No 23 billet. Bomb & rifle ammunition exploding freely. When every great personal effort to get the fire under Mayor Burnett M.C. slightly wounded by bomb splinter in right hand. Following casualties were incurred in fight 21/22	orly.

KILLED: -   Capt. T. FOSTER, 2/Lt. S.G. WHITAKER, 2/Lt. R.V. COTTERELL, 2/Lt. F.S. CREASY,
WOUNDED: - Lieut A.P. WHITEHEAD, 2/Lt A.E. HUSBAND, 2/Lt W.S. BACON, 2/Lt W.P. RHODES, 2/Lt J.A. GREEN,
            2/Lt C.A. SCOTT,
WOUNDED & MISSING: - 2/Lt. A.S. BOURNE, 2/Lt. A.J. BROWNE, 2/Lt. J.S. STEPHENS,
WOUNDED at DUTY: - Capt. G.B. LANGTON, 2/Lt. T.H. SMITH.
OTHER RANKS: - KILLED: - 26. WOUNDED: - 58. MISSING: - 133. WOUNDED at DUTY: - 1.
TOTAL CASUALTIES: - OFFICERS: - 15. OTHER RANKS: - 218.

Army Form C. 2118.

WAR DIARY
or
INTELLIGENCE SUMMARY.
(Erase heading not required.)

Instructions regarding War Diaries and Intelligence Summaries are contained in F. S. Regs., Part II. and the Staff Manual respectively. Title pages will be prepared in manuscript.

Place	Date	Hour	Summary of Events and Information	Remarks and references to Appendices
BEAUDRICOURT	26.4.17		Battalion bathing. General cleaning up.	APP3
"	27.4.17	5.P.M. 5.30P.	2/Lt. S. BAKER granted leave to PARIS. Brigadier visits C.O. Reinforcements arrive. 1 Officer and 34 O.R's.	APP3
"	28.4.17	3.30P.M 6.30P.	Training. Platoon and Coy. drill. G.O.C. (19th Div.) visits P.O. (10.30 am). Football match v 5/Nd F.A. result Staffords 4. F.A. 3. C.O. visits Bat. Hd. Qrs.	APP3
"	29.4.17	10.30P.M	Church parade 11.30 am. Football in afternoon. 2 Officers and 150 O.R's rejoin from Corps Depôt. Warning orders received to move on 2nd May. Spare kits etc. to be stacked in teachers.	APP3
"	30.4.17	10.15 a.m 5.P.M	Warning order of yesterday cancelled. Prepare to move on May 1st Court of Inquiry re fire in D.O.23 killed reassembles. Operation orders received to move to Beaudry at 2 P.M. 1st May 1917.	APP3

B.P. Bennett Major
2/Lt South Staffs Regt

Ref. Map.
51 B. N.W.
& PEEVES.

OPERATION ORDERS BY.
LIEUT.COLONEL. W.A.J.BARKER D.S.O.
COMDG. 8th. Bn. South Staffordshire Regiment.
22-4-17.

1. INFORMATION.

A General Advance will take place tomorrow the 23rd. inst, zero hour will be notified later.

Battalion will assemble as detailed below, and will attack the enemy trenches immediately to its front, simultaneously attacks will be made by the 7th Borders and 29th Division on our right and 51st Division on our left.

The 10th Sherwood Foresters will be in support to the 7th Borders, and the 7th Lincolns to the 8th South Staffords.

2. OBJECTIVE.

Trench system in I 25 c and the blue line, boundaries in the first trench system to be crossed are, the Canal to the North, and the junction of RIFLE and BAYONET trenches to the South (RIFLE TRENCH exclusive)

The BLUE LINE runs North and South through I 26 a N.9. - a 8 9 - I 26 c. 7.7. - G 2,2. (including work and quarries in I 26 c. 7.7.)

3. ASSEMBLY.

The Battalion will assemble in the Assembly Trenches North of LONE COPSE at 5 a.m. "D" & "C" Coys in Assembly trench H.30 d.3.1. to H.30 b.7.2. "B" & "A" Coys in Assembly trench H.30 d.0.2. to H.30 a.B.0.

Boundary between Coys East and West line through H.30.d.4.7.

4. FORMATION OF ATTACK.

The Battalion will attack in four waves, "D" & "C" Coys will attack in two waves, each wave to consist of two. lines, 15 yards between lines and 100 yards between waves.

"B" & "A" Coys in support, will advance in two waves, each wave to consist of four platoons moving by sections in single file, 200 yards in rear of 2nd wave of "D" & "C" Coys. The extension in this case will be about 10 yards between men.

Five (5) minutes before zero time, all Coys will be faced up on the proper alignment. If there is no shelling the first wave of each Coy in front of its trench, the second wave behind the trench. Os.C. Coys will be in positions where they can actually start their first waves off in time, falling in with their second waves as they come along

Both "C" & "A" Coys will detail a special section to watch their left flanks, and to investigate the bank which runs along the southern shore of the lake.

On or before arrival at the cross roads at I 25 d 70.95. O.C. C Coy will push out one or two platoons, as required, half left to get into line with his leading platoons.

5. ASSAULT.

The assault will be carried out by following the barrage as closely as possible throughout the attack, and rushing all German trenches where met with.

6. ARTILLERY PROGRAMME.

This will be notified separately later.

7. STOKES MORTARS

Two Stokes Mortars under 2/Lt. TYRRELL will be established during the night at the Northern end of the jumping off trench in I 30.d. They will assist in guarding the left flank of the Battalion, and as each objective is gained will move forward in rear of the Battalion. If the situation allows Os.C. Coys will on request from 2/Lt.TYRRELL supply him with a few men to carry up ammunition from one fire position to another.

8. MACHINE GUNS.

Orders to the two Machine Guns attached to the Battalion will be given separately.

2.

9. SIGNALLERS. The Battalion Signalling Officer will run a line from the advanced Bde. Hd.Qrs at H 23 b.3.1. to the present "C" Coy Hd.Qrs H.29 b.5.3.) This Hd.Qrs will be report Centre, A wire will be run from this Hd.Qrs tonight as far as the assembly trench and will be continued to Bayonet Trench near the junction of Rifle Trench as the attack progresses.
Visual must be used as much as possible.

10. CONSOLIDATION. "C" & "D" Coys will consolidate on the Eastern or Forward slope of the Blue Line objective. The quarries near PELVES Mill will be the right hand post of "C" Coy.
"B" & "A" Coys if not drawn into the front line during the action will consolidate in platoon posts on the reverse side of the slope. All posts should be of the Z pattern. The most intense digging will be used. The road running on top of the ridge should be avoided as it has telegraph posts on it and is an easy Artillery mark.

11. FLARES. Flares in groups of twos or threes will be lighted by the advanced troops of "C" & "D" Coys when they have taken their objective or should they receive a check.
These flares are only to be lighted when called for by aeroplanes by the claxon horn or Very Light, and will probably be required at 7 a.m.

12. EVACUATION OF WOUNDED & PRISONERS. All Stretcher Bearers will remain with Hd.Qrs until after Bayonet Trench has been captured. They will then be used as circumstances arise. The M.O. will establish an forward Dressing Station under the high Bank Near LONE COPSE.
The leading Coys will take no steps as regards prisoners with the exception that they are all disarmed and driven into the open towards the rear two Coys.
1 N.C.O. from "A" and 1 from "B" will be detailed to collect these prisoners. An escort of 1 man for every 10 prisoners will be supplied. They will be marched direct to Bde. Hd.Qrs., handed over, receipts taken and the escorts will then rejoin their Coys.
2/Lt. GREEN will arrange about collecting papers and investigating any dugouts there may be in the various trenches
Suvenir hunting is a CourtMartial offence, and all ranks must be warned that if they take part in this they are gravely imperilling the success of the operation.

13. DETAILS.
a. Every man will carry 180 rounds of S.A.A.
b. " " " " his own bomb and if necessary when the objective is gained, platoon Officers will have them collected.
c. Rifle Grenades will be collected in Sandbags, and handed over to the Rifle Grenadier Sections.
d. Tools 60% of the Coys will carry tools in the proportion of half picks and half shovels.
e. Waterbottles will be filled under Coy arrangements before 10 p.m. tonight. The C.O. is making efforts to get tea sugar and milk up so that the men can have a hot drink about 12 midnight. Any Coy arrangements made in this respect still hold good. If tea as above is obtained it will be supplementary
f. Individuals carrying Very Lights and Pistols must be known to the O.C.Coy and should become casualties these should be collected.
S.O.S. 2 green or 2 reds not both, preferably reds.
g. Wirecutters detailed to leading platoons.
h. BARRAGES. Should the enemy put down barrages, the safest position is forward of the barrage towards the enemy.

14. REPORTS. The report Centre is "C" Coy Hd.Qrs dugout which all runners of all Coys must know.
As the Battalion advances a wire will be run out following the C.O. but should he be missed, the orderly will go to the report centre where he will be directed.

15. These orders will be communicated to and studied by all ranks, and the C.O. hopes and expects that in carrying them out the 8th South Staffords will maintain the high reputation they now hold.

24-4-17.

Dear Collins,

I have just heard from the C.R.A. 33rd Division that all his men are full of admiration at the most gallant way in which the South Staffords attacked Bayonet Trench yesterday.

All the F.O.O.'s who saw it describe it as a magnificient show.

Yours,

Philip Wheatley.
(C.R.A. 17th Division).

Dear General,

Forwarded for communication to O.C. South Staffords.

Yours,

26-4-17.   R.G.Collins,

D.A.G.
Back.

Herewith War Diary of the Battalion under my Command for month of May 1917.

W.J. Parker Lt Col
Comg 8th So Staff Rgt

WAR DIARY or INTELLIGENCE SUMMARY

Army Form C. 2118

J. S. Stafford
Vol 23

Place	Date	Hour	Summary of Events and Information	Remarks and references to Appendices
BEAUDRICOURT	1.5.17	9 am	Orders received to be ready to entrain at 2 P.M. Battalion marched from BEAUDRICOURT TO GRAND-RULLECOURT for Y	
		2 P.M.	Entrained at L.I.B. Battalion detrained at 5-30 P.M.	
		11 P.M.	Operation orders to move on the 3rd not received.	
" HUTS "	2.5.17		Reorganizing sections. Physical Training. Platoon drill etc.	RMB
	3.5.17	3.45 am	Zero hour 4th and 7th Divisions attack	RMB
		7.15 am	Batt. ready to move.	
ST. NICHOLAS CAMP		7.31 am	Leave Y huts for ST. NICHOLAS CAMP arrive 9-50 am and under orders to move at 2 hours notice to reinforce either the 4th and 9th Division. C.O. proceed on leave to England	RMB
	4.5.17	4 P.M.	Wire received "No prepare moved by 4th and 9th Divisions 2 hours notice to move is cancelled	
			General cleaning up of camp. Coy training etc. Till further orders.	
		6.30 P.M.	The Brigadier visits Major BURNETT	RMB
		8 P.M.	Ammunition dumps on fire in ARRAS. Boots steel outside of town and vicinity of camp	
	5.5.17		Physical Training etc. and bathing in the river SCARPE	
		4.30 P.M.	Thunderstorm. 2/Lts Wilson and Wells reconnoitre new road track to ATHIES	RMB
		9 P.M.	Heavy enemy bombardment. Shelling close to camp	
	6.5.19	7.45 am	Working party of 1 Officer and 50 O.R's to work under Corps Sgn. Officers at railway bridge H.14.a.0.2.	
		10 am	Church parade on parade ground East of camp.	
		12.30 P.M.	6 other ranks proceed to BOB DÉPÔT en route to base camp BOULOGNE on ?	T.23
		5 P.M.	Warning orders for operation on 12th received	
		5.30 P.M.	C.O. has at offices in M.G. Tak with reference to orders received	RMB
	7.5.19	10 am	Final Pres. of Camp Lewis Gunners and bombers being formed. O.C. Coys take platoon this is in not reading and continue bathing.	

Court of Enquiry re. Pte EVANS held. Capt. MASSY President.

WAR DIARY
or
INTELLIGENCE SUMMARY.

Army Form C. 2118.

Place	Date	Hour	Summary of Events and Information	Remarks and references to Appendices
ST. NICHOLAS CAMP.	7.5.17	12 noon	Wire from Bde. stating that working parties would be called upon daily. C.O. addresses the Batt: re working parties and the importance of work to be accomplished.	R.B.
		5 p.m.		
	8.5.17	9.30 p.m.	Order to detail a working party of 4 Officers and 251 O.R's ranks for 8" work till 2 p.m.	R.B.
		6.45 am	1st Working party of 2 Officers and 100 O.R's. Eng. fat: work till 2 p.m.	
		12.45 p.m	2nd party of 2 Officers and 100 O.R's went till 8 p.m.	
			Work continues burying of cables, 4000 yards in rear of lines	
		1 p.m.	Another working party of 3 Officers and 100 O.R's reported	
		6 p.m.	Operation orders for operations on 11th and 12th received	
			51st Bde. to engage to 19th Div: Commander also on above. C.O. interviews all Co. Commanders on out front line.	R.B.
	9.5.17	10.30 p.m	Heavy enemy bombardment on our front line. Batt: leaving 2 S's and Lewis hats of 5 Officers and 260 O.R's relief received	R.B.
		11.30 a.m	Party of 1 Officer and 50 men reported	
		9 p.m.	50th and 52nd Bdes arrive forward. Remainder 00's received	R.B.
	10.5.17		Training. No working parties required	
	11.5.17	7.30 p.m.	19th Div: attack CEMETERY - CHEMICAL WORKS - RAILWAY BUILDINGS. CAM - CROW - CROOK Trenches. All objectives taken. 350 prisoners	R.B.
	12.5.17	6.30 a.m	19th Div attack CUPID - CURLY - CHARLIE - W1157	

M.H. Bennett Maj.
D. Smith J. Koffe R.I.

Army Form C. 2118.

WAR DIARY
or
INTELLIGENCE SUMMARY.
(Erase heading not required.)

Place	Date	Hour	Summary of Events and Information	Remarks and references to Appendices
ST. NICHOLAS CAMP	13.5.17	9 am	Battalion Training	APB
		1 pm	Bathing in CANAL east of Camp	
	14.5.17		Usual Training	
		11:30 am	Orders received to relieve LINCOLNS in RAILWAY CUTTING (H.9 & 8.6)	
		12 noon	above orders cancelled.	
		2 pm	Orders again received to relieve in RAILWAY CUTTING.	
		4 pm	Batt. operation orders issued.	
		7.45 pm	H.Q. and A Coy leave Camp and proceed to RAILWAY CUTTING	
		8.40 pm	Arrival in CUTTING, occupy LINCOLNS Quarters	APB
	15.5.17		Orders received to relieve LANCASHIRE FUSILIERS in GREEN LINE (H.6.0)	
			operation orders issued.	
			Arrival in GREEN LINE and find no relief in taking place.	
			C.O. on phone to Bde. H.Q. found 200 yds in rear of LANCASHIRE	
		2.30 pm	FUSILIERS H.Q.	APB
		5.30 pm	Batt: relief Completed. Right Quiet.	
		9.30 pm		
GREEN LINE		10. pm		
	16.5.17	3-45 am	Boche attack SORSET Regt. in front line and gain a footing.	
		7.30 am	Orders to take Batt H.Q received.	
			C.O. proceeds to Bde to take Batt H.Q to Bde in advance.	
		8.15 am	Orders from C.O. to counter-attack CUSHION TRENCH	
			attack postponed until 9-30 am	
		8.45 am	A, B, and D Coys ordered to assemble in CADIZ TRENCH.	
		9.30 am	attack starts. D.G. Leading, A Coy arriving and supports	C. R.M. Burgess Major
				D⁰ Smith Major R⁰

Army Form C. 2118.

WAR DIARY
or
INTELLIGENCE SUMMARY.
(Erase heading not required.)

Instructions regarding War Diaries and Intelligence Summaries are contained in F. S. Regs., Part II. and the Staff Manual respectively. Title pages will be prepared in manuscript.

Place	Date	Hour	Summary of Events and Information	Remarks and references to Appendices
CADIZ TRENCH	16.5.17	10.5.D a.m.	Message from O.C. B Coy that CUSHION TRENCH is reoccupied. O.C. reports the above to Bde H.Q.	
		11.25 am	C Coy not yet arrived from BROWN LINE, C.O. reports this to Bde.	
"		11.30 am	Report from Capt MASSY (O.C. D Coy) received for more L.G's and supports. Wire from Bde asking what time to decide for attack on CURLY and CUPID.	
		2 P.M.	Barrage of 4 min: write heavies asked for.	
		2.30 P.M.	Ordered to stand fast. Attack postponed. 2 H BORDERS to attack at 9.30 P.M.	
		3.30 P.M.	Ration party of 60 men sent to GREEN LINE for rations.	
		3.40 P.M.	Barrage for 2 H BORDERS put down. BORDERS not yet arrived, and attack is cancelled.	
		9.30 P.M.	C.O. 2 H BORDERS asks if attack can be carried out by ourselves. No reply from Bde. CADIZ	
		9.45 P.M.	Batt relieved by BORDERS in trenches, and on relief proceed to GREEN LINE.	
		10 P.M.	Relief complete. O. C. C Coy returns from CUSA Trench with 1 prisoner.	RPB
GREEN LINE	17.5.17	4.30 am	Orders for 1 Coy to go as close support to BORDERS and B Coy goes up and over effort to O.C. 2 BORDERS in CADIZ Trench. 30 men from C Coy sent to release jack from CADIZ Trench.	
		9 P.M.	A Coy tortorin.. Carried by B Coy.	

A5834 W.W.4973 M687 750,000 8/16- D.D. & L. Ltd. Forms/C.2118/13.

McBerwick Major
3 H South Staffs R.

Army Form C. 2118.

WAR DIARY
or
INTELLIGENCE SUMMARY.
(Erase heading not required.)

Instructions regarding War Diaries and Intelligence Summaries are contained in F. S. Regs., Part II. and the Staff Manual respectively. Title pages will be prepared in manuscript.

Place	Date	Hour	Summary of Events and Information	Remarks and references to Appendices
GREEN LINE	17.5.17	11. P.m.	Party of 1 Officer and 45 men to carry S.A.A. To Front Line	App B
	18.5.19	9. a.m.	Orders from Bde to move H.Q.rs into GREEN LINE Bde H.Q.rs to SUNKEN Rd	
		10 a.m.	1/4th WELLS sent to recover the GREEN LINE for Batt: Hd. Q.rs in	
		8.15 Pm	1 Officer 1 Sergt. 1 Cpl. and 60 men to carry bombs for BORDER Regt in	
			CADR. TRENCH	
		9.45 P.m	Carrying party of 2 Officers 100 O.R's ordered	App B
	19.5.17		Slight shelling by enemy throughout the day.	
			Enemy quiet in the morning	
		2.15 P.m.	One N.C.O. and 5 men to report to Bde bombing Officer	
			all S.A.A. and bombs collected in GREEN LINE and dumped	
		3.15 P.m.	Leave reopens. 1 Officer and 3 O.R's proceed on leave. (Officer Lt HARE)	
			Usual carrying parties provided.	
		9.20 P.	Heavy bombardment by enemy on south side of canal.	App B
		10.30 P.m	C.S.M. COADY (S.G.) killed by shell fire.	
	20.5.19	9 am	Three enemy aeroplanes over GREEN LINE engaged by own and	
			other Officer	
		3. P.m	O.O's received. Batt: to be relieved by 7th EAST YORKS.	
		4. P.m	Advance party sent down to RAILWAY CUTTING.	
		5.1 P.m	Advance party of 7th EAST YORKS arrive at RAILWAY CUTTING.	
		10. P.m.	C.O of EAST YORKS arrives and takes over.	
RAILWAY CUTTING	21.5.17	10. a.m.	G.O.C interviews Batt: Commanders.	App B
		2. P.m	Rations arrive at RAILWAY CUTTING.	
		4. P.m	Major of PLOUVAIN received and issued to Companies	
	22.5.17	9 a.m	O.O's received to effect that 51st Bde attacks in pro forma	
		12.4h	P.O. (Col. BARKER) arrives and visits Brigades.	
		1.30 P.m	Operation orders received Batt: to relieve BORDERS in GREEN LINE.	

Army Form C. 2118.

WAR DIARY
or
INTELLIGENCE SUMMARY.

(Erase heading not required.)

Instructions regarding War Diaries and Intelligence Summaries are contained in F. S. Regs., Part II. and the Staff Manual respectively. Title pages will be prepared in manuscript.

Place	Date	Hour	Summary of Events and Information	Remarks and references to Appendices
RAILWAY CUTTING	22.5.19	2.15 P.m	Advance party relieved for GREEN LINE under 2/Lt SMITH	
		3.30 P.m	Operation orders issued to Companies	
		5.10 P.m	Rations arrive.	
		6 P.m	C.O. interviews Coy Commanders.	
		7.10 P.m	Party of 3 officers and 130 O.R.s relieved.	
		8.45 P.m	C.O. leaves for GREEN LINE.	
		9.30 P.m	Arrival at BORDER. Hot grog in LEMON TRENCH in GREEN LINE	
		11.8 P.m	Relief complete.	
		11.25 P.m	Enemy shells with 5.9s. Found Hot Q? 1 Left and 1 man wounded by shell fire in GREEN LINE. Situation quiet, working parties provided.	RPB
GREEN LINE	23.6.19	3 P.m	Lt BARKER and Brigadier arrive in GREEN LINE.	
		5 P.m	Orders received for 1 Coy to relieve 1 Coy of SANE in CADIZ and 1 Coy in support to SASH in CADIZ TRENCH.	
		9.45 P.m	Rations arrive.	
		10 P.m	Capt. LANGTON and 2/Lt S BAKER arrive with reinforcements.	
		12 mid	12 BINCHE maps issued. 1 killed and 2 wounded S Lesl Fus connections.	RPB
	24.6.19	10.20 a	C.O. and 2/Lt WILSON leave for front line	
		1.35 P.m	Operation orders for 3 relief received	
		1.40 a	Return of C.O. from front line	
		3 P.m	Operation orders issued to Companies	
		6 P.m	Bde Major visits C.O. Capt LANGTON and 2/Lt S BAKER take over front line.	
		9.30 P.m	C.O. and Hot Q? depart base for CADIZ TRENCH.	

A.5834. Wt.W.4973 M687. 750,000 8/16 D. D. & L. Ltd. Forms/C.2118/13.

WAR DIARY or INTELLIGENCE SUMMARY

Army Form C. 2118.

Place	Date	Hour	Summary of Events and Information	Remarks and references to Appendices
CADIZ TRENCH	25.5.17	1 a.m.	C.O. and adjt at 10th Yorks leave for GREEN LINE	
		1.45 a.m.	C.O. leaves for tour of front line and to arrange patrols	
		2.20 a.m.	Lt. BAKER and 4/Pt. S. BAKER also 2 servants wounded by rifle grenade.	
		2.45 a.m.	Major BURNETT goes up to front line with 2/Lt WILSON	
		4.45 a.m.	Casualties clear of CADIZ TRENCH	
		5.30 a.m.		
		9.30 a.m.	C. Company carry 20,000 rounds S.A.A and 40 boxes of bombs from TANK DUMP to Hd. Qrs.	
		12 noon	Brigade Major visits Hd. Q'rs. no casualties	
		2.30 p.m.	Steering round. C.O. visit reference to raids.	
		4.30 p.m.	T.M.B officer visits. C.O. leave to patrol CHAPLIN TRENCH	RP.B.
		10 p.m.	Patrol of 1 officer and 6 men return to raids	
		12 mn.	Patrols active	
			C.O. writes order for raid	
26.5.17		4.30 a.m.	Enemy shelling front line with 5.9's.	
		1 p.m.	T.M.B and M.G.C. officers at disposal of C.O. for raid	
		2.10 p.m.	C. G. frontage shelled heavily by enemy (3 casualties)	
		4 p.m.	C.O. leaves for tour of front line, Coplain Abraham to	
		5 p.m.	2/Lt KELSEY, 2/Lt NUTT, 2/Lt GLEED	
		9.30 p.m.	Major BURNETT goes to front line to supervise raiding party	
		10.15 p.m.	2/Lt WELLS takes command "C Coy" who carry ladders up to CUTE TRENCH	
29.5.17		12.30 a.m.	One minute bombardment on enemy front line commenced	RP.B.
		1 a.m.	2/Lt GLEED reach CHAPLIN TRENCH and find same unoccupied	
		1.30 a.m.	If damage required from Major BURNETT "GLEED" reach CHAPLIN tank	
		2 a.m.	Party going forward "attack failed" 2/Lt MIXER killed 15 O.R casualties	
		4 a.m.	Major BURNETT returns and reports to C.O.	
		3 a.m.	C.O. sends full report to Bde.	

R.P. Burnett Major
2nd South Staffs Regt

WAR DIARY
or
INTELLIGENCE SUMMARY.

(Erase heading not required.)

Army Form C. 2118.

Instructions regarding War Diaries and Intelligence Summaries are contained in F. S. Regs., Part II. and the Staff Manual respectively. Title pages will be prepared in manuscript.

Place	Date	Hour	Summary of Events and Information	Remarks and references to Appendices
CADIZ TRENCH	27.5.17	12 noon 1.P.m.	G.S.O.2. and Bde Major visit C.P. in CADIZ Trench. Operation orders issued. Batt being relieved by 7th BORDER regiment. Two platoons of D Coy remain in CADIZ Trench.	
		3.30 P.m.	2/Lt HYDER's body taken to Cemetery.	1243.
		9.30 P.m.	Boreas Nd Qr. Company arrive.	
GREEN LINE	28.5.17	1.15 am 3 am.	Relief completed. Batt. reported present in GREEN LINE.	1243.
			Party of 1 officer 35 men to report to R.E.	
"	29.5.17	10 am.	Strong points manned. No.1 at junction of LUCID and HERON with C.T.'s 3. No 2. (L.G. in SUNKEN road about 11.a.6.3.	
			No.1 held by D Coy. (2 platoons) No.2 by A Coy (L.G.) Considerable shelling round LEMON TRENCH (L.P. killed) C.P. Coys for Batt. Hd qrs.	
		10.30 am		
		11.30 am	O.C. 10th LINCOLNS arrive to take over line.	
		2. P.m.	Heavy enemy shelling of GREEN LINE Tunnel Tsd HOI Qrs	
		2.30 P.m.	Hd Qrs orderlies dug-out blown in, 5 orderlies wounded (slightly)	1243.
		3. P.m.	Operation orders received for move to take over.	
		9.30 P.m.		
	30.5.17	10.45 am	Advance party of 10th LINCOLNS arrive to take over.	
		12.15 P.m.	Guides to take over at St. NICHOLAS CAMP sent down.	1243.
		9.3.12	C.P.O. and Hd Qrs. Coy of 10th LINCOLNS arrive & take over in GREEN LINE.	
		10. P.m.	Relief completed	
ST. NICHOLAS CAMP.	31.5.17	3.25 am	Battalion reported present in camp.	
		4 am.	Aviation notice for men at gun arrived.	
		8 am.	Transport cook by road for MONDICOURT.	
		8.30 am.	2/Lt WILSON and N.C.O. sent to arrange extremes for Battalion	
		9 am.	Batt. entrain for MONDICOURT.	1243.

A 5834 Wt. W4973/M687 750,000 8/16 D. D. & L. Ltd. Forms/C.2118/13.

> 8TH (S) BATTALION,
> SOUTH STAFFS.
> REGIMENT.
>
> No. 1282
> Date 2/7/17

D.A.G.

3rd. Echelon.

Herewith War Diary of 8th Battalion South Staffordshire Regiment for month of June 1917.

[signature]
       Major.
    for. Lt. Colonel.
Comdg 8th South Staffs. Regt.

18 Staff Rgt
Vol 24

T.23?

WAR DIARY
or
INTELLIGENCE SUMMARY
(Erase heading not required.)

Army Form C. 2118.

Place	Date	Hour	Summary of Events and Information	Remarks and references to Appendices
MONDICOURT	1.6.17		Battalion bathing, issue of clean clothing.	
"	"	9.30am	Brigadier visits P.O.	
"	"	10.15am	P.O. interviews all Officers in Hd.Qts mess.	
"	"	2.30p.	Brigadiers and P.O's at Divisional Conference.	APB.
"	2.6.17	9 am	Battalion inoculated at 51st F.A.	APB.
"	3.6.17		Resting after inoculation.	
"	4.6.17		General reorganisation of Battalion.	APB.
"	5.6.17		Training commenced, all specialists under their respective officers.	
"	"	8 am	1 Officer and 20 men to work on clearing up show ground.	APB.
"	6.6.17		Training of Companies and specialists continued	
"	"		firing on range.	
"	"	12.30p.	Lieut Bennett attends "Tank" demonstration at WAILLY.	
"	"	3.15p.	All Officers in Hd.Qts mess on map reading under P.O.	
"	"	4.30p.	Box respirator inspection by Divi: Gas Officer.	

M⸺ Bennett Major
2nd North R.

Army Form C. 2118.

WAR DIARY
or
INTELLIGENCE SUMMARY.
(Erase heading not required.)

Instructions regarding War Diaries and Intelligence Summaries are contained in F. S. Regs., Part II. and the Staff Manual respectively. Title pages will be prepared in manuscript.

Place	Date	Hour	Summary of Events and Information	Remarks and references to Appendices
MONDICOURT	7.6.17		Divisional horse show. Entries. (Major Burnett, Capt. Gray, and Lt. Hare.)	
"	"		Training until 12 noon. Reinforcements arrive, 1 Officer/105 and 13 other ranks.	12/3
"	8.6.17	6.30a	Brigade route march in morning. Training in afternoon.	12/3
"	9.6.17		Battalion training in morning. Afternoon off.	12/3
"	10.6.17	11 am	Church Parade on B Coy's parade ground.	12/3
"	11.6.17		Training. Arrangements for Batt. Sports made. 10th Sherwood Foresters sports in afternoon.	12/3
"	12.6.17		Battalion Sports on horse show ground N.E. of MONDICOURT. Slight rain during afternoon.	12/3
"	13.6.17		Normal training. Lecture to all Officers by C.O. on "Not P.F. Fires".	12/3
"	14.6.17		Brigade route march in morning. 1 Officer and 5 other ranks reinforcements.	12/3
"	15.6.17		Battalion practiced attack "in" at HURTIBISE FARM.	12/3

M.J. Burnett Major
8th South Staffs Regt

Army Form C. 2118.

WAR DIARY
or
INTELLIGENCE SUMMARY.
(Erase heading not required.)

Instructions regarding War Diaries and Intelligence Summaries are contained in F. S. Regs., Part II. and the Staff Manual respectively. Title pages will be prepared in manuscript.

Place	Date	Hour	Summary of Events and Information	Remarks and references to Appendices
MONDICOURT	15.6.19		Capt Barlow to command "A" Company.	
"	"	6 P.m.	All officers take "lectures" prior to Company parade at 10.30 P.m.	BP13
"	16.6.19		Usual Training.	
"	"		R.O. 8/4303b Pte Davis C.H. and 11/11621 Pte Bo Hugh J. was also the Military Medal. Regimental teams in training for Brigade Sports on 23rd inst.	BP13
"	17.6.19	11 am	Church Parade.	
"	"		P.O. Boyd, Bennet, Training for Brigade Sports. Capt Massey to Horse practice for Lloyd Lindsay race.	BP13
"	18.6.19		Usual Training of Battalion until 3 P.M. C.O. rode Brigade arrangements made for practice attack on following day.	
"	"	3 P.m.	Brigade Headquarters afternoon.	

BP13 Bennet Major
8th South Staffs Reg.

WAR DIARY or INTELLIGENCE SUMMARY.

Army Form C. 2118.

Instructions regarding War Diaries and Intelligence Summaries are contained in F. S. Regs., Part II and the Staff Manual respectively. Title pages will be prepared in manuscript.

(Erase heading not required.)

Place	Date	Hour	Summary of Events and Information	Remarks and references to Appendices
MONDICOURT	19.6.17		Brigade to practise attack at HURTEBISE FARM. Attack postponed owing to bad weather. Battalion carried out an attack on same ground, heavy thunderstorm during morning.	
"	20.6.17		Brigade attack jumped for the 19th. Carried out. Battalion bathing and paying out in afternoon.	
"	21.6.17		Bn. Left for St. NICHOLAS camp by bus. Battalion marched out of MONDICOURT at 7-45 am, reaching entraining point on ARRAS - DOULLENS road at V.29.b.15 Entrained at 8-45 am. Arrived at detraining point RONDE POINT ARRAS	
St. NICHOLAS	21.6.17		at 10.45 am. Arrived St. NICHOLAS 11-35 am. Rest in afternoon.	
"	22.6.17		Battalion training in vicinity of camp. Working party of 1 officer and 50 O.R's to be found daily. Brigadier to see all C.O's at Bde.	
"	23.6.17	1 P.m.	Anti Aircraft Lewis Gun position built 100 yards EAST of camp. Post manned by 1 L.G. and team. Training carried on in vicinity of camp. Battalion bathing. (Hot day)	
"	24.6.17		Training. Working party of 6 Officers and 300 O.R's to dig cable trench in rear of Bayonet Trench. H.o.R from 11 P.M - 2.30 am.	

Army Form C. 2118.

WAR DIARY
or
INTELLIGENCE SUMMARY.
(Erase heading not required.)

Instructions regarding War Diaries and Intelligence Summaries are contained in F. S. Regs., Part II. and the Staff Manual respectively. Title pages will be prepared in manuscript.

Place	Date	Hour	Summary of Events and Information	Remarks and references to Appendices
St. Nicholas	26.8.17		Church Parade in field east of camp. Battalion bathing parties.	APP3
"	27.8.17		Usual training. Working party of 6 officers 300 ORs for Cable lines. Party returns from work.	APP3
"	"	4.15 am	2/Lt MILLER goes on leave to England. Brigadier visits P.O. in Camp. So training in morning. P.O. and Adj go up to there to takes ORs after receiving orders to relieve 9th YORKS in front line on 29th. Return from line 7 p.m. P.O. interviews all Coy. Commanders and arranges for them to take ORs line on following day. Working party of 6 officers & 150 ORs on Cable lines	APP3
"	28.8.17	9 pm	3 officers and 150 ORs of 3/4th R.W. KENT Regt. attached to Battalion for working party. Heues proved to Fort line. Act. Bg. Commanders and 2/Lt 00's for relief issued to Coys.	APP3
"	29.8.17		A.M. place 1 Coy. 3/4 R.W. KENT Regt. relieve 7th YORKS in front line. B. Coy. (Staffs) to relieve A Coy. (Yorks) in front line (CUTHBERT) trench. "C" Coy. (Staffs) to relieve C Coy. (Yorks) on App.	APP3

WAR DIARY
or
INTELLIGENCE SUMMARY.
(Erase heading not required.)

Army Form C. 2118.

Place	Date	Hour	Summary of Events and Information	Remarks and references to Appendices
	29.6.17		A 2nd line (CHARLIE). D Co (Staff) to relieve B Co (Yorks) on right of 2nd line (CHARLIE). A Co (Staff) to relieve D Co (Yorks) in 3rd line (CUBA) Battalion Exp. camp at 9 P.m. Delayed for 2 hours at TANK DUMP (GREEN LINE) by own gun limbers. Relief complete by 4.30 am 30th. Casualties during relief 4 O.R's killed and 4 wounded. The above casualties include 2 R.M. Kents killed and 2 wounded. Boch shell heavily with gas trench mortars.	B.B.
FRONT LINE	30.6.17	4.30 a	Relief complete.	
		5.30 a	P.O. goes round the line.	
		7.15 a	C.O. returns. Boch shelling with gas shells. Trenches in bad state.	
		8.S.R.	C.O. goes round to visit Coys.	

J.R Burnett Major
O.C 8. Staff Reg.
8th

Army Form C. 2118.

WAR DIARY
or
INTELLIGENCE SUMMARY.
(Erase heading not required.)

Instructions regarding War Diaries and Intelligence Summaries are contained in F.S. Regs., Part II. and the Staff Manual respectively. Title pages will be prepared in manuscript.

Place	Date	Hour	Summary of Events and Information	Remarks and references to Appendices
FRONT LINE N. of SCARPE	1/7/17	2.30 a.m.	Both quiet. Night hence mostly shelling in CUBA TRENCH (no casualties) acc. Coys. heavily trench mortared during evening. Many casualties.	Miss Chapman
		3.10 a.m.		
		5 a.m.	Both fool arrivin. Nothing important.	
		10.30 a.m.	Liaison officer and 2/Lt A.G. News pleased to try and ascertain position of T.M. which has been causing the trouble.	R.T.B.
			C.O. goes round the line, accompanied by Major WILSON R.E.	
	2/7/17	12.1 noon	Fine and hot. Great amount of work to be done in trenches. C.O. makes two tours of the line. Brigadier General visits C.O.	1948
			Ration party shelled (1 man and 1 mule killed) 1 mule wounded. C.O. turns the line. Our patrol of 1 officer and our O.R.'s came in contact with enemy raiding party of about 40 men. Our patrol attacked with rifle grenades and bombs and dispersed enemy.	
	3/7/17		Major BURNETT arrives at Bn. Hd. Qrs. back from leave. Test S.O.S. Brigadier General gave round the line, calls in and stops to lunch. Much artillery and R.G. fire on our right during the night.	T 24

Lt/Col Burnett Lyle
2nd South Staff. Rgt.

Army Form C. 2118.

WAR DIARY
or
INTELLIGENCE SUMMARY.

(Erase heading not required.)

Instructions regarding War Diaries and Intelligence
Summaries are contained in F. S. Regs., Part II.
and the Staff Manual respectively. Title pages
will be prepared in manuscript.

Place	Date	Hour	Summary of Events and Information	Remarks and references to Appendices
TRENCHES	4/1/17	2.30am	2/Lt ACTON Wounded. Situation quiet	
		5 am	Work and patrol reports received from Coys. Nothing of importance to report.	
		9 am	One name submitted to Bde for Special Leave.	
		9.45am	Brigade Major arrives at Bn. Hd qrs to go round the line with the C.O.	
		3 pm	C.O. returns from the Line.	
		10 pm	Rations arrive and issued to Coys.	
		10.30 pm	2/Lt WAGSTAFF joins Batt. from Corps Depôt, and is posted to D Coy.	
		10.45 pm	D Coy of R.W.K's (attached) relieved	2493
		12 m.n.	Major BURNETT goes round the Line	
5/1/17		1.30am	Heavy T.M's on our Front Line. Artillery engaged and T.M's silenced.	
		1.45am	Relief of R.W.K's (by) complete.	
		2.30 am	Situation all quiet.	
		4.30am	Major BURNETT returns from Line	
		5.30am	Report from Capt. NEWSEY that enemy working party was attacked and driven off. A fire balloon of the enemy drifts into our front Line.	
		6 am	4 Boche aeroplanes flying very low over Batt: Hd qrs.	

A/Lt.[illegible] Signs.
2nd West Kent Regt.

2353 Wt. W3544/1454 750,000 5/15 D. D. & L. A.D.S.S. Forms/C 2118.

Army Form C. 2118.

WAR DIARY
or
INTELLIGENCE SUMMARY.
(Erase heading not required.)

Instructions regarding War Diaries and Intelligence Summaries are contained in F.S. Regs., Part II. and the Staff Manual respectively. Title pages will be prepared in manuscript.

Place	Date	Hour	Summary of Events and Information	Remarks and references to Appendices
TRENCHES	5/9/17	8 a.m.	All very quiet.	
		11.20 a.m.	C.O. goes round Front Line.	
		3.10 p.m.	P.O. of 7th Lincolns arrives to arrange details of to-morrow's relief.	RPB.
	6/9/17		Enemy very quiet in the morning. Batt. relieved in Front Line and proceed to GREEN LINE. Batt. reported present in GREEN LINE at 12 midnight.	RPB.
	7/9/17	11.30 a.m.	C.O. interviews all Coy Commanders.	
		12.15 p.m.	Message from Bde. that C.O. is to be prepared with trench demolition on Monday.	
		2. p.m.	Coys commence work in GREEN LINE. All quiet on the front.	12PB.
	8/9/17	9 a.m.	Coys start work, party of 1 N.C.O. and 20 men to dig-in way out at TANK DUMP	
		10 a.m.	Brigadier visits C.O.	
		12.10 p.m.	C.O. accompanies Brigadier to Bde. and stays lunch on his way down to Camp.	12PB.
	9/9/17		Party of 2.30 officers to be found for R.E.'s for carrying. Very quiet all day. Major BURNETT in command during C.O.'s absence. Slight shelling round Batt. Hd. Qrs. Waiting for list of 190 things to be found. Brigadier General makes a tour of the line.	

W.H.Burnett Major
2nd Lincs. Staff Regt.

Army Form C. 2118.

WAR DIARY
or
INTELLIGENCE SUMMARY.

(Erase heading not required.)

Instructions regarding War Diaries and Intelligence Summaries are contained in F.S. Regs., Part II. and the Staff Manual respectively. Title pages will be prepared in manuscript.

Place	Date	Hour	Summary of Events and Information	Remarks and references to Appendices
TRENCHES (GREEN LINE)	10/7/17		Heavy shelling round Batt: H.d Qrs. C.O. returns. All Coys to close in to make accommodation for 1 Coy of MIDDLESEX regt.	
	11/7/17		Working parties of 136 for R.E's. to be found by Batt. All quiet on the Batt. front during the day. Go at work all day. Much air activity in evening	APP.3
	12/7/17		Brigadier comes round the line. Working parties of 200 strong to be found Enemy raid Bombing Post. Batt. stands-to.	APP.3
	13/7/17		Every quiet during the day. Several enemy aeroplanes over our lines in the evening. Working parties of 190 strong to be found.	APP.A
GREEN LINE	14/7/17		C.O.s, Commanders, and Brigadier go round the line. Very pleased with work done by Battalion. 1st Borders to make a raid on enemy trenches to-night. Divisional General visits Batt. H.Q.rs. Two working parties to be found.	APP.3
"	15/7/17	1.20am	Every very quiet all day. Batt: relieved in GREEN LINE by 10th Lancashire Fusiliers. Relief complete. Go march independently to same camp at ST. NICHOLAS as vacated by the Batt. on night of 29-30th.	
ST. NICHOLAS	16/7/17		General clean up and Bathing parade.	APP.3 Appendices forwd. to Sealt Staff HQ

Army Form C. 2118.

WAR DIARY
or
INTELLIGENCE SUMMARY.

(Erase heading not required.)

Instructions regarding War Diaries and Intelligence Summaries are contained in F.S. Regs., Part II. and the Staff Manual respectively. Title pages will be prepared in manuscript.

Place	Date	Hour	Summary of Events and Information	Remarks and references to Appendices
ST NICHOLAS	17/9/17		Training carried on by Coys. Rapid wiring, physical training, Bayonet fighting. "HP" Cinema show gives free entertainment to the Batt. in the afternoon.	APB.
"	18/9/17		Batt. route march. Short Scheme carried out during march.	APB.
"	19/9/17		Usual training in afternoon. Coys bathing in the morning. Major General visits cook-houses and camp very satisfactory. Lecture to all officers of Bde by Lt. Col. BIRCH 17th Div on Battle of MESSINES.	APB.
"	20/9/17		Usual training carried out by Coys during morning. All officers and N.C.O's under C.O. on writing reports.	APB.
"	21/9/17	10.10am	C.O. and adjutant proceed up the line to visit 7th EAST YORKS. Lecture by Brigadier to all officers of 13th Bde on "Trench warfare".	
		2.pm	Usual training by Coys. Rapid wiring etc.	
"	22/9/17		Bn Church parade, Route Marching of St. NICHOLAS Camp, Bde. drilled no casuals held. Lt. WILSON proceeds up to GREEN LINE for the purpose of erecting notice boards having numbers of dug-outs. (a) Commanders proceed up the line to take over.	APB.

M Bennett Major
Cmdg 9th West Riding Regt

Army Form C. 2118.

WAR DIARY
or
INTELLIGENCE SUMMARY.
(Erase heading not required.)

Instructions regarding War Diaries and Intelligence Summaries are contained in F. S. Regs., Part II. and the Staff Manual respectively. Title pages will be prepared in manuscript.

Place	Date	Hour	Summary of Events and Information	Remarks and references to Appendices
FRONT LINE	23.7.17.		Battalion relieves 7th EAST. YORKS in the front line trenches. Left camp at 8.35 p.m. relief complete 12.30 a.m.	1298.
"	24.7.17.		Brigadier visits line, and calls at Bat'n Hd. Qrs on way back. Enemy very quiet during the day. Heavy shelling south of our front during night.	1298.
"	25.7.17.		All quiet during day. Great deal of work to be done in order to get line in good condition. "C" Coy. in support to supply all ration parties.	
CHEMICAL MIN-SECTOR	26.7.17.		Lt. Col. BARKER D.S.O. assumes command of 5.1st Inf'y Bde intact. Brigadier is on leave. Major BURNETT M.C. assumes command of Battalion. Enemy quiet. One man of "B" Coy. died of wounds.	1298.
"	27.7.17.		Lt. Col. BARKER D.S.O. visits Battalion sector accompanied by Bde Major. Enemy trench mortars our front line heavily. Our artillery retaliating.	
"	28.7.17.		Enemy very quiet during morning. Our artillery registers on enemy positions in afternoon prior to raid by 7th E. YORKS (to take place on our front at 12.30 a.m. (29th).	1298.

Capt. J. M. Burnett Major
Commdg. 23rd South Staffs Reg.

2353 Wt. W3544/1454 700,000 5/15 D. D. & L. A.D.S.S. Forms/C 2118.

Army Form C. 2118.

WAR DIARY
or
INTELLIGENCE SUMMARY.
(Erase heading not required.)

Place	Date	Hour	Summary of Events and Information	Remarks and references to Appendices
FRONT LINE	29/9/17	12-30 am	Sent out p/s J/A E. YORKS raid. Very successful result. 14 prisoners taken. 5 brought to Batt. Hd.qrs in CAD12 trench. 2 of these being wounded. H.Col. KING calls on his way back from the B.C.G.S. accompanied by Lt.Col. BAKER D.S.O. is met by Major BURNETT on the right of Batt. sector and tours the Line. Arrive back in CAD12 trench 11-40 am. Every shelling our front line trenches most of the day with 4.2's. trenches	B.M.B.
	30/9/17	9 am		
	31/9/17		Quiet in at several points. Light quiet. Enemy quiet during day, rain in evening. Col. BIRCH (G.S.O.I) and Major WILSON visit Battalion Hd.qrs in CAD12 trench at 6 P.m. Night quiet and very wet.	B.M.B. E.M.Burnett Major 1st South Staffs Regt

2353 Wt. W2544/1454 700,000 5/15 D. D. & L.   A.D.S.S. Forms/C. 2118.

Army Form C. 2118.

WAR DIARY
or
INTELLIGENCE SUMMARY.
(Erase heading not required.)

A.S. Staff Vol 2

Place	Date	Hour	Summary of Events and Information	Remarks and references to Appendices
CHEMICAL SUB-SECTOR	1.8.17.		Enemy very quiet during the morning. Slight shelling with T.M's in the afternoon. Heavy rain. Lt. Col. BARKER (comdg. 51st Infy Bde) visits Battalion HeadQrs at Batt: Hd Qrs on way back. Battalion relieved in front line by 7th LINCOLNSHIRE Regt. "C" and "D" Coys move back to GAVRELLE SWITCH, and "A" and "B" Coys + Batt: Hd Qrs in the RAILWAY CUTTING H.8.C.0.3.	AAB.
"	2.8.17.	9-10 am	Battalion complete in GAVRELLE SWITCH and RAILWAY CUTTING. Great deal of work to be done by C and D Coys in GAVRELLE SWITCH. While Battalion out on working parties during the night. P.C. visits C and D Coys in GAVRELLE SWITCH.	AAB.
"	3.8.17.		Enemy very quiet. 4 enemy planes fly over the cutting, but are driven off by A.A. fire. Usual parties to be found at night.	AAB.
"	4.8.17.		Two Lover Otros issued to the Battalion for use in RAILWAY CUTTING. All quiet during the day. Usual working parties at night.	AAB.
RAILWAY CUTTING	5.8.17.		Battalion arrive about 2.30 P.M. Very quiet all day in the cutting.	AAB.
"	6.8.17.		P.C. visits two Coys in GAVRELLE SWITCH. Whole Battalion out on working parties during the night.	AAB.
"	7.8.17.		Brigadier General returns from leave and resumes command of the Bde.	AAB. [signature]

Army Form C. 2118.

WAR DIARY
or
INTELLIGENCE SUMMARY.
(Erase heading not required.)

Instructions regarding War Diaries and Intelligence Summaries are contained in F. S. Regs., Part II. and the Staff Manual respectively. Title pages will be prepared in manuscript.

Place	Date	Hour	Summary of Events and Information	Remarks and references to Appendices
RAILWAY CUTTING	7.8.19.		Lt. Col. BARKER D.S.O. rejoins the Battalion.	1298.
"	8.8.19		Usual working parties out until 2.30 a.m. Lt. Col. BARKER D.S.O. proceeds on leave to ENGLAND. Major R.P. TURNETT M.C. assumes command of the Battalion. The P.O. of the 9th Duke of Wellington's comes up to arrange relief. Relief to commence at 11 P.M. Battalion relieved by 12 m.	1298.
"	9.8.19.		Battalion arrives in LANCASTER CAMP about 2.30 a.m. C/O bathing and generally cleaning up. Inspections of arms, kit etc: held by Coy. Commanders.	298.
"	10.8.19.		C/O commence training. Bayonet training to be carried out in morning. Games in afternoon. Live entertainment at Cinema for the Battalion all C/o attend	1298
"	11.8.19		Rapid wiring demonstration by 51st Bde Depot. C/o carry on usual training in morning. Football in afternoon.	1298.
"	12.8.19		C.O. with C and D Coy Commanders go to ground N.W. of ANZIN prior to practising attack. Physical Training, Bayonet fighting, Rapid wiring etc: carried on by C/o. Enemy shell met observation balloon and force it to descend.	

Signed,
[signature]
3rd South Staffs Regt

Army Form C. 2118.

WAR DIARY
or
INTELLIGENCE SUMMARY.
(Erase heading not required.)

Instructions regarding War Diaries and Intelligence Summaries are contained in F. S. Regs., Part II. and the Staff Manual respectively. Title pages will be prepared in manuscript.

Place	Date	Hour	Summary of Events and Information	Remarks and references to Appendices
LANCASTER CAMP.	13.8.19		Battalion route march and practice attack on ground N.W. of ANZIN. Bde football in afternoon. Every shell camp and dot mine at R.N. Divisional Dump.	M.B.
"	14.8.19		Coys bathing in order D.C.B.A Coys. When not bathing, normal training carried out with P.O. visits 13th rifle ranges. Coys firing on the MONT ranges, ARRAS in the afternoon.	M.B.
"	15.8.19		Coys firing on the long range, TSUTTE de TIR from 7 a.m. to 12 noon. P.O. goes up the line to take over from 6th DORSETS, GREENLAND HILL SECTOR. Heavy rain. Coy Commanders go to take over from Coy Commanders of 6th DORSETS.	M.B.
"	16.8.19	2 a.m.	Final of Bde football Competition. S.L.I. ? BORDER Regt. v. D Coy. 2nd S.Staffs. 1. Result. BORDERS 2. S.Staffs 1. Battalion relieve 6th DORSETS in front line. Very quiet during relief.	M.B.
FRONT LINE.	17.8.19	12.35 a.m. 2.30 P.m	Relief complete. P.O. goes round the line at 10 o'clock. Coy Commander visit Batt. Helpers. P.O of ? H.INGRAMS Corner to arrange about R.E carrying parties. Patrols active in N.L.m. YUKON posts used for	M.B.

Army Form C. 2118.

WAR DIARY
or
INTELLIGENCE SUMMARY.
(Erase heading not required.)

Instructions regarding War Diaries and Intelligence Summaries are contained in F.S. Regs., Part II. and the Staff Manual respectively. Title pages will be prepared in manuscript.

Place	Date	Hour	Summary of Events and Information	Remarks and references to Appendices
FRONT LINE	17.8.17		Carrying up rations, found unsatisfactory	
	18.8.17		Enemy T.Ms very heavy during the night. No casualties. C.O. goes round the line. Artillery bursts during the afternoon on our front.	AAB
	19.8.17		Brigade route Battalion 2000. very temp satisfactory. Hiring of suffered line to be completed by August 24th. C.O. came back from leave. Rations arrive about 9.45 P.M. and issued to Coys.	AAB
	20.8.17		Major BURNETT (C.O.) goes round the line accompanied by Intelligence Officer. All very quiet.	AAB
	21.8.17		Lt.Col. BIRCH (9.O.D.I) rode Batt. Hd.Qrs. and remarks on count state of the well. Very good writings done by the Battalion. Coys when round of case - RESERVE (Drawing Station) Several tracks dug up by S. Col. and returned at I 7 d. 97. PLOUVAIN 12.12.000) C.O. returns from leave and resumes command of the Battalion.	AAB
	22.8.17		Enemy shell front line heavily with gas T.Ms. (3 casualties)	AAB

Army Form C. 2118.

WAR DIARY
or
INTELLIGENCE SUMMARY.
(Erase heading not required.)

Place	Date	Hour	Summary of Events and Information	Remarks and references to Appendices
GREENLAND HILL SECTOR	22.8.17		Bale out for release of gas T.M. This was postponed	189B
	23.8.17		Divisional Gas R.C.O sent up to investigate gas sent over by enemy last night. C.O. goes round the line accompanied by the Brigadier. Battalion relieved by the 7th LINCOLN'S in the	
		2 P.m.	Front line. Day light relief commencing at 2. P.m. Relief	
		5-15 P.m	Complete. Battalion moves back into support	
		5-15 P.m	GAVRELLE SWITCH (HUDSON TRENCH). 3/4th BETHUNY gassed during relief and sent down the line. Much work to be done in HUDSON TRENCH.	B.B.
GAVRELLE SWITCH	24.8.17		Enemy shell Batt: Hd qrs in HUDSON TRENCH during the night (no casualties) Brigadier visits Batt. Working parties of 200 men to be found. Rations arrive 7.45 P.m. Close change of clothing issued to every N.C.O and man. Regimental Canteen moved up into GAVRELLE SWITCH. Working parties return about 1.30 am.	193

W Worenzetty Lt
o.c. 7 Lincolns

Army Form C. 2118.

WAR DIARY
or
INTELLIGENCE SUMMARY.
(Erase heading not required.)

Instructions regarding War Diaries and Intelligence Summaries are contained in F.S. Regs., Part II. and the Staff Manual respectively. Title pages will be prepared in manuscript.

Place	Date	Hour	Summary of Events and Information	Remarks and references to Appendices
HUDSON TRENCH	25.8.19		C.O. gave round the line. Very quiet on the front all day.	1115
	26.8.19		all Coy working in their own sectors during the day. Carrying party of 1 Offr and 60 O.R's to be found for the 9th Lincolns in the afternoon. Brigadier came round. C.O. dines at Bde. Hd qrs.	1115
"	27.8.19		Heavy rain in the morning. Capt. C.I. MASSY M.C. attached to Bde. Hd qrs as assistant Bde. Major. C.O. motor cycles home at 12 noon. Very quiet in afternoon and evening.	1115
"	28.8.19		Cos carry on work in own areas. Continuation of rain and wash-house etc's. Heavy rain all day. Working parties of 220 OR's route found by the Battalion.	1115
"	29.8.19		Enemy very quiet during the morning. Major BURNETT M.C. detailed as President of Court Martial held tomorrow at Bde Depot. Raining all day. Enemy shell round of CHILI AVENUE in afternoon.	1115
"	"	9.45pm	Rations arrive at 9.45pm	1115

Attaccurate Coppy
8th J. Wolffe Lt

WAR DIARY
or
INTELLIGENCE SUMMARY

Army Form C. 2118.

Place	Date	Hour	Summary of Events and Information	Remarks and references to Appendices
HUDSON TRENCH	30.8.17		About 1.45 p.m. enemy shell A.B.C. Coy area with 5.9's. 6 direct hits on trench. A Coy Officers Mess blown in. A Coy cookhouse and C Coy Officers Mess blown in. One Lewis Gun of A Coy destroyed by shell fire. 10 casualties.	NMB
"	31.8.17		Coy at work in own Coy area repairing damages to trenches etc. Enemy fire quiet all day. Usual working parties found. Rations came up and moved to Coy.	

M.L.Bryant Major R.E.
i/c 212st NMFA R.

2.9.17

M.L.Parker Ltcol.
Comg 1st South Staff Regt.
2/9/17

D.A.G.
Base.

> 8TH (S) BATTALION.
> SOUTH STAFFS.
> REGIMENT.
> No. 1577
> Date. 1-10-17

Herewith War Diary of 8th Battalion
South Staffordshire Regiment, for the
month of September 1917.

WJParker
Lieut. Colonel.
Comdg. 8th. Bn. South. Stafford. Regt.

Army Form C. 2118.

S S Stafford Regt S I
17
Vol 27

WAR DIARY
or
INTELLIGENCE SUMMARY.
(Erase heading not required.)

Instructions regarding War Diaries and Intelligence Summaries are contained in F. S. Regs., Part II. and the Staff Manual respectively. Title pages will be prepared in manuscript.

Place	Date	Hour	Summary of Events and Information	Remarks and references to Appendices
HUDSON TRENCH.	1.9.17		Representative of the 3/4th Royal Welsh Fusrs comes up to take over line. C.O. visits Hd.q.rs of 7th Leicestershire Regt. Enemy very quiet on our front. Battalion relieved by the 3/4th R.W.K's in the GAVRELLE SWITCH, HUDSON TRENCH LANCASTER	
"		10.45P.m	Relief complete. Coys march back independently to St. NICHOLAS CAMP. C.O. and Batt. Hd. Q.rs officers rode back from TANK DUMP. Working party of 3 officers and 110 O.R's to work at ATHIES under 2.Z. cable section. Party return to camp at 1-30 a.m on lorries.	RWB.
LANCASTER CAMP	2.9.17		Battalion bathing in the morning. Football (Result) Drawn. Officers versus Sergeants in afternoon.	RWB.
"	3.9.17.		General cleaning up and inspections by Companies. Football in afternoon. S.Staff versus 5/3rd T.M.B.'s Result S.S 5. T.M.B 2.	RWB.
"	4.9.17		C.O. and two Coy Commanders attend a gas demonstration at Div: Gas School.	
		10-12P	Battalion bathing. Those not bathing, Coys to carry out usual training. Football in afternoon S.Staffs v Bde Hd.q.r Result S.Staffs 1 Bde Hd.q.r 1 T.26 nil.	

B/Major Brewitt Major
2nd South Stafford Regt
2 South Staffs Regt

Army Form C. 2118.

WAR DIARY
or
INTELLIGENCE SUMMARY.
(Erase heading not required.)

Instructions regarding War Diaries and Intelligence Summaries are contained in F. S. Regs., Part II. and the Staff Manual respectively. Title pages will be prepared in manuscript.

Place	Date	Hour	Summary of Events and Information	Remarks and references to Appendices
LANCASTER CAMP.	5.9.17		C.O. and two Coy. Commanders attending Gas Course at Div: Hd. Q'rs. Coys carry on usual training up to 12 noon. Firing on MOAT RANGE from 12 noon to 3 P.M. Football in the afternoon.	
"	6.9.17		Battalion Route march and Tactical Exercise combined during the morning. Scheme carried out on ground east of ANZIN (new formation for attack) Battalion return about 1.15 P.M.	
"	7.9.17		Usual training during the morning. Battalion find Bde Guard of 1 2.N.O and 8 men. Afternoon. 2/Lieut P. Staffs. 10th SHERWOOD. Football in the afternoon. 2/Lieut I. Sherwoods. Nil. FORESTERS. 2/Lieut I. Sherwoods. Nil.	
"	8.9.17		C.O. goes up the line at 9.0 am to take over from 10th WEST YORKSHIRE Regt. returning at 1.0 P.M. Battalion route match match match Major R.P. BURNETT M.C. During march. Batt: proceeds artillery formation. Batt: return to camp about 12.45 P.M. Football in afternoon.	

M P Burnett Major
2/Lieut Staffs

WAR DIARY
or
INTELLIGENCE SUMMARY.
(Erase heading not required.)

Army Form C. 2118.

Place	Date	Hour	Summary of Events and Information	Remarks and references to Appendices
LANCASTER CAMP.	9.9.17		Church Parade in the morning at 10 am. C.O. interviews all Coy Commanders. Coys. send up 1 officer and 1 B.P.O. to take over from the 10th West Yorks Rgt. Battalion relieves 10th West Yorks in front line CHEMICAL WORKS SECTOR. LEFT BATTALION SUB-SECTOR.	
"	"	11.25 p.m.	Relief complete.	BMB
FRONT LINE CHEMICAL WORKS SECTOR.	10.9.17		C.O. attends a Court of Inquiry in the RAILWAY CUTTING. Major BURNETT goes round the line. Enemy aeroplane flies very low over our lines. Coys Commanders visit Batt Hd qrs.	
"	"	6.20 p.m.	C.O. returns to Batt Hd qrs. Capt. GASTON (M.O.) wounded on his way Batt Hd qrs to DRESSING STATION in the QUARRY. Rations brought up on mules. Impossible to get ration any further forward of QUARRY on account of enemy M.G. fire.	

M.P. Burnett Maj. for Lt Col
8th South Staffs Rgt

Place	Date	Hour	Summary of Events and Information	Remarks and references to Appendices
CHEMICAL WORKS SECTOR	11.9.17		C.O. goes round the line at 9 am. Bde. Major and Major of 20th Coy R.E.'s visit Batt. HQ at 1-30 P.M. C.O. returns at 1-30 P.M. Enemy very quiet on our front during the day. Enemy aircraft fairly active over our line in the afternoon. Major R.P. BURNETT goes round the line. Rations arrive at QUARRY DUMP at 8-45 p.m. and Rations arrive at Coy. are carried to Coys. All quiet throughout the night.	
"	12.9.17		C.O. goes round line about 9-30 am and makes arrangements for a fighting patrol of 1 Officer and 13 OR's to attempt to enter WART TRENCH tonight. Patrol leaves our trench at 11 p.m. and about reaches Boch wire but are seen and fired on. Bombs were also thrown at our patrol which was forced to withdraw. Casualties 1 OR Killed and 2 OR's wounded. Patrol found from a Coy. C.O. returns from line about 2-30 am	1898

M Browning Major
9th Batt.

Place	Date	Hour	Summary of Events and Information	Remarks and references to Appendices
FRONT LINE CHEMICAL WORKS SECTOR	13.9.16		Enemy very quiet during the morning. Major BONNETT Report the Bde B.G.O. and Major O'Brien met Batt. Hd qrs C.O. toured the line in the afternoon. Enemy planes attempted to cross our lines at low altitude but no damage. Hostile A.A. and M.G. fire. One of our planes brought down in our lines. Pilots alive and returned to Coys.	
"	14.9.16	8.30am	Major GIBSON detailed as President of F.G.C.M. to be held at 51st Bde. Depot St. NICHOLAS. Rain in the morning.	MB.
		11 am	Lt. Col. KIRK of the artillery visits Batt. Hd Qrs.	OB.
	15.9.16	11 am	Major BONNETT detailed as President of F.G.C.M. to be held at Bde Depot at St NICHOLAS. Enemy shell FAMPOUX during the morning. C.O. goes round the line about 12.15 pm and returns at 2.15 pm. Enemy very quiet during the afternoon. C.O. goes round the line with the Brigadier. Arrangements made for raid to be carried out by the Battalion on our right (SHERWOODS) SOUTH of Ry. Enemy registers on C.T's and selected spots in our area. Several 5-9's put into CHEMICAL WORKS in the morning. Except for T.M's on front line, enemy very quiet in afternoon. Major BONNETT return from Cmt trailed Gas tries for front line.	CMB
	16.9.16	9 pm		
		9.30 pm	Enemy put down very heavy barrage of T.M's and 5.9's on front line	

A.M.Bonnett Major
1st Scott. Rifles

Army Form C. 2118.

WAR DIARY
or
INTELLIGENCE SUMMARY.
(Erase heading not required.)

Place	Date	Hour	Summary of Events and Information	Remarks and references to Appendices
FRONT LINE CHEMICAL WORKS SECTOR	16.9.19	9.25 p.m.	Enemy quiet again.	
			1 Lewis gun destroyed by shell fire during raid.	
		12 md.	Zero hour for second raid carried out by the DONCASTER Regt. in left sector.	
		12.9 am	Enemy barrage put about on our sector. Another L.G. badly damaged by shell fire. Casualties for both raids N.O.R's killed 2 wounded. Enemy very quiet for remainder of night.	W.B.
"	17.9.19	10 a.m.	C.O. goes round the line. Back flare our own lines very low altitude. Enemy barrage put down on our left. Enemy fairly quiet on any front during the day. C.O. takes command of Bde for a few hours during absence of Brigadier.	
	18.9.19		Arrangements made with incoming Division to relay to-night. Operation Orders issued.	W.B.
		12 noon	Lewis Guns Summo returned.	
		6.30 P.m	Relief commences.	
		7 P.m	Relief complete. Dispositions as under.	
		9 P.m	1 Coy in CADIZ RESERVE 1 Coy in COLT RESERVE 1 Coy in LEMON TRENCH 2 Coys in SUNKEN ROAD (TANK DUMP) Batt Hdqrs in SUNKEN ROAD (TANK DUMP)	

A.S34. Wt. W4973 M687 750,000 8/16 D. D. & L. Ltd. Forms/C.2118/13.

WAR DIARY
or
INTELLIGENCE SUMMARY.

Army Form C. 2118.

Place	Date	Hour	Summary of Events and Information	Remarks and references to Appendices
RESERVE LINE (LEMON TRENCH)	19.9.17		195 other ranks to be found by Battalion for working parties. C.O. gave orders to clean to camp and latrines at 9.30 p.m.	
"	20.9.17		C.O. gave revised Band D. Coy area. Working parties as yesterday to be found by Battalion. Brigadier General visited Batt. Hd qrs. Aerial activity on both sides all day.	208
"	21.9.17		Usual Working parties. C.O. Commanders and B.G.G.S. 1st Battalion Hol. g'rs and wish us goodbye on Battalion leaving the Corps. Aerial activity throughout the day.	209B
"	22.9.17		Usual working parties found by Battalion. Brigadier visits Batt Hd qrs about 10.30 am C.O. accompanied Brigadier round the line P.O. acft officers and N.C.O.s of 21st 5th Batt. Royal Warwicks come up to take over sector	211B
"	23.9.17	6 p.m.	30 working parties for B and D Coy. line of relief for B and D Coy. visited Bde to also Major Burnett went to Transport Lines	

WAR DIARY
or
INTELLIGENCE SUMMARY.

Army Form C. 2118.

Place	Date	Hour	Summary of Events and Information	Remarks and references to Appendices
YMAELE SWITCH	23.9.17		Transport Officer in charge and took over billets.	
		4.30 pm	A and C Coy relief complete.	
		2 pm	B and D Coy two Lewis Gunners relieved	
		10 pm	Battalion relief complete	
		11.10 pm	Batt. Hd Qrs. arrive in ARRAS enters Head Quarters at 9 Rue CHATEAUDUN. All Coy billetted in Prison.	
ARRAS	24.9.17		Batt. complete in billets at 12.30 am.	1918.
		10.10 am	Batt. march out of ARRAS. ⇒ to SIMEN COURT via DAINVILLE - BERNEVILLE arrival at SIMENCOURT	
SIMENCOURT		3.30 pm	Draft of 170 arrive. 2/Lt H.V. SMITH arrives with draft and is posted to C Coy.	1918.
"	26.9.17	10.15 am	C.O. attends G.C.M. at BERNEVILLE. Draft of 159 O.R.s arrive between 3 pm and 7 pm	
		6 pm	C.O. returns. Draft inspected by C.O. at 7 pm. Draft consists of H2 R.F.C. men transferred from Balloon section also men from 1st & 2nd & 6th & 7th & 8th & 9th Battns R.F.	

M Burgess Lt.Col.
For 7/R.F.

Army Form C. 2118.

WAR DIARY
or
INTELLIGENCE SUMMARY.
(Erase heading not required.)

Instructions regarding War Diaries and Intelligence Summaries are contained in F.S. Regs., Part II. and the Staff Manual respectively. Title pages will be prepared in manuscript.

Place	Date	Hour	Summary of Events and Information	Remarks and references to Appendices
BEAUDRICOURT	26/9/19	9.30am	Batt march out of SIMENCOURT to BEAUDRICOURT via GOUY-en-ARTOIS BARLY SOMBRIN - SUS-St. LEGER	
		2.30 pm	Batt fall in for march to dinner in field east of SUS-St. LEGER	
		3.30 pm	Batt proceed and had BEAUDRICOURT 5.30 pm. No Coy parades on the march	
		11.30 pm	Last night training to in afternoon. COs conference over B.C. Grp	NMB
	27/9/19	9.30am	Training. Tactics including firing on tapes	
		4 p.	Musketry, squad drill, Bob Leopfright	
		10.30am	Brigadier and Bde. Sniper visit Battalion	
		2 Pm	CO's conference at Hd Qr IVERGNY	NMB
		4 Pm	Lt. BIROM (G.S.O.I.) visits B. Hq.	
	28/9/19		Training as for 27th. During leisure hours Battery at coy ranges. Football on etc. Coys	
	29/9/19		Training on 27-28. CO met Coy Commanders	
	30/9/19		Inter Company round at coys. football match between right & left half Battn. (about)	NMBuryess Maj 2nd S.S. Ny/9/19

WAR DIARY
or
INTELLIGENCE SUMMARY.
(Erase heading not required.)

Army Form C. 2118.

J C Stafford
5/1/7
Vol 28

T. 27

Place	Date 1917	Hour	Summary of Events and Information	Remarks and references to Appendices
BEAUDRICOURT	OCT 1st	10am 11 12 noon 2 to 4 pm	Battalion practice the attack over flagged area. Usual training carried on by Coy's during the afternoon, including Inspection, Inspection of Bayonet fighting etc., etc. From R.P.B. arrived M.C., 2nd in Command of the Battalion proceeds to England for C.O.'s course at Aldershot, making of three months. 2/Lieut Burges, attached to Bn. for Duty, proceeds to join the Royal Flying Corps.	faa
ditto	2nd	11am	The Battalion accompanied the 51st Brigade on a Field Day which Brigade does practice attack over flagged area.	
ditto	3rd	12.30pm 3pm 9am 12 noon	Practice attack finished and Battalions march home independently. Battalion again practices the attack, in conjunction with the other Battalions of 51st Inf Brigade. Brigadier General inspects Inspection of Arms, Equipment, Kit, Box Respirators etc., carried out by Coy's during the morning. Warning Order received that Battalion is to be prepared to move tomorrow 4.th.	faa
ditto	4th	4.30am 6am	Reveille. Battalion marches from BEAUDRICOURT via SUS-ST-LEGER-SOUASTRE to SOUTH	Stafford Lt Col

Army Form C. 2118.

WAR DIARY
or
INTELLIGENCE SUMMARY.
(Erase heading not required.)

Instructions regarding War Diaries and Intelligence Summaries are contained in F.S. Regs., Part II. and the Staff Manual respectively. Title pages will be prepared in manuscript.

Place	Date	Hour	Summary of Events and Information	Remarks and references to Appendices
SAULTY	4th	9 am	Battalion arrived at SAULTY Station.	
			The Regt Transport leaves BEAUDRICOURT at 4.30 am.	
			Batt'n entrain at SAULTY Station and leave at 9.45 am, for PESELHOEK, 2 miles N of POPERINGHE. Train via DOULLENS - FREVENT - ST POL - LILLERS - HAZEBROUCK. Detrain at 11.30 pm and march to SUEZ CAMP, PROVEN AREA.	
	5th	1.30 am	Battalion arrives at SUEZ CAMP at 1.30 am and transport at 2.0 am.	
		7.30 am	'B' Coy arrive at PESELHOEK	
		10 am	'B' Coy arrive at SUEZ CAMP	
			Operation Orders for move to HERZEELE received.	
HERZEELE.		2 pm	Battalion march out of SUEZ CAMP to HERZEELE via PROVEN - HOUTKERQUE. Accommodation at HERZEELE very limited. Battn Hd Qrs at farm E7041 1/5 Corps.	
		5.0 pm	Activities over an area of about 1½ miles. Lorries arrive and are issued to Coy's.	
HERZEELE.	6th	10 am	The Commanding Officer rides round to see all coys.	
		2 pm to 4 pm	Training includes Inspections, Musketry, Bayonet fighting, Physical Training &c.	
		5 pm	C.O. attended conference at 575th Brigade Headquarters	
		"	Lieut Armstrong, Tadjt. returns from leave, and takes over from Lieut Wilson.	

J. Armstrong Lt
Staff S. Staff Regt.

WAR DIARY or INTELLIGENCE SUMMARY.

Army Form C. 2118.

(Erase heading not required.)

Place	Date	Hour	Summary of Events and Information	Remarks and references to Appendices
HERZEELE	7th	9 a.m.	N.C.O. accompanied the Brigadier General, 51st Brigade, to the forward area for reconnoitring purposes.	
		10 a.m. to 12 noon	Coys under Major W. Gibson, M.C., practiced the attack during the absence of C.O.	
		3.45 p.m.	Commanding Officer returns.	
			Weather very wet & dull the whole day	
		8.45 p.m. 10.15	Coy's under Major Gibson on night operations. (Forming up on taped lines.) Night operations cease. Operation Order for move to ST SIXTE area received.	
— do —	8th		During the morning Battalion is busy packing up and preparing for move.	
		10.45 a.m.	Lecture by C.O. to all officers and N.C.O's, on forthcoming operations.	
		12.30 p.m.	Coys & Transport parade ready to move off.	
		1.0 p.m.	Battalion marches from HERZEELE to SUEZ CAMP (ROUEN Area).	
		4.45 p.m.	The Battalion arrives at SUEZ CAMP (ST SIXTE) EAST of PROVEN. Orders received that whole Brigade is expecting to move early tomorrow morning. Suez Camp in a very muddy condition. Rain all night.	
SUEZ CAMP	9th	3 a.m.	Operation Orders for move received.	
		6.30 a.m.	Battalion parade and marches to to INTERNATIONAL CORNER	

8 Staffordshire Regt

Army Form C. 2118.

WAR DIARY
or
INTELLIGENCE SUMMARY.
(Erase heading not required.)

Instructions regarding War Diaries and Intelligence Summaries are contained in F. S. Regs., Part II. and the Staff Manual respectively. Title pages will be prepared in manuscript.

Place	Date	Hour	Summary of Events and Information	Remarks and references to Appendices
WHITEMILL CAMP (ELVERDINGHE)	9/7/17 CONTD	8am	Battalion entrains at INTERNATIONAL CORNER for ELVERDINGHE.	
		8.25am	Transport proceeds by road to ELVERDINGHE.	
		8.45am	Entrains at ELVERDINGHE and march to WHITEMILL CAMP.	
		9.30am	Arrive at WHITEMILL CAMP at 8.45am.	
		9.50am	Transport arrives.	
			Commanding Officer and all Coy commanders reconnaitre Headquarters lines. Learn that both British and French captured 1st Objectives and guards Division their 2nd objective. Great number of prisoners taken. Remainder of day spent in issuing S.A.A., flares, sandbags, rations etc. in preparation for move to front line.	
		3.30pm	Passwords for Brigade Report learns made known by Gibson	
			ZERO DAY. Orders received for the Battn to relieve front line by 8.00am on ZERO+2 days. Battn spends the night in ELVERDINGHE (WHITEMILL CAMP).	
ditto	10/7/17		Camp bombed by enemy aeroplanes during the night. No casualties.	
		9-3am	C.O and all Company Commanders reconnaitre route to front line. C.O.'s horse killed and 4 others wounded slightly.	

S A Whinney D
S A Stafford Regt.

Army Form C. 2118.

WAR DIARY
or
INTELLIGENCE SUMMARY.
(Erase heading not required.)

Instructions regarding War Diaries and Intelligence Summaries are contained in F. S. Regs., Part II. and the Staff Manual respectively. Title pages will be prepared in manuscript.

Place	Date	Hour	Summary of Events and Information	Remarks and references to Appendices
WHITTEMQUE CAMP	10TH CORPS	9.am to 11.30am	Coys paraded in Battle Kit for inspection. Warning Order issued. Battn. to be ready to move forward at 3.30pm	
		2 pm	Operation Orders received. Battn. to move quietly at VULCAN CROSSING at 5.45pm	
		2.30pm	C.O sees all Coy commanders	
		4.0pm	Battalion moves off for front line	
		5.45pm	Arrive at VULCAN CROSSING and pick up Lewis guns and rations. Guides met got	
			Arrival	
		6.30pm	Guides arrived at Battn, after rations are issued moved off by coys. Battn. HQ Orn. established in Pill Box at NAQOR CROSSING. All coys dug in in new	
			Battn. HQ Orn.	
			Heavy shelling by the enemy during relief. Several casualties including 2/Lieuts Costley + Harding, Wounded.	
		6.0am	Relief completed reported to Brigade Headquarters. During the night 10/11th two Lewis guns were destroyed by shell fire.	faa
IN SUPPORT NAQOR CROSSING	11TH	12 noon	Very heavy shelling round Battn. HQ. Orn. 2 officers and 32 other rank Casualties. C.O sees all Coy Commanders in B.m. Orn Rx. another 300000 rds. No	
		3pm	down to wire operation orders. Major Pedder commanding 7th Lincolns meets C.O to make arrangements	H.Smith. Lt. S Staffs/Infantry?

WAR DIARY or INTELLIGENCE SUMMARY

Place	Date	Hour	Summary of Events and Information	Remarks and references to Appendices
	11TH (CONTD)		Attack. Both CO's decide to establish out posts and sent Pat. Bois. gear in rear of Company Hdrs. on the Railway. U.12.d.45.72. SCARP-BAIZE 1:10,000	
		5.30p	1st Coy moves off to relieve 7th Lincolns in front line. "A", "B" + "D" Coys in front line. "C" Coy remain in same position and move forward later	
		12 M.N.	Lieut Wilson detailed to lay the tapes from which the Battn will jump off for the attack tomorrow.	
	12TH	2.0 am	C.O. and Adjutant go out to West Coy and also to reconnoitre jumping off line. Heavy rain during the night and Hullah Col. shews very cheerful.	
			ZERO hour at 5.25 am. Coys to form up on tape line at 4.45 am. 30pm. The C.O. Adjutant and Battn HdQrs. move up in rear of jumping off line	
		at 5.0 am	All Coys lined up ready for attack by 5.5 am. Report on attack from 4.25 am (2 m.s.t.) is attached. Casualties during the attack 7 Officers and 153 other ranks (including C.O. 2/Lt Col w.a.t. Baker. D.S.O. and 2/Lt Wilson.) Unknown 50 + 100 prisoners taken by 6 & 8 Staffordshire Regt. in the attack.	Yes Yes Yes

J.R.M. Wright
8th Bn. N. Staffordshire Regt.

Army Form C. 2118.

WAR DIARY
or
INTELLIGENCE SUMMARY.
(Erase heading not required.)

Instructions regarding War Diaries and Intelligence Summaries are contained in F. S. Regs., Part II. and the Staff Manual respectively. Title pages will be prepared in manuscript.

Place	Date	Hour	Summary of Events and Information	Remarks and references to Appendices
FRONT LINE	13TH		It was impossible to obtain communication with any owing to absence of any runner until 9-0 am this morning. The Brigade Major visited Battn. HQ and the situation as far as it is known was explained to him. During the whole of the 13th the Boche put down an intense Barrage in rear areas but speared attention to the Pit. B.s in which B. was. Sea issue had been established. There were more killed and many more wounded thro' enemy photography.	filed
		12 noon		
		6·30p	O.o is found severely wounded, by 2Lt. Glover and this been posted, it is uncertain and sent up to keep him in shelter. Officer commanding Lt.Col. D. S. Barker arrives in the Om.n. has worked in division and to is made alternate arrangements and found his officers to go down.	
	14TH	5·15am	Heavy Shelling continued round HA OR. O.O is sent down to the Dressing Station. Warning Order received that 51st Bn. is going to be relieved tonight. Arrangements made for guides to meet relieving units from the time the C.O. was wounded, until nearly the Battalion was commenced to be relieved Major J. Armstrong, all the officers with the exception of the signalling officer being [?]	filed

S. P. Hoffmeister Capt.

WAR DIARY or INTELLIGENCE SUMMARY

Army Form C. 2118.

Place	Date	Hour	Summary of Events and Information	Remarks and references to Appendices
FRONT LINE	14TH (Cont'd)		2nd & 3rd Coy officers known to have been killed or wounded. Representatives of the relieving unit (1st [?] 1st Yorkshire Regt) arrive to take over.	
		3 [?]	3 guides per Coy went to meet 10th West Yorks at Brigade relay post about 1500 yards in rear of Bn Hd Qrs.	
		9.0 pm	C.O. 10th [?] Yorkshire Regt arrives at Bn Hd Qrs. Relief went well, very smoothly and our reporting Corporals to Bn Hd.	
			Out at 4.45 am on 15th inst. During the operations the total casualties of the Battn amounted to 18 officers (4 killed + 14 wounded) and 340 other ranks (killed + wounded)	J.A.A.
	15TH		The Battn marched to PILKEM by Coys.	
		5.30 am	Battn arrived at PILKEM where they were met by Major Gibson M.C. who took over command. Hot Cocoa & Biscuits were served to the men immediately they arrived.	
		10.0 am	Breakfast was served	
		12.30pm	The Battn by Coys PILKEM marched to camp in CARIBOU. 4 G.S. wagons were provided for stragglers. Battn arrived at CARIBOU camp and proceeded in by the Right Bank. 1st Monmouth Regt & 1st Staffordshire Regt	J.A.A.

Army Form C. 2118.

WAR DIARY
or
INTELLIGENCE SUMMARY.

(Erase heading not required.)

Instructions regarding War Diaries and Intelligence Summaries are contained in F.S. Regs., Part II. and the Staff Manual respectively. Title pages will be prepared in manuscript.

Place	Date	Hour	Summary of Events and Information	Remarks and references to Appendices
CARIBOU CAMP.	15TH Contd		Rest of the day was spent in CARIBOU CAMP. Cleaning up of Arms, Equipment & Clothing etc.	
		6.0 pm	To clear from 151st Inf Brigade Depot signed the Battalion G.O.C. 17th Division speaks to N.C.O's of the Bn. and congratulates them on the splendid work done during recent operations. Orders received that Battn will entrain at ELVERDINGHE for PROVEN tomorrow 16th inst.	J.A.O.
,,	16TH	10.23 am	Battalion marches from CARIBOU CAMP to ELVERDINGHE where they entrained	
		12.0 pm	Entrained for PROVEN.	
		12.45 pm	Battalion detrained at PROVEN and marched to PIDDINGTON CAMP. P.I. area.	J.A.O.
		2.0 pm	Arrived at PIDDINGTON CAMP (Canvas). Transport not yet arrived	
		4.0 pm	Regtl Transport turned up at Camp and Tea & Dinner were issued to the men.	
PIDDINGTON CAMP	17TH	9.0 am	C.O. (Major D Egerton M.C.) sees all Coy commanders re reorganization of Coys	

J Armstrong Lt
O.C. Staffordshire Regt.

Army Form C. 2118.

WAR DIARY
or
INTELLIGENCE SUMMARY.
(Erase heading not required.)

Instructions regarding War Diaries and Intelligence Summaries are contained in F. S. Regs., Part II. and the Staff Manual respectively. Title pages will be prepared in manuscript.

Place	Date	Hour	Summary of Events and Information	Remarks and references to Appendices
PIDDINGTON CAMP	17th Contd		Coy spent in re-organising Coys. Inspection of Arms, Kit, Equipment etc. Notifications that Major S. Darby, M.C. is to take over command of the Batt. from the 18th inst.	file
— ditto —	18th		Training by Coys in the morning, Inspections etc. A. + C. Coys played B + D Coys at football in the afternoon. A+C Coys 1 goal	
		3.0pm	B + D Coys Nil. Lieut Burch. 17th D reviews orders Batt. Ad. Bag.	
		4.0pm	2/Lts Murphy & Henderson rejoin the Battalion from Corps Depot.	
		6.0pm	Major S Darby, M.C. arrived and takes over Command of the Battn from Major W Gibson M.C.	file
— ditto —	19th	9.0am	Party of 7 Officers and 60 other ranks formed by the 13 Coy for work unknown the R.F.C. at the R.F.C. Camp.	
		2.0pm	Remainder of the Battalion carry on general training in the morning. Kit inspections & football.	
		4.0pm		
		5.0pm	150, Officers + men, go to the 17th D reviewed Cinema.	
		10pm	Orders received for Battalion to move at 6 a.m. tomorrow by road to	

LICQUETS.

J Armstrong Lt
& Lt/Adjutant Reg.
8 Staffordshire Regt.

Army Form C. 2118.

WAR DIARY
or
INTELLIGENCE SUMMARY.
(Erase heading not required.)

Instructions regarding War Diaries and Intelligence
Summaries are contained in F. S. Regs., Part II.
and the Staff Manual respectively. Title pages
will be prepared in manuscript.

Place	Date	Hour	Summary of Events and Information	Remarks and references to Appendices
PIDDINGTON CAMP	20TH	6.0 a.m	Transport moved off for LICQUES.	
			5.15 by Brigade Pavillion Orders for move of Battn. to be to LICQUES on morning of 21st inst. received.	
		3.0 p.m	Major McGreer starts a class for N.C.O's who have had no previous training in open warfare and camp but is immediately thrown off by A.A.	
			Enemy aeroplane flew over camp but is immediately thrown off by A.A.	
	21ST.	7.15 a.m	The Battalion fall in and is told off in parties of 25 ready for entraining.	
		7.45 a.m	Arrive at the entraining point on the POPERINGHE-PROVEN ROAD.	
		8.15 a.m	Battn entrains and moves off to LICQUES.	
		6.15 p.m	Battn arrive at LICQUES. Very good Billets.	
LICQUES	22ND		Day spent in generally cleaning up Arms, Clothing etc ready to commence training tomorrow.	
		10.0	C.O. goes round Billets.	
	23RD	11.30 a.m	Very wet weather training carried on in Billets. C.O. goes to Brigade Headquarters.	

Shrewsbury L.I.
& Staffs Regt

WAR DIARY
INTELLIGENCE SUMMARY.
(Erase heading not required.)

Army Form C. 2118.

Place	Date	Hour	Summary of Events and Information	Remarks and references to Appendices
LICQUES	23RD	2.30pm	Conference of all officers in Headquarters Mess on methods of training for the attack.	R.W.
- ditto -	24d	2.30pm	Moving order received for part of transport to proceed by road to PROVEN Area.	
		8am	G.S. Wagons move off to PROVEN area	
		9am to 1pm	Company training, training in the attack. Battalion will now Major W. Gibson M.C.	
		10.30pm	Operation Orders received for the Battalion to move to PROVEN (P.5 Area)	A.W.
- ditto -	25d	8am	Battalion moved by road from LICQUES to AUDRUICK. Dinners served on the road.	
		5.30pm	Battalion entrained at AUDRUICK & detrained at PROVEN at 11.30pm	R.W.
PROVEN PATIALA CAMP	26.4	12.30am	Battalion arrived at PATIALA CAMP.	
		12noon	Operation Orders received for Battalion to move to BOESINGHE	
		2pm	Inspection of Box Respirators, P.H. Helmets, Ammunition etc for further parade.	
			4 Officers from 7th Border Regt. attached temporarily to this Battalion	R.W.
-ditto-	27th	9am	Battalion fell in ready to move off to PROVEN Station	
			Brigade Depot personnel remained at PATIALA CAMP under Major W. Gibson. M.C.	R.W.
		4.30pm	Battalion entrained at PROVEN Station for BOESINGHE	R.W.

R.J. Wells Lt
2nd S. Staff R.

Army Form C. 2118.

WAR DIARY
or
INTELLIGENCE SUMMARY.
(Erase heading not required.)

Instructions regarding War Diaries and Intelligence Summaries are contained in F. S. Regs., Part II. and the Staff Manual respectively. Title pages will be prepared in manuscript.

Place	Date	Hour	Summary of Events and Information	Remarks and references to Appendices
BOESINGHE	27th	10.40am	Detrained at BOESINGHE. Battalion marched from the Station to BOESINGHE CAMP & arrived there at 11.45am.	
		5.0pm	Companies fell in & moved to BABOON CAMP arrived there at 8pm. All Companies are in Dugouts. C.D & Halgin are in Nissen huts	R.W.
BABOON CAMP	28th		Companies "Standing To" alternately for 2 hours each ready to move forward at a moments notice if called upon by Divisional troops.	
		1.30pm	D Company stood to. Party of 1 officer & 50 men to work under the R.E. This party was not required. Returned to camp at 7pm. Enemy shelled in vicinity of camp. No damage done.	R.W.
			Battalion in Reserve.	
-ditto-	29th		Companies "Standing To" as yesterday. However the Battalion rested the whole day.	R.W.
	30th	7.30am	Battalion paraded & marched to BOESINGHE Station, arrived there at 8.30 am.	
		9.40am	Entrained at BOESINGHE Station for PROVEN.	
		10.20am	Detrained at PROVEN & marched to PATIALA CAMP (T.5.a.a.a.) arrived there at 10.50 am.	R.V. Wells 2/Lt. Sgd S. Staff. R.

Army Form C. 2118.

WAR DIARY
or
INTELLIGENCE SUMMARY
(Erase heading not required).

Place	Date	Hour	Summary of Events and Information	Remarks and references to Appendices
PATIALA CAMP PROVEN	30th		Breakfast served on arrival in Camp. Battalion resting the whole day.	D.R.
-ditto-	31st	9am	Battalion Muster Parade, all specialists transport & cooks with their Companies. General cleaning up; rifle & equipment inspection	D.R.
		6pm	Warning Order received for Battalion to move to WURMHOUD ('B' area)	
		11:50pm	Operation Orders for move received.	

Stacke
Lieut Col
Commanding 6th the South Staffs Regt.

REPORT ON THE ADVANCE OF THE 8th BATTALION SOUTH STAFFORDSHIRE REGT
IN THE ATTACK ON THE MORNING OF THE 12th OCTOBER 1917.

FORMING UP. At 4.25 a.m. on Oct. 12th 1917, the 8th South Staffordshire Regt, formed up on a tape stretching between the points U 12 d 76 95 and U 12 b 42 70 facing a direction of about 43° true bearing.

POSITIONS. "B" Coy. (2/Lt.R.W.A.GLEED.) on the right and "A" Coy (Capt.O.BARLOW.M.C.) on the left in the front line.
"D" Coy. (Capt.P.A.W.CAME.) right support and "C" Coy. (Capt.L.J.KELSEY) left support.

ADVANCE.
At 5.25 a.m. the barrage came down 200 yards in front of and parallel to the tape line.
The Battalion at once moved forward.
FORMATIONS. The first half of each platoon of the two leading Coys were extended and formed one wave of two lines. The men being extended to about 8 paces. The second half of each of the leading Coys formed a "line of half platoons in file"
The two supporting Coys follow in Artillery Formation of platoons in file. The depth of ground covered by the Battalion was about 90 yards and the frontage of about 380 yards.
At 5.31 a.m. the two leading Coys halted on a line U 12 b 95 12 to U 12 b 62 95. The supporting Coys closed up behind them.
At 5.33 a.m. had the battalion resumed the advance closely following the barrage which at this moment lifted 100 yards. The advance continued at the rate of 8 mins per 100 yards until at 6 a.m. the left Coy("A") reached its first objective. It appears that by this time the left Coy "A" had closed in a little to their right.
All the Officers of this Coys became Casualties before the first objective was reached, and "C" Coys supporting them had only one Officer left. "B" & "D" Coys had each two or three Officers. The retreating enemy made off in an Easterly direction for the Railway, and "A" Coy being without Officers lost direction to some extent in following the the enemy. The right Coy("B") were very close to the barrage and had to hold back a little while "A" Coy advanced and here again "A" Coy appears to have closed to the right.
At 6.5 a.m. the right Coy ("B") reached their first objective.
There was now a decided gap in the line on the left of Battalion which appears to have been increased after the first objective was reached. At this stage Capt.Came of "D" Coy seeing a gap on the left of "A" Coy took up one platoon on a left incline to fill this gap. At the same time Col.BARKER observing the gap sent forward one platoon of "C" Coy under Sgt.Simms for the same purpose. This however was not done until the whole Battalion had passed to the left of ADEN HOUSE. Immediately after detailing the platoon of "C" Coy to move forward, Col.BARKER was seriously Wounded. "B" Coy had now one Officer left, "C" Coy one Officer and "D" Coy 2 Officers. The right of "B" Coy pushed on and reached their final objective i.e. TURENNE CROSSING. This was at 6.37 a.m.
The left of "B" Coy hung back to keep in line with "A" Coy who were held up on the road behind ADEN HOUSE. Then right of "A" Coy rested on point V 1 c 74 37.

CONSOLIDATION. The Battalion then consolidated on the South Side of the TURENNE CROSSING - ANGLE POINT ROAD. At 6.40 a.m. the right of "A" Coy was withdrawn about 50 yards for this purpose.
Line ran across the railway at TURENNE CROSSING and along the road to point V 1 C 41 22. On this line "A" & "B" Coys with 1 Platoon from "C" Coy and 1 Platoon from "D" Coy, consolidated in an irregular line of shell holes. The remaining three platoons of "C" and three of "D" Coy formed another irregular line of posts about 150 yards in rear.
Casualties 6.45 a.m. About 200 Other Ranks, by noon there remained only the Adjutant, the Signalling Officer and 1 Coy Officer
At 9.30 p.m. on the 12th the C.O. of the 1st Grenadier Guards came to the Adjutant Lt.ARMSTRONG, who was in Command of the Battalion and told him he had orders to clear the ground, in conjunction with the Border Regt, between ANGLE POINT, EGYPT HO and the Railway. He asked Lt.ARMSTRONG to warn his Coys which he did, but they reported that nothing happened.

About noon on the 13th Major.Irwin Commanding the 7th Border Regt. called at Bn. Hd.Qrs. and told Lt.ARmstrong that he had to meet the C.O. of the 1st Grenadier Guards, with reference to the clearing up of ADEN HOUSE. The latter however did not turn up. Major.Irwin then sent for one of his Coy Commanders and gave him instructions to take ADEN HOUSE with 1 Officer and 35 Other Ranks. This party was shelled on their way up about 2.30 a.m. on the 14th inst, and they returned without having done anyhhing.

RELIEF. The Battalion was relieved about 4,45 a.m. on the 14th and the dispositions handed over were as indicated on page 1. There was a gap of about 200 yards between the left of the Battalion and the right of the 1st Grenadier Guards.

A copy of Lt.Armstrong's final report of his position is attached hereto..

It would appear that the loss ofd direction after passing the first objective and the consequent failure of the left of the Battalion the reach the final objective are due to the following causes.

(1) The extremely heavy casualties to Officers in the early stages of the attack, and that there was no Officer to Command "A" Coy(the left Coy in the front line) when the first objective was reached.

(2) That the few Officers left did not realize that as the attack progressed the frontage of the Battalion had to be increased from 340 yards at the jumping off tape to about 550 yards on the final objective.

(3) The retreat of the enemy across our front to the railway drew platoons without officers after them, and so a gap was left on the left flank, and the right became congested.

The Battalion was in touch with the 1st Grenadier Guards when they left the jumping off tape. During the whole of the 12th it was impossible to obtain communication with the front line owing to the accuracy of enemy snipers. Reports as to the position of the line could only be based on information received from Casualties passing to the rear. Though the first reports of the position of the front line proved inaccurate I do not consider that this was any fault of the Adjutant's. He was Commanding the Battalion with only one Company Officer remaining and that one wounded. He would have been unwise to attempt to reconnoitre the front line during daylight, after every Orderly he had sent 15 in all had been sniped.

In my opinion he carried on remarkably well under the most difficuly circumstances. He informs me that he several times asked for some reinforcement Officers to be sent up but none arrived.

(Sd) W. GIBSON.

15-10-17.

MAJOR.
Commanding. 8th. Bn. South Staffordshire Regt.

"A" Form.
MESSAGES AND SIGNALS.

Army Form C. 2121 (in pads of 100).
No. of Message ......

Prefix ... Code ... m.	Words	Charge	This message is on a/c of:	Recd. at .... m.
Office of Origin and Service Instructions.				Date ....
	Sent		.... Service.	From ....
	At .... m.			
	To			
	By		(Signature of "Franking Officer.")	By ....

TO { HOBBY

Sender's Number.	Day of Month.	In reply to Number.	AAA
* SR 21.	13th		

Line was as follows and not as previously reported aaa TURENNE CROSSING on a line running W.S.W. to V.1.c.2.2 aaa Gap of 200x between our left and GOOD'S right.

From: HOIST.
Place:
Time: 5.25 pm

The above may be forwarded as now corrected.

(Z) (Sd) J Armstrong Lt
Signature of Addressor or person authorised to telegraph in his name.

D.A.G.

Base.

8TH (S) BATT.
SOUTH STAFFS.
REGIMENT.
No. 1867/1
Date 1-2-7

Herewith War Diary for the Battalion under my
Command from November 1st to November 30th. 1917.

S. Danby.

Lieut.Colonel.
Comdg. 8th. Bn. South Staffordshire Regt.

Army Form C. 2118.

1/5 Staffordshire Regt November 1917

WAR DIARY
or
INTELLIGENCE SUMMARY
(Erase heading not required.)

Vol 29

Place	Date	Hour	Summary of Events and Information	Remarks and references to Appendices
PATIALA CAMP PROVEN	Nov 1	10.20am	Battalion fell in ready to move off to WORMHOUDT B' Area. Thompson to inspan 200 yds in rear of each company. Route:- PROVEN - HOUTKERQUE - HERZEELE - WORMHOUD f Division moved en route at 1.15pm. 3 miles east of WORMHOUDT	
	4.15pm	Companies arrived at their billets in the new area, they being very scattered & four from Battalion Headquarters. Major S. Dawbarn R.C. authorised to wear the Badges of Lt Colonel commanding the Battalion.	PM
WORMHOUDT	Nov 2	10am	The C.O. & 2 in Command visited the companies in their billets companies carried out inspections f Box Respirators P.H. Helmets &c &c. The Military Bross is awarded the following officers for gallantry in the field :- Capt Jacobs R.A.M.C. Lieut J.A. Dennistoun Lieut R.W.G. Reid	
			The D.C.M. is awarded to unaccounced N.C.O.- Sgt Ward H.	
			The following Medals is awarded to the following men:- Sgt Walker W.L. L/Cpl Thompson J.K. Pte Middleton W.S. Pte Moore T. (2nd Btn)	PW

R1 (reed) 7th
35 Staff R

Army Form C. 2118.

WAR DIARY
or
INTELLIGENCE SUMMARY.
(Erase heading not required.)

2/0.5 Staffordshire Regt
November 1917

Instructions regarding War Diaries and Intelligence Summaries are contained in F. S. Regs., Part II. and the Staff Manual respectively. Title pages will be prepared in manuscript.

Place	Date	Hour	Summary of Events and Information	Remarks and references to Appendices
WORMHOUDT	Nov 2	5 pm	A Company H.Q. Company moved from their billets as these had been handed over to another unit. A Company now billets was 4 km from Battalion Headquarters.	R.W.
ditto	Nov 3	10.30 am	The C.O. & 2nd in Command visited the Companies in their new billets. The baths at WORMHOUDT were allotted to the Battalion for the whole day.	
		3 pm	The pack animals & transport were inspected at Brigade Headquarters by the acting Brigadier, Lt-Col Metcalfe, C.M.G. D.S.O. 1st Lincolnshire Regt.	R.W.
ditto	Nov 4	10 am	Church Parade.	R.W.
		11 am	The C.O. & Adjutant visited Brigade at ZERMEZEELE.	
ditto	Nov 5	9 am	Companies training independently.	
		12.30 pm	Bombing Companies in the attack, special attention being paid to the taking of strong points and "pillboxes".	
		10 pm	Warning Order received for the Battalion to move to TROYEN, PLOEGSTEERT on the 8th inst.	R.W.

R.I. Wells 2/Lt
2/0.5. Staff R.

Army Form C. 2118.

WAR DIARY
or
INTELLIGENCE SUMMARY.

(Erase heading not required.)

E & S. Staffordshire Regt.

November 1917

Place	Date	Hour	Summary of Events and Information	Remarks and references to Appendices
WORMHOUDT	Nov 6		Lt Col S. Darby. M.C. having proceeded on leave to Paris, Major W. Gibson M.C. took over command of the Battalion.	
		9am to 4pm	Battalion Route march.	
		9am to 12.30pm	Major W. Gibson, M.C. holds class for senior N.C.O's. Sightmeal served at 12.30pm	P.T.O.
		12.30pm	8 Officers join the Battalion from Corps Depot as reinforcements & are taken on the strength.	
ditto	Nov 7	10am	Operation Orders received for the Battalion to move to PROVEN P.I. Area. Weather very wet. Training in Billets. Major W. Gibson, M.C. holds class for senior N.C.O.'s.	R.W.
		9am to 12.30pm		
			T/Lieut J. A. Armstrong appointed Acquitant of the Battalion, the appointment to date from 11.3.17, vice T/Capt G.C.R. Coleridge M.C.	
ditto	Nov 8	9.30am	Battalion ordered to be clear of the WORMHOUDT Area by 9am. Battalion paraded ready to move off. Route - WORMHOUDT - HERZEELE - HOUTKERQUE - PROVEN.	R.W.
		1.30pm	Arrived at PIDDINGTON CAMP, PROVEN, having been delayed by congestion on the road.	R.W.

R. J. Webb 2/Lt
E & S. Staff. R.

Army Form C. 2118.

5 MBn 5. Staffordshire Regt

WAR DIARY
or
INTELLIGENCE SUMMARY.
(Erase heading not required.)

November 1917.

Instructions regarding War Diaries and Intelligence Summaries are contained in F. S. Regs., Part II. and the Staff Manual respectively. Title pages will be prepared in manuscript.

Place	Date	Hour	Summary of Events and Information	Remarks and references to Appendices
PRODINGTON CAMP	Nov 8		Dinners served on arrival. Camp in a very muddy condition	R.W.
PROVEN	Nov 9	8.30am to 10am	} Physical Training, Rifle & Equipment Inspection.	
		10am	} Cleaning up of camp. Building of splinter proof walls around tents	
		12.30pm	}	
		2pm	} Foot inspection parade	
		2.30pm	}	R.W.
- ditto -	Nov 10	8.30am to noon	Cleaning up of camp. Building of splinter proof walls round tents.	
		10am	Warning Order received for 5th Bde to move into Tournai Camps on the 11th inst	R.W.
		5pm	Movement Order cancelled.	
- ditto -	Nov 11	10am	Church Parade in Hangar of No 2, Squadron. R.F.C. PROVEN. Four service held under cover for 10½ months. Lt. Col. S. Darnby. M.C. having returned from Leave, resumed command of the Battalion.	R.W.
- ditto -	Nov 12	9am to 1pm	} Company training separately, special attention being given to Box Respirator Drill. } Senior N.C.O's class under Major W. Gibson. M.C.	R.W.

R. J. Leeds, 2nd Lt
N/5 Staff. R

Army Form C. 2118.

WAR DIARY
or
INTELLIGENCE SUMMARY

S.K.S. Staffordshire Regt
November 1917

(Erase heading not required.)

Instructions regarding War Diaries and Intelligence Summaries are contained in F.S. Regs., Part II. and the Staff Manual respectively. Title pages will be prepared in manuscript.

Place	Date	Hour	Summary of Events and Information	Remarks and references to Appendices
PIDDINGTON CAMP PROVEN	Nov 12	11am	The C.O. sees all Officers & discusses Intell. Work in the Trenches.	
		12.30pm	Visit by the Divisional Commander & the Brigadier.	
		2pm	Draft of 135 OR arrived from Corps Depot.	
ditto	Nov 13	10am	Battalion paraded ready to march to PROVEN Station.	
		1pm	Entrained for ELVERDINGHE	
		2.30pm	(Vervoerd of BRIDGE CAMP (Huts) ELVERDINGHE	
BRIDGE CAMP ELVERDINGHE	Nov 14	9am	Companies training; extended order drill, Box Respirator Drill.	
		12.30pm		
		2-4pm	The Medical Officer inspected the feet of the Battalion.	
ditto	Nov 15	9am	Companies training; platoon rifle drill musketry	
		12.30		
		2-2.30pm	Foot inspection parades.	
		2.30 3	Digging & the trenches in case of bombardment by enemy on retiring	
		8.30pm		

The following additional awards have been granted to the Battalion:—
Sergt Sanders E.
L/Sergt Foster G.C. } Military Medal
Pte Woodward A. }

R.A. Bells 9/v
P.O.S. Staff R.

Army Form C. 2118.

WAR DIARY
or
INTELLIGENCE SUMMARY.

(Erase heading not required.)

8th S. Staffordshire Regt.
November 1917.

Place	Date	Hour	Summary of Events and Information	Remarks and references to Appendices
BRIDGE CAMP ELVERDINGHE	Nov 16		Companies carried out ordinary training. The C.O. visited the 18th W. Yorkshire Regt in Reserve at HUDDLESTON CAMP. The Battalion found a working party of 3 Officers & 150 O.Ranks for work under the R.E's Builder J. Burrage	R.W.
ditto	Nov 17		Companies carried out ordinary training. Company Commanders visited 10th W. Yorkshire Regt in Reserve to obtain information about the front line & the methods of holding it. Working party of 3 Officers & 150 Other Ranks provided for the R.E's	R.W.
ditto	Nov 18	11am	Church Parade. The C.O. & Adjutant visited the Battalion Head Qrs of 10th W.Yorkshire Regt in the front line. Working party of 3 Officers & 150 Other ranks, bringing up cable for the R.E's.	R.W.
	Nov 19	7.45 am	Battalion paraded ready to move to the front line.	
		10 am	Reached HUDDLESTON CAMP where a rest of 1 hour was given & climbing were served. 3 days rations were issued. Lewis gun & rations being slung up in a separate sandbag (Gumboots thigh were also carried) to one company only, for experimental purposes	R.W.

E.L. Russell Lt Col
8th S. Staffords Regt.

WAR DIARY
or
INTELLIGENCE SUMMARY.
(Erase heading not required.)

Army Form C. 2118.

5 & 5 Staff reshuffling
November 1917

Place	Date	Hour	Summary of Events and Information	Remarks and references to Appendices
	Nov 19	2.30pm	Moved off from HUDDLESTON CAMP to relieve 10th W. Yorkshire Regt. in the Front line, TRANQUILLE Nº - 17 METRE HILL SECTOR. 6 Companies in front line, 2 companies in support. Heavy barrage on tracks in and in the neighbourhood of LANGEMARCK turning relief any thing but easy. Reached in passing through this barrage. Relief was complete at 5.30pm Head quarters in SOUPENIR = 0am ("Pillbox")	R.W.
Front line	Nov 20	6am	Our artillery put down a heavy barrage on German line. Throwing no retaliation to this.	
		7.30am	8 enemy aeroplanes observed over our lines, firing bursts from them	
		8.30am	Machine guns on troops in the line.	
		9.30am		
		9.45am	Visit from Major Daniels, 10th Sherwood Foresters	
			Hostile artillery slight, except on back areas where it was severe.	
		6.30pm	The C.O. goes round the line. An Inter-Company relief was carried out, C&D Coys relieving A&B Coys in the front line. Relief complete 2am 21st. Very dark wet night. Arrangements had been made for delivering hot soup to the troops, but the transport was unable to get up on the barrage made.	R.I. Weea Lt. F.O. S. Staff. R

WAR DIARY
INTELLIGENCE SUMMARY

Army Form C. 2118.

8.A.S. Staffordshire Regt
November 1917.

Place	Date	Hour	Summary of Events and Information	Remarks and references to Appendices
Front line	Nov 20		The River BROEMBEEK had been blown up by shellfire	R.W.
ditto	Nov 21	7:30am	Water brought up by the Transport to Bn.H.Q., the bridge over R BROEMBEEK having been repaired during the night.	
		8:30am	Major Petche D.S.O. & Company Commanders from 7th Lincolnshire Regt. came up to take over.	
		9:30am	The O/Brigadier, Lt.Col Metcalfe, C.M.G., D.S.O. & the Brigade Major visited Bn. H.Q.	
		6pm	Pack animals reached H.Q. with hot soup & tea in special containers. These were delivered equally to companies, but these the containers were not found satisfactory as the soup & tea were cold on arrival.	
			The weather was but troops during the day, enemy artillery not light.	R.W.
			The undermentioned Officers joined the Bn:- Major T.S.B. Fitzwarine-Smith, Capt. J.S.W. Murray, 2/Lt J.A. Green, 2/Lt C. Scott M.C., 2/Lt R.J. Bruce, 2/Lt S.A. Pownall.	
ditto	Nov 22		Enemy artillery not very active during day.	
		10:30am	First twenty of Major Teary R.E.	
		4pm	Advance party of 7th Lincolnshire Regt arrived to relieve	R.W.

R.I. Weller Lt
8/S. Staff. R.

Army Form C. 2118.

1/5 Staffordshire Regt.
November 1917

WAR DIARY
or
INTELLIGENCE SUMMARY
(Erase heading not required.)

Instructions regarding War Diaries and Intelligence Summaries are contained in F.S. Regs., Part II. and the Staff Manual respectively. Title pages will be prepared in manuscript.

Place	Date	Hour	Summary of Events and Information	Remarks and references to Appendices
	Nov 22		The Battalion moved into Reserve at HUDDLESTON CAMP. Relief of Companies proceeded smoothly. Relief completed 9pm. Enemy artillery very quiet during relief. Casualties during tour in front line 10 killed, 50 wounded, mostly from enemy shelling during minor raids on the line.	RW
HUDDLESTON CAMP.	Nov 23		Battalion in Reserve.	
		2.30am	Warning order received from HOULTHURST FOREST expected German attack at 5.30 am on division. Officer was sent to Rear Brigade HQ at 4am, but no attack was launched.	
		1pm	The C.O. & Adjutant visited Rear Brigade HQ. Sgt Lockley (D Coy) & Sgt Clews (B Coy) awarded the D.C.M. for gallantry in action (12th Oct).	RW
ditto	Nov 24	8.30am–3pm	Battn. attached to the Battalion for the whole day. Working party of 7 officers & 300 O.R. proceeded to the R.E.s	RW

R. Wells &
2nd S. Staff. R.

Army Form C. 2118.

8th S. Staffordshire Regt.

November 1917

WAR DIARY
or
INTELLIGENCE SUMMARY.
(Erase heading not required.)

Instructions regarding War Diaries and Intelligence Summaries are contained in F. S. Regs., Part II. and the Staff Manual respectively. Title pages will be prepared in manuscript.

Place	Date	Hour	Summary of Events and Information	Remarks and references to Appendices
HEDDLESTON CAMP & CARIBOU CAMP	Nov 25	7 pm	Battalion relieved in Reserve by 3/4 W. Kent Regt. marched to CARIBOU CAMP, near ELVEDEN HALL, arriving there 5.45pm. Bivouacked on arrival.	RW
CARIBOU CAMP	Nov 26	2 pm	General cleaning up, inspection of rifles, equipment, clothing etc. The M.O. inspected the feet of the Battalion (2Lt. S.J. HILL (M.R. Borden) returned from hospital	RW
ditto	Nov 27		Weather improved during the morning. Training in huts, musketry etc. Lt. F. KITE & 2Lt. H.M. THOMAS joined Battalion	RW
ditto	Nov 28		Ordinary training parade in morning	
		12-12.30	C.O's. Parade	
		2-3	Junior N.C.O's. working under R.S.M. & men signing French vocabulary. Training under small arm instructor	1/4
		2-4	Men signing french training in Bayonet fighting at Poste Hébert	1/4
		3.15	Football match against 10th SHERWOODS. Match drawn 3-3	
do	Nov 29		Parades as for 28th with addition of foot midnight inspection 2-3 pm	1/4
do	Nov 30		Parades as for 29th	1/4

J. Stanley
Lt. Col.
Comdg. 8th Bn. S. Staffordshire Regt.

WAR DIARY

or

~~INTELLIGENCE SUMMARY~~

(Erase heading not required.)

Army Form C. 2118.

Dec/17 6th Br. No. Staff Regt.

Place	Date 1917	Hour	Summary of Events and Information	Remarks and references to Appendices
CARIBOU CAMP	1 Dec.	10 am 4 pm	Inspection of Battalion by Brigadier at 10 am. Battalion complimented on work, etc. Battalion marched to BRIDGE CAMP, near ELVERDINGHE, via DROMORE CORNER and ELVERDINGHE.	
BRIDGE CAMP	2 Dec.	6.30 am	Orders of march from "A" "B" "C" "D" Companies with 5 min. intervals. Working party of Recruits proceeded to England on leave in the morning. Working party of 6 Officers and 300 O.R. provided to CADDIE SUPPORT TRENCH. Party returned in afternoon. Major W. Gibson, M.C. and Lt. F.J. Adams returned from leave.	
BRIDGE CAMP	3 Dec.	9.45 am	Received warning order of move to PROVEN area. Company parades, cleaning of kit + huts from 9 am to 1 pm.	
BRIDGE CAMP	4 Dec.	9.45 am	Battalion marched to POODLE + PITCHCOTT CAMPS, near PROVEN, in other Rank Huts. "B", "C", "D", "A" Coy, at 9.45 am. Route via ELVERDINGHE, DROMORE CORNER, DE WIPPE CABARET CORNER.	
POODLE and PITCHCOTT CAMPS	5 Dec.	9–12	Company parades + cleaning up from 9 am till 12 noon. Inter-Company football matches in afternoon, in which "D" Coy beat "C" Coy 3–1, + "B" Coy beat "A" Coy 3–1.	
POODLE and PITCHCOTT CAMPS	6 Dec.	9–12 12–1	Company parades + practices lining up for attack from 9 am till 12 noon. Battalion parade. In a football match in the afternoon, a team from "A" + "B" Coys drew with a team from "C" + "D" Coys 1–1. Draw retained for return to LICQUES area.	
POODLE and PITCHCOTT CAMPS	7 Dec.	2 am 2–4 pm 4.30 pm	Men bathing in the morning at COUTHOVE. Mr. Thomas + 13 O.R. joined with Battalion. Battalion route march. Billeting party of 1 Offr + 10 O.R. proceeded to LICQUES area. Afternoon etc. gtr. to Staffs Regt.	

Army Form C. 2118.

WAR DIARY
~~INTELLIGENCE SUMMARY~~ War/ 8th Bn. do Staff Regt

(Erase heading not required.)

Place	Date 1917	Hour	Summary of Events and Information	Remarks and references to Appendices
POPERINGHE and PITCHCOTT CAMPS	8 Dec		Company parades, lining up for attack and Battalion parade in morning. N.C.O's & "duds" parade in afternoon. In a football match in the afternoon the Batt. drew (2-2) with a team from the 9th Squadron R.F.C.	J.E.G
— Ditto —	9 Dec.		Transport, two limbers & cookers detailed to accompany the Battalion, marched off to LICQUES, under the T.O. Battalion, after 3 hours wait in rain, entrained at PROVEN & detrained at AUDRICQ at 8.30 pm; marched from AUDRICQ at 8 pm & arrived in billets at 1 am. H.Q., 'A' & 'B' Coy. billeted at LICQUES, 'C' & 'D' Coy. at HERBINGHEN.	J.E.G
LICQUES	10 Dec.	3.30 pm	Batt. received warning order of move on 11th.	J.E.G
	11 Dec.		General day of rest; foot-inspections & washing of feet. Battalion marched off from LICQUES at 10.30 am, & arrived in new area about 2 pm. 'A' & 'B' Coy. in LA RONVILLE, H.Q., 'C' & 'D' Coy, with transport, in MENTQUE - NORTBÉCOURT.	J.E.G
LICQUES				
MENTQUE	12 Dec.		Company parades & cleaning up; Battalion parade under 12 hours notice. Football in afternoon; 'C'+'D' Coy. (2) v. 'A' + 'B' Coy. (0)	9fGreen Lt. 8th Bn. Staff Regt. J.E.G

Army Form C. 2118.

WAR DIARY
or
INTELLIGENCE SUMMARY.   8th Bn. No. Staffs. Regt.
(Erase heading not required.)

Place	Date 1917	Hour	Summary of Events and Information	Remarks and references to Appendices
MENTQUE	13 Dec		Company & Specialist parades in morning. Battalion given notice to be ready to move off in 1 hour. Operation orders received in afternoon for move to new area. Football match in afternoon in which "D" Coy beat "C" Coy 5-0.	
- ditto -		4.30pm	"C" Company moves off to WIZERNES to act as loading party at railway.	
- ditto -	14 Dec		Foot inspection in morning.	
		2.0 pm	Battalion marched off to WIZERNES in order H.Q., "D" Coy, Remt. "A" & "B" Coys. arriving & entraining at 7.0 pm. Train left at 9.0 pm.	
O 16 a. CAMP. BARASTRE	15 Dec		Battalion detrained at BAPAUME at 9.0 am and marched to O 16 a. CAMP. BARASTRE, arriving at 11.50 am. Remainder of day given up to rest.	
- ditto -	16 Dec	10 am	Church parade in camp. Battalion under orders to move on 2 hours notice. Football in afternoon, versus 10th Sherwoods. Result 1-1.	
- ditto -	17 Dec		Day of Company Parades. C.O's conference at 5 pm.	
- ditto -	18 Dec		Company parades & Battalion scheme in morning. Footballing & football in afternoon. Officers, v. 8th Co. Staff (2) & Rgt. H.Q. (O); "D" Coy (4) v. "C" (1) 8 th S. Staff. Regt	

Army Form C. 2118.

WAR DIARY
or
INTELLIGENCE SUMMARY.
(Erase heading not required.)

Unit 8th Bn. So. Staff. Regt.

Place	Date	Hour	Summary of Events and Information	Remarks and references to Appendices
OIGA CAMP BARASTRE	19 Dec.	9am to 10am	Physical Training 9am to 10am. C.O.'s conference with Company Commanders, on forthcoming Bde. scheme. Brigade scheme in the afternoon from 2 to 3.15. Warning order received of probable move in morning of 20th	
— do —	20 Dec	10am	Battalion marched to OLD BRITISH FRONT LINE on N of HAVRINCOURT WOOD, K 31 c, a, + K 32 a, a (FRANCE 57c). Warning order of move to front line trenches received in the afternoon	
HAVRINCOURT WOOD.	21 Dec	4pm	Reconnoitring party of officers proceeded to front line trenches in morning. Battalion marched into line at 4 pm to trenches in K 10 a,4,11c + 16 b,d (sheet 57 c FRANCE) [Bn. HQrs. in WHITEHALL K.15 a. 85.30] + relieved the 8th BN. LONDON REGT.	
In line	22 Dec		Day quiet. Work done on general improvement of trenches + wire. New trench started joining front line with forward line of Bn. on left	
In line	23 Dec		Another quiet day in the line. Work again done on wiring and improving front and support lines of former position in K10 a + K 11 c. i.e. OWEN TRENCH	
— do —	24 Dec		Quiet day. Work as for 23rd. Warning order received of relief on 25th	
— do —	25 Dec		Battalion relieved in the line by 7th Bn LINCOLNSHIRE REGT. and proceeded to Bn. Support in TANK TRENCH + TANK SUPPORT, K 21 a, c (FRANCE 57c)	

Aftroun Lt
6th So. Staff. Regt

Army Form C. 2118.

WAR DIARY
or
INTELLIGENCE SUMMARY.

(Erase heading not required.)   8th Bn. So. Staff. Regt.   December 1917

Place	Date 1917	Hour	Summary of Events and Information	Remarks and references to Appendices
TANK TRENCH 4th in SUPPORT	26 Dec		Situation quiet. Day spent in improvement of trenches, cutting firesteps etc. Party of 2 Officers + 100 O.R. working in support line of front system (K.10.a, 11.c FRANCE 57c) at night + 1 Officer + 50 O.R. on carrying party.	J.G.
—ditto—	27 Dec		Work and working parties as for 26.12.17. Day quiet.	J.G.
—ditto—	28 Dec		Quiet day. Work and parties as for 27.12.17 except that the party of 2 Officers + 150 O.R. carried up wiring material before commencing digging.	J.G.
—ditto—	29 Dec		Working parties as for 28.12.17, except that party of 2 Officers + 150 O.R. was increased to 2 Officers + 150 O.R. and was used solely as party for carrying wiring material for 11 Fld Coy R.E.	J.G.
—ditto—	30 Dec		Operation orders received from Brigade Hqrs. Battalion standing-to in morning owing to attack in neighbourhood of LA VACQUERIE salient. Battalion relieved in evening by 9th Bn. D. of Wellingtons (W. Riding Regt) & 5/2nd Inf. Bde + moved back to OLD BRITISH FRONT LINE from K.31.c.2.1 & Q.3.a.3.2. (FRANCE, 57c). 51st Inf. Bde became Bde in support. Relieved to 14th Division.	J.G.
OLD BRITISH FRONT LINE	31 Dec		Battalion bathing by half companies at RUYAULCOURT. Day quiet on Divisional front.	J.G.

A. Green Lt.
6th Bn. So. Staff. Regt.

W. Gibson Major
for O.C. 8th Bn. So. Staff Regt.

D.a.S.
Succ

Herewith War Diary
for the month of January
1918.

[signature]
Comdg 8th South Staffs

Army Form C. 2118.

WAR DIARY
of
INTELLIGENCE SUMMARY.
(Erase heading not required)

Jan. 1918   8th Bn South Staffordshire Regiment

Place	Date 1918	Hour	Summary of Events and Information	Remarks and references to Appendices
OLD BRITISH FR. LINE	1 Jan	—	Quiet day. Nothing for men. Bn. bathing at RUYAULCOURT	1/2
— ditto —	2 Jan	—	men of Battalion given their Christmas dinner	1/2
— ditto —	3 Jan	—	Battalion relieved 13th Bn Royal Fusiliers & part of 1st Bn Royal Berkshire Regiment in front line K8a.90.40 — K9b.20.40. Enemy attacked at 4.30 pm as Bn. were moving up and captured 1st Royal Fusilier posts at K9b.20.90, K9b.50.90, K10a.20.90, K10a.60.80 & K10b.20.55. Counter-attack (on posts K9b.20.90 — K9b.50.90) by 1st R Berks was unsuccessful.	1/4
then line K8a.90.40 — K9b.20.40	4 Jan	—	Day quiet. Part of new line (from CANAL at K9b.20.40 to K9.095.90) taken over by 10th Sherwood Foresters	1/4
to line K8a.90.40 — K9.095.90	5 Jan	—	Quiet day. Working of interest to report	2/4
— ditto —	6 Jan	—	Quiet day. Rain at noon.	3/4
— ditto —	7 Jan	—	Quiet day. Nothing to report.	7/4

Reeve Lt.
8th S Staff Regt.

WAR DIARY
INTELLIGENCE SUMMARY.

8th Bn 1st /5th Staffs Regt.

Jan 1918.

Place	Date 1918	Hour	Summary of Events and Information	Remarks and references to Appendices
ditto	8 Jan		REF. MAP. FRANCE 57c. Another quiet day in line. Ordinary trench routine & working parties.	/14
ditto	9 Jan		Quiet day. Battalion relieved in line by 4th Bn Lincolnshire Regiment and moved back into Bde Support. TANK TRENCH, TANK SUPPORT, HUNT AVENUE + ALBANY AVENUE (K14 b, K15 a, c.) Bn Hqrs on HERMIES road at K13 d 80.30	/14
Bde. Support	10 Jan		Bn standing to on aeroplane alarm during morning. No unusual front	/14
ditto	11 Jan		1 Platoon of "D" Company moved into STAGG STREET to form a strong point at K14 b 40.40. Working parties out in evening Day quiet. Rain	/14
ditto	12 Jan		Day quiet in support. Nothing of interest except usual working parties.	/14
ditto	13 Jan		Day quiet. Ordinary trench routine & working parties	/14
ditto	14 Jan		Battalion moved up into line and relieved 4th Lincolns in left sector K80.90.40 – K9 a95.90	/14
In line	15 Jan		Relief complete at 3.30 am owing to extremely bad state of trenches	/14

J.R. Green Lt
8th Bn 1/5th Staffs Regt

Army Form C. 2118.

WAR DIARY
INTELLIGENCE SUMMARY.
(Erase heading not required.)

8th Bn. A. & S. Staffs. Regt.

Jan 1918.

Place	Date 1918	Hour	Summary of Events and Information	Remarks and references to Appendices
In line	16 Jan		REF. MAP. FRANCE 57c. Quiet day in line. Men occupied in making dugouts & posts in trenches habitable.	
—ditto—	17 Jan		Inter-company relief in evening. 'C' Coy relieved 'A' Coy in line K9a 95.90 — K8b 80.70. 'D' Coy relieved 'B' Coy in line K8&80.75 — K8a 90.40.	
—ditto—	18 Jan		Day quiet. No operations to report. 2/Lt. H.U. Smith 'killed in action'.	
—ditto—	19 Jan	2.15am	Heavy enemy bombardment of Battalion sector from 2.15am to 2.35am. Battalion stood to line by 10th Bn Lancashire Fusiliers. On relief Bn entrained at WINDY CORNER, HERMIES, & proceeded to SAUNDERS CAMP, HAPLINCOURT. 2/Lt. A. RAMSDEN wounded in action.	
SAUNDERS CAMP HAPLINCOURT	20 Jan		Men bathing at HAPLINCOURT, otherwise day given up to rest and cleaning of clothes & equipment.	
—ditto—	21 Jan		Working party of 250 working at HERMIES under R.E. Transport bathing at HAPLINCOURT.	
—ditto—	22 Jan		Day spent in cleaning up. Parade under company arrangements in morning. Football match in afternoon. Result 'A'&'C' 2 v 'B'+'D' 2.	

J.F. Green Lt.
8th Bn A. & S. Staffs. Regt.

Army Form C. 2118.

WAR DIARY
or
INTELLIGENCE SUMMARY.

(Erase heading not required.)

8th Bn. No. Staff. Regt.

Place	Date	Hour	Summary of Events and Information	Remarks and references to Appendices
	Jan 1918		REF. MAP. FRANCE 57C	
SANDERS CAMP	23 Jan		Working party of 250 working under R.E.s at HERMIES. Subaltern officers before camp reported to Bde. Hqrs. for discussion on patrolling.	
ditto	24 Jan		Company underwent special foot treatment at HERRICK Camp during the morning. Subalterns discussion on patrolling at Bde. Hqr. in morning. In a football match in the afternoon the Battalion beat 51st Bde. Hqrs. 3-0.	
ditto	25 Jan		51st Bde. moved up into line, the Battalion moving into Bde. Reserve in K.32 & Q.2 (HAVRINCOURT WOOD) to relieve 10th W. YORKS. Men improving accommodation in occupied trenches.	
K.32, Q.2	26 Jan		Party of 8 Officers & 300 O.R. working under 93rd Fld.Coy R.E on front line system, digging c.t. in K.14.	
ditto	27 Jan		Working party of 6 Officers & 270 O.R. working as for 25th inst. Major R.P. Burnett M.C. instructed to turn in badges of rank of Lt.-Col. H. Col. S. Darby M.C. receiving orders to take over command of 12th Manchesters on his return from a course on the 5th February.	
ditto	28 Jan		Work as for 28th inst.	

R.P. to Staff C. of S.

Army Form C. 2118.

WAR DIARY
or
INTELLIGENCE SUMMARY.

(Erase heading not required.)

8th Bn. A. Staff Regt

Jan 1918

Place	Date	Hour	Summary of Events and Information	Remarks and references to Appendices
K32, Q2	29 Jan		Lt-Col R.P. Bennett took over command of the Battalion. Working parties as for 28th inst. Day quiet on Bn. front. Bivouacs, shelters + trenches occupied by the Battalion cleaned + improved. Special working parties of 6 officers + 270 O.R. as for 29th.	KB
ditto	30 Jan		Battalion underwent special foot treatment at K31.a.00 during the morning.	
ditto	31 Jan		Battalion relieved 7th LINCS. REGT. in front line K11.a.00.70 – K10a.75.25 with 'B' Company on left front, 'B' Company on centre front, 'A' Company on right front + 'C' Company in support. Relief complete by 9.5 pm. Battalion commenced work done whilst in Bde Reserve. Quiet night spent in line, patrols having no encounter with the enemy.	KB

MPBennett Lt-Col
Cmdg 8th Bn. A. Staff Regt.

McKissen C
8th Bn. A. Staff Regt

WAR DIARY / INTELLIGENCE SUMMARY

Army Form C. 2118

8th Bn Ls Staff Regt.

WK 32

Place	Date 1918	Hour	Summary of Events and Information REF. MAP. FRANCE 57C & areal sheet BOURSIES 1/10,000	Remarks and references to Appendices
In line K10a 10,25 – K11c 00,00	1 Feb		Quiet day in line. No operations to report	/18
– do –	2 Feb		Quiet day. Orders received to detail drafts as follows, for 7th Bn to Staff: 2 Officers + 50 O.R.: for 2/6th Bn to Staff 5 Officers + 100 O.R.	/18 /19
– do –	3 Feb		Quiet day in line.	
– do –	4 Feb	1am	Enemy raided bombing post at K10b 22.42. Attack was beaten off by our Lewis Gun fire. The leader & about 20 men being seen to fall. 3 men succeeded in entering bombing stop but were immediately bombed out. 1 of our men was missing. Remainder of day quiet.	/19
– do –	5 Feb		Enemy heavily bombarded our lines in the early morning, but no raid or attack took place. Remainder of day quiet. Warning order for relief received.	/19 /31
– do –	6 Feb		Battalion relieved in evening by 7th Bn Lincolns & proceeded by train from Q2a 1.5 to SANDERS CAMP (Q4)	/18
SANDERS CAMP	7 Feb		Day of cleaning up. Working party of 5 Officers + 271 O.R. trained to HERMIES in evening for work in K15 + 16.	/19

J.A. Green Lt Col
8th Ln Staffs

Army Form C. 2118.

WAR DIARY
or
INTELLIGENCE SUMMARY.

8th Bn. A. & S. Staff Regt

(Erase heading not required.)

Instructions regarding War Diaries and Intelligence Summaries are contained in F. S. Regs. Part II and the Staff Manual respectively. Title pages will be prepared in manuscript.

Feb. 1918

Place	Date 1918 Feb.	Hour	Summary of Events and Information	Remarks and references to Appendices
SAPIGNERS CAMP.	8		Men working in HAPLINCOURT in morning + afternoon. Battalion dinner in evening for all ranks	
-ditto-	9		Officers dinner in evening with following guests:- Lt Col Metcalfe, 1st Lines. (a/Brigadier) Major W. Gilson, 8th Lo Staff (act. 10th Stewarts), Capt E. N. Walker (Bn. Major) Capt Als Allan (Staff Captain) Working party of 4 officers +200 O.R. travel to HERMIES in evening	1/9
-ditto-	10		for work in K15 + 16.16.	1/9
-ditto-	11		Draft for 17th Lo Staff left in morning at 10am (Nos 2+66) Company parades in morning football, etc, in afternoon. Parades under company arrangement in morning the 41st Div R.F.A. beat the Battn team 5-4 after a very fast game	1/9
-ditto-	12		Draft for 2/6th Lo Staff left in morning (No 127.16), entraining at FREMICOURT.	1/9
-ditto-	13		Company parades in morning football, etc in afternoon	1/9
-ditto-	14		Ordinary morning parades afternoon devoted to football	1/4

WAR DIARY or INTELLIGENCE SUMMARY

Army Form C.

8th Bn. W. Yorks. Regt.

Feb 1918

Place	Date	Hour	Summary of Events and Information	Remarks and references to Appendices
SANDERS CAMP	16/16		Parades in morning under Company arrangements. Football in afternoon.	
- ditto -	17		Day of rest. Voluntary Church Parade in morning. In the afternoon a football match between the Warrants & Officers of the Battalion resulted in a win for the latter 3-0.	
- ditto -	18.		Company parades in morning. A football in the afternoon the Bn. defeated the 8th R.F.A. 2-1.	
- ditto -	19		All work during day under Company arrangements. Afternoon usual devoted to football etc.	
- ditto -	20		Usual morning parades with football in afternoon	
- ditto -	21		Parades in morning. Afternoon given over to recreation	
- ditto -	22		— ditto —	
- ditto -	23		Remainder of Brigade moved to VITTORIA & SALAMANCA camps. BARASHES being found for them by the remnants of the 9th YORKS, 3/4 R.W. KENTS from 17th the HOWE & NELSON Battalions & the 63rd (R.N.) Division. Reorganisation carried out. Bn. now consists of: (A. Coy.) 1st — from 6th E. Surrey Regt.	

www.ingramcontent.com/pod-product-compliance
Lightning Source LLC
Chambersburg PA
CBHW080903230426
43664CB00016B/2714